ALSO BY FRED GRAHAM

The Self-Inflicted Wound

THE
ALIAS
PROGRAM

THE ALIAS PROGRAM

Fred Graham

LITTLE, BROWN AND COMPANY . . . . BOSTON—TORONTO

т09/77

Second Printing

Portions of this book were first published in slightly different form in *New York* magazine.

LIBRARY OF CONGRESS CATALOGING IN PUBLICATION DATA
Graham, Fred P
  The alias program.

  1. Organized crime—United States—Prevention.
2. Witnesses—United States—Case studies. 3. United
States. Dept. of Justice. I. Title.
HV6791.G7 1977 364 77-23392
ISBN 0-316-32298-9

Published simultaneously in Canada
by Little, Brown & Company (Canada) Limited

PRINTED IN THE UNITED STATES OF AMERICA

for Lucile

Oh, what a tangled web we weave,
When first we practice to deceive!

Sir Walter Scott

Contents

1. Paul Maris 3
2. "Mr. X" 15
3. Witness 33
4. Officer and Gentleman 56
5. Tycoon 97
6. Overreacher 118
7. Fugitive 145
8. Quarry 165
9. Businessman 185
10. Nontaxpayer 199
11. Gerald Martin Zelmanowitz 220
12. Plaintiff 231
13. Visitor 236
    Afterword 239

This story is true.

Unfortunately.

THE
ALIAS
PROGRAM

1.............................Paul Maris

It was the day of what people in the garment industry in San Francisco would later call the "Good Friday Massacre," but Friday, April 20, 1973, began on the upbeat for Paul Maris. He woke up feeling very rich and secure. Lillian Maris stayed in bed — she would follow him to the plant later — so in the quiet of his morning routine he began his day as he frequently had in the recent years of his success, savoring the elegance of his apartment.

Maris knew that many of his more conservative friends considered his apartment building a bit tacky. It was the newest, tallest building perched high on the brow of fashionable Pacific Heights, facing down toward San Francisco Bay. He knew it suffered by comparison with the more settled elegance of the structures around it. The apartment building stood twelve stories high at the corner of Washington and Laguna Streets, much taller and sleeker than the private mansions around it. Across the street was a well-trimmed park, where a few adults walked dogs, but where children seldom played. "Miami Modern," the neighbors called his building's architecture, with its slightly convex facade lined with balconies, and, at the main entrance just in front of the turnaround carport, two huge crouching plaster lions.

Maris smiled about that as he gazed over his breakfast coffee down at Alcatraz and the Bay. He and Lillian were comfortable in the wall-to-wall affluence of the building. Their antiques had been shipped out from storage in New Jersey, and he felt at home with them and with his prized Chagall on the wall. Besides, others couldn't appreciate the inner comfort he drew from two other features of the building. One was an around-the-clock doorman on guard at the entrance, and the other was a protected garage underground, reached only by elevators from above, keeping the automobiles tamper-proof at night.

His feeling of well-being wavered a few minutes later, as Maris stepped out of the elevator and climbed behind the wheel of his white Rolls-Royce. Just before he turned the key Maris felt the old, familiar, breathtaking moment of fear. With a sudden rush, the old terror began

3

to flow back — of the bomb crashing up from underneath, always tearing out his testicles and blasting away his buttocks. It was a fear he had felt many times before, but with decreasing frequency in the recent busy years.

Maris did what he always forced himself to do: he quickly turned the key to get the moment past. Nothing happened but the churning of the motor, and the fear drained away quickly as he drove out into the bright morning.

Driving down the hill toward the heart of the city and the Paul Maris Company, he wondered what had brought back his old fear. It might have been the insecurity of being fired as president of the Paul Maris Company by the board of directors five weeks earlier. But immediately after that, an astonishing thing had happened. The employees of the Paul Maris Company had begun to walk out in protest — first the executives and secretaries, then the salesmen, then the designers of all three ladies' wear lines, and finally even the Oriental women who worked at the knitting machines, cutting boards, and sewing machines.

The ladies' walkout impressed Maris in a secret way that none of them could know; his mother had worked at jobs very much like theirs in the garment district of New York when he was a boy. Her wages were so meager that he could remember her keeping a pan of water bubbling on the stove on Sunday afternoons, so that the women who dropped by would think dinner was cooking. He knew how badly every hour of a seamstress's pay was needed. The workers continued to stream out until, of the 350 employees of the company, a person could count those left in the building on the fingers of both hands.

The board of directors had screamed "management strike" and had accused Maris of using threats to force workers to join the walkout and of taking clothes designs and customer lists with him. But the walkout lasted, and within a week the board had caved in. Despite the protests that Maris was spending too lavishly to keep up with his rising sales, the board had given him a new contract as president. In return, he had promised to cut costs and to meet his payrolls without further credit. But in a rapidly growing company, economies came hard. Maris had taken the phone out of his Rolls and had trimmed elsewhere, but still he couldn't seem to make ends meet. He had been forced to admit several days before that he wouldn't be able to make the payroll on Good Friday without more credit. Milton Stewart, the chairman of the board, had been surprisingly subdued about that, Maris thought.

It seemed to Maris that the current squeeze was mostly a matter of temporary bad luck. It had begun with one of his bold ideas. Each summer, American fashion writers flock to Paris to get the annual word on styles at the *prêt-à-porter* fashion show at the Porte de Versailles. When they got there in May of 1972, they had been surprised to find an American fashion house showing its wares — the Paul Maris Company. It was a daring stroke, and perfectly timed — the casual knits and sports clothes featured by Maris were just becoming the rage of Europe. Maris let it be known that he was the first American house to have a booth at the Porte de Versailles (a competitor compared the feat to "getting an invitation to a $100-a-plate fundraiser for George McGovern"), and California newspapers ran picture stories with such headlines as "Our Paul Maris Is a Hit in Paris."

But, in fact, Paris had been too much a hit with Paul Maris. He had been greatly impressed with the acrid colors that were the rage in Europe, but that hadn't yet caught on in the United States. So the Maris "holiday line" that came out at Christmas had been heavy in such colors as electric pink and glowing chartreuse. The trouble was that the new Maris "color story" was all wrong for the soft colors that other American manufacturers were featuring. His knit tops clashed with most of the skirts and slacks that women had in their wardrobes, and the Maris holiday line was a disaster. But for the spring line, Maris had gone back to the soft colors and sporty fashions that had been his mainstay. This time the timing was good, because women were increasingly wearing jeans, and they were buying his knit tops to wear with them. The spring line promised to be a smash and Maris was confident that it was only a matter of time before the firm would be in the black.

Maris parked in his usual spot behind the large square cream-colored building beneath the elevated approach to the Bay Bridge — a bland structure, except for the bold lettering above the entrance: PAUL MARIS COMPANY. He seemed surprisingly young to be the man behind that name: lean and mod in his narrow suit, poodle-cut dark reddish mop, a few freckles around clear green eyes. The frequent articles about him in the press quoted his age as thirty-eight, and they often remarked that he looked younger than that. One article described him as "a man who is fortyish but looks thirtyish," and many of the people around him suspected that the low estimate was probably nearer to the truth. But Maris was flamboyant and mysterious in so many ways that nobody thought much about the oddity of a man who claimed to be older than he looked.

He took the elevator up, past the "Factory Store" that he operated on the second floor, past the huge knitting machines on the third floor, to the fourth floor, where the clatter of the factory was well cushioned in a finely appointed executive suite of offices.

Maris waved at the receptionist on the way in and gazed longer at his secretary, Kat Walker. Tall, lithe, brown-haired, wide-eyed Kat Walker. It was a name that fit her perfectly, but Maris knew it was an invention. Her name was Janet, and she had been married to a struggling musician in Manhattan, Ronald Crosby. His musical career had seemed to be going nowhere, and then one day, in a punchy, what-the-hell mood, they solemnly decided that no New Yorker named Ronald could make it big in country ballads. So they dreamed up the name Jerry Jeff Walker and to go with her new last name she picked the name Kat — and became Kat Walker. Whether there was magic in his new name or new wife, Jerry Jeff began to sense music in an experience he had had earlier in a New Orleans jail. He had spent the shank of a high-spirited weekend in a cell being entertained by a vagrant Negro street dancer, and now Jerry Jeff Walker was inspired to write a haunting song about him, called "Mr. Bojangles." It made Jerry Jeff a star and also very busy, and eventually he and Kat were divorced.

Kat Walker drifted to San Francisco and into the fringes of liberal politics, where Paul Maris was operating in his spare time as the organizing force behind referendum drives to limit the height of high-rise buildings and to save Alcatraz Island from commercial developers. Environmentalism was the rage then among the political idealists of San Francisco, but their leadership was often long on zeal and short on organization. Paul Maris was a singular exception. As the volunteers gathered on weekends to circulate petitions for signatures, it was Maris who provided the direction and energy that made things happen. It was Maris who told people where to go, Maris who saw to it that there were tables and chairs at busy corners, and Maris who appeared later with sandwiches and coffee for the volunteers. And when they needed to catch the public's attention at the end, it was Maris who brought in the clowns, the skywriting airplanes, and the other hoopla that put the campaign over the top. Kat was twenty-three years old then, and was much impressed with this demonstration of leadership and of apparent idealism. She ended up as Paul's personal secretary at the Paul Maris Company.

Kat often served to reassure Paul Maris that many people other than he were not just what they seemed to be. But that morning, as he slid behind his huge desk, Maris felt no qualms.

Not bad, he thought — considering that he was not Paul Maris at all, but Gerald Martin Zelmanowitz, a high-school dropout from Brooklyn and three-times-convicted criminal who had never held a legitimate job before in his life.

Paul Maris began his day's work.

Meanwhile, down the hill from the Maris apartment house, on a quiet, tree-lined residential street, an unusual scene was starting to form. Cars began to line up into a waiting caravan in front of a dignified beige town house, and teams of men — many wearing blue jumpsuits and carrying long nightsticks — began to file inside. There they milled around as they received their orders from the man who ran this unusual establishment, Harold K. Lipset, private investigator.

Hal Lipset was a balding, paunchy, myopic man who for almost thirty years had been San Francisco's most famous private detective. He operated out of the first floor of the big Victorian house, a relic of the Golden Age of the Barbary Coast. It had twenty-three rooms, impressive high ceilings, and an exquisite Japanese garden in the rear. But the building's dominating feature was a room to the right of the main entrance, where persons entering could not fail to glimpse banks of tape recorders, radios, and other, more mysterious, electronic gear.

For in the folklore of the real and fictional private eyes of the world, Hal Lipset had gained some degree of an international reputation as a "private ear." An urbane man who enjoyed operas, symphonies, and the friendship of many celebrities, Lipset had a decade before let the license lapse on his pistol, and had begun carrying instead an expensive and versatile tape recorder. In those days there were few laws against wiretapping and bugging, and he became known as an investigator who could learn more by electronic arts than by the more physical tactics of real and fictional private detectives.

Lipset also had a genius for the public relations aspects of electronic snoopery. In 1965, when Senator Edward Long of Missouri was casting about for some means to dramatize to the public the dangerous headlong development of eavesdropping technology, it was Lipset who came up with the gimmick that said it all. He built and demonstrated at a Senate hearing an olive with a tiny transmitter in the center and an antenna for a toothpick — and the bugged olive-in-the-martini has been the symbol of electronic surveillance ever since.

Just a few days before Good Friday of 1973, Lipset had received national notoriety of a more dubious sort, when he suddenly resigned as special investigator for the Senate Watergate Committee's investigation into the bugging of the Democratic National Committee headquarters. Lipset had been hired by the committee's chief counsel, Sam Dash, a former district attorney of Philadelphia, who had once written a book on wiretapping and who had known Lipset for many years. It never became clear why the Senate committee needed all this eavesdropping expertise to investigate what was essentially a story of political abuse. For the red-faced Senators had quickly learned that Lipset himself had once been convicted of bugging a room in the Plaza Hotel in New York — where electronic eavesdropping had long been illegal — and Lipset had quickly resigned and returned to San Francisco.

But Lipset had come back to a lucrative assignment, the like of which San Francisco had never seen before. His mission was no less than to stage a corporate coup d'état, to recruit a platoon of men to surprise and physically oust the top-level management of a corporation from its premises. He was told that the reason for such unprecedented tactics was that the target was an unusual man: Paul Maris, a mercurial and charismatic corporate president, who had brought the business to a standstill earlier when an attempt had been made to remove him by orthodox means.

On hand this morning, in Lipset's Victorian lair, was Lipset's client, Milton Stewart, the chairman of the board of the Paul Maris Company and president and chief operating officer of its sole financial backer,

On Good Friday, 1973, Harold K. Lipset, San Francisco's celebrated private detective, led a raid to oust Paul Maris from the presidency of the company bearing his name.

the Creative Capital Company of New York. Lipset concluded that New Yorkers must play rough in business, because never before had he been hired to use paramilitary tactics to enforce a corporate shake-up. He had about thirty men — private investigators borrowed from other agencies, free-lance detectives, off-duty watchmen, and former cops — and each was given a specific assignment to carry out when the time came to invade the building. Meanwhile, an attorney was at the courthouse, meeting with a judge in his chambers. The lawyer had a thick stack of temporary restraining orders already prepared, alleging that Maris and his supporters in the management could cause irreparable damage to the corporation unless they were ordered out of the building to stay. The papers included a recitation of the walkout and alleged removal of records following Maris's previous dismissal, and the judge was persuaded. He signed the orders. Shortly before noon the lawyer arrived at Lipset's house, with the court orders in his hand.

Milton Stewart was still not satisfied. He was afraid that there might be violence. As he put it to reporters when it was all over later that day: "When there is a significant change involving a substantial number of people, who knows who will get uptight about what?" But to Lipset, Stewart was more specific. He was worried about Maris, who he said was tricky and excitable.

Lipset agreed that they should assign one of the men to stick with Stewart as his bodyguard during the raid. The natural choice was Charles Thompson, a free-lance private investigator who looked like heavyweight champion Ezzard Charles in his prime. Thompson was a veteran former San Francisco cop. But he had also, for a short time, been a narcotics agent for the Justice Department's Bureau of Narcotics and Dangerous Drugs. Thus it happened that the man who was assigned to stay close to the center of events during the raid was the one member of the raiding party who could observe those events with a background of knowledge of the inner secrets of the Department of Justice.

In 1976 Milton Stewart became president of the National Small Business Association. As chairman of the board of the Paul Maris Company in 1973, he mounted the coup against Maris.

It was a few minutes after noon when the men in blue burst into the factory and swept through the building. They calmed the ladies who were shopping in the factory store and then led them outside, explaining that "an emergency" was in progress. Guards were posted at all exits, and the employees were told to stay quietly at their places. Then Lipset and twenty of his men each stepped up to a selected member of the Maris staff, handed each one an envelope containing a restraining order addressed to him, and chanted something like this: "You are hereby served with an order of the superior court, commanding you to immediately leave the premises of the Paul Maris Company, and restraining you from taking anything with you as you leave."

Then each victim was escorted down the stairs and out the door, where they found themselves empty-handed, on the sidewalk, without even the personal effects from their desks. The last to go were Kat Walker and Paul Maris. Lipset personally did the honors for Maris, and he described it later to the press: "He was a lamb. He didn't get rough, fortunately."

Maris was quiet, but he was obviously not cowed. "See you in court, Stewart," he said, as he passed Milton Stewart on the way out the door.

Later that weekend, Stewart and his lawyers dug through the company's files for the elusive record of how and where so much money could have gone. The sequence of events later became jumbled in their memories, but one of the attorneys, William R. Chandler, recalled that at one point a personnel clerk emerged from the files, with a sheaf of papers and a triumphant shout: "Look at this!"

It was a roster of company employees, which included Paul Maris, his wife, Lillian, who had handled advertising, and her father and mother, Joseph and Evelyn Miller, and Lillian's daughter and her husband, Cynthia and Norman Roth. The clerk pointed out their Social Security numbers: each began with the same seven digits; 218-64-59. Paul Maris had 218-64-5910, followed by Cynthia Roth, 5911; Evelyn Miller, 5912; Joseph Miller, 5997; Norman Roth, 5998; Lillian Maris, 5999. The personnel clerk said he'd never seen anything like it — six members of the same family, of different ages, with almost sequential Social Security numbers. Milton Stewart decided to ask Hal Lipset to drop by again on Monday.

Lipset was as puzzled as the others by the Social Security numbers. Since numbers are assigned consecutively as applications come in, it was inexplicable that the Millers, in their late sixties, would have almost sequential numbers with their daughter, in her mid-forties, her husband, some eight years younger, and the even younger Roths.

"Who is this Paul Maris?" Lipset asked. Stewart replied that about a year earlier, he had begun to ask himself the same thing. When Creative Capital had first begun to invest in the company in April of 1971, it was known as the Alvin Duskin Company and Maris was its live-wire secretary-treasurer. Stewart had been so impressed with him that he engineered Maris's rise to the presidency of the company, and insisted that the firm be given Maris's name. Stewart felt strongly that a women's clothing house should have a strong public identification with its leading personality through the company name. Maris had opposed this; he wanted the new company name to be "San Francisco Gold." The board of directors had insisted on the name "Paul Maris Company," and Stewart had thought it a little odd that Maris, who was a forceful, domineering man, should have fought so hard to keep the company from taking his name.

In the succeeding year there had been a few other oddities. When Maris was made president, he refused to have his picture taken for the ads in the trade press announcing the change. He rarely spoke about his past, other than to mumble something about intelligence work in the army. His résumé said he was a native of Philadelphia, but all of his contacts and relatives seemed to be from New Jersey.

Nobody had paid much attention to this until the spring of 1972, when Creative Capital realized that under Maris's management it had been required to make massive investments to meet operating deficits, but that Maris had not invested $100,000 himself, as he had agreed to do. Maris had refused to give more details about his background — he said it was classified because of his status as an officer in the Army Security Agency reserve — but he did give as a reference Thomas Campion, a partner in a major law firm in Newark, New Jersey. A call to Campion seemed to bear Maris out. Campion spoke admiringly of Maris as "one of the most brilliant men I've ever met," and confirmed that Maris had been in classified work for the government.

13

Creative Capital was getting in too deep to let it go at that, so in July of 1972 it had quietly retained Proudfoot Reports, Inc., a prestigious New York private investigative agency, to check out Maris's background. When the report arrived, it could not have done more to lay the doubts to rest. In six neatly typed pages it confirmed the personal, educational, and military background stated in the résumé that Maris had submitted when he had first joined the company. It even added credentials not included in the résumé — that Maris had been promoted to major in the reserves and had done special assignments for the Department of State and the Atomic Energy Commission.

The report quoted unnamed bankers and businessmen as speaking of Maris in such terms as "a high degree of integrity and business acumen," "every confidence in the subject's integrity and ability," and "an able executive, trustworthy in every respect and much admired by those with whom he has business relationships." The report concluded: "Nowhere in the conduct of this inquiry was anything learned or developed which would reflect unfavorably upon the business or personal background of the subject."

Stewart flipped the Proudfoot report, the résumé, and the Social Security roster to Lipset, and waited for him to pronounce judgment.

Lipset recalled later that two items in the résumé caught his eye. One was that it was uncharacteristically modest of any business executive to state, as Maris had done, that he was the owner of a company called Sound Enterprises, Inc., and yet not to give the address or even the city or state where it was located. The other was that Maris's army duty was listed as "cryptographer," but his rank as captain. Lipset had never known a cryptographer to be an officer; they were always enlisted men.

"He's a phony. It doesn't add up," Lipset told Stewart. "I'm going to do some more checking."

2..................................."Mr. X"

There had been an atmosphere about the United States Courthouse in Newark, New Jersey, on March 12, 1969, that told everyone with a feel for the place that something unusual was going on. At about midmorning United States marshals cleared everyone from the corridors of the fourth floor, so that nobody could see the person who was hustled under heavy guard up a back elevator and into the grand jury room. Grand jury testimony is always held in a guarded room, with all of the participants sworn to secrecy on pain of imprisonment (except the witnesses, who are usually either accusers or targets, and thus usually have their own reasons for keeping their testimony secret). But what was taking place before the grand jury that day was more secret than any testimony that had ever been given in that courthouse before.

When the twenty-three grand jurors entered the room they could tell immediately that something extraordinary was about to happen. They took their usual places in the classroomlike seats that faced forward toward the raised podium where the witness usually sat behind a small table. But this time the witness chair was empty. To the left of it, the entire corner of the room had been blocked off by a tall, cream-colored screen that angled across the room. Facing the grand jurors was the United States attorney for New Jersey, David M. Satz, Jr., and his chief assistant, Donald Horowitz. Satz was usually very informal in his dealings with the grand jurors, but this time he stood before them and made a little speech. He said that something unprecedented in his experience was about to happen. The grand jury was about to hear evidence against criminals so vicious that the witness's life would be in danger if his identity were even suspected. So even the usual severe grand jury secrecy would not be enough. This witness would testify as "Mr. X," and he would not be seen or identified during his testimony.

Then Horowitz began the questioning:

" 'Mr. X,' do you know Angelo DeCarlo?"

It quickly became apparent to the grand jurors why such precautions were being taken. "Mr. X" spoke in a low half-whisper to disguise his voice, and for good reason — he was bearing witness against Angelo "Gyp" DeCarlo, a Mafia capo for the late Vito Genovese and a gangland enforcer who had ruled the rackets of northern New Jersey for years with murderous brutality.

The witness explained that eighteen months earlier he had undertaken a business deal with a Newark insurance man named Louis Saperstein. (In the style of most legal testimony, the witness left out details of human — but not legal — significance: the facts that Saperstein's links with the Mafia had surfaced two decades before, during the Kefauver crime hearings, that he had once been convicted of labor racketeering, and that he had survived an attempted gangland execution in which he had been shot four times in the head.) "Mr. X" said that he and Saperstein had been involved in an intricate international financial shuffle called arbitrage. The witness explained that he was an expert at arbitraging securities — that is, buying and selling the same stocks almost simultaneously on American and foreign stock exchanges and making money on the slight differences between the stock prices in the various countries. It was complicated by the fact that in 1960 Congress had, in an effort to stop the outflow of dollars and gold from the United States, imposed an interest equalization tax of 18 percent on the gross sale price of any security purchased overseas by an American from a person other than a United States citizen, and then resold in the United States. The problem was that profit margins in arbitrage deals were usually far narrower than 18 percent. Thus arbitrage was usually practical only if the transactions could be conducted in such a way as to avoid the interest equalization tax — that is, illegally. "Mr. X" was also an expert at that; the forging of documents to make it appear that the stocks purchased overseas had previously been owned by Americans, and the bribing of IRS agents not to notice the forgeries.

This is where Louis Saperstein came in. Through his contacts he could tap the large sums of cash required to make arbitrage profitable, cash from sources who would not care that the methods being used were against the law. In other words, Mafia money.

The voice behind the screen told the grand jurors that in the fall of 1967, Saperstein had taken "Mr. X" to a restaurant near Mountainside, New Jersey, to a structure in the rear called The Barn, known far and wide as Gyp DeCarlo's hangout. A deal was struck. DeCarlo and two other fixtures of the New Jersey mob, Daniel "Red" Cecere and Joe "Indian Joe" Polverino put up $100,000 to expand the arbitrage operation, and were cut in for a one-half share. Over the next sixteen trading days, "Mr. X" made $85,000 in profits. Then the IRS smelled something rotten in the complex web of transactions, and froze a securities trading account at the Hayden Stone brokerage house in New York, an account which proved to be a link in the arbitrage chain.

With the source of profits frozen, it turned out that Saperstein was in deep trouble with DeCarlo, Cecere, and Polverino. He had already owed them $50,000, on which he was paying the loan shark's rate of $1\frac{1}{2}$ percent per week. When this rate of interest — "vigorish," they called it — was applied also to the money they had invested in the arbitrage scheme, Saperstein was being squeezed for $1,725 each week, in cash. The arbitrage deal had been designed to get Saperstein out from under his debts, but over the succeeding weeks and months, the loan sharks began to realize that he was sinking even deeper. "Mr. X" managed to unfreeze the trading account, but in the process he discovered that Saperstein had milked almost one-third of the principal to pay his vigorish. There was not enough money left to support a successful arbitrage operation, but still Saperstein was caught on the weekly vigorish treadmill. "Mr. X" said he loaned and advanced money to Saperstein as long as he could, and when he could provide no more cash, Saperstein disappeared.

On September 12, 1968, Saperstein surfaced again, telephoning "Mr. X" from the New York Hilton Hotel, where Saperstein was registered under a false name. He was sputtering with fright, saying his debt had ballooned to $250,000, that he hadn't a ghost of a chance to pay, and that he feared for his life and the safety of his family. They arranged to meet at noon the next day in the lobby of the hotel.

They did, but "Mr. X" had not come alone. He was accompanied by Red Cecere and an "assistant" named Lenny. For a moment, Saperstein tried to turn and run, but at the last instant the Hilton was spared a pell-mell chase of New Jersey mafiosi pursuing their terrified victim through the lobby. Cecere seized one of Saperstein's arms and Lenny the other, and before Saperstein could start screaming Cecere calmed him, saying everything would be all right: "We just want to talk to you."

They went up to Saperstein's room, and while he was packing for the trip back to Jersey, he made what turned out to be prophetic offer: if they would promise not to hurt his family, he would take out a $100,000 insurance policy, make the gangsters his beneficiaries, and jump out the window.

They talked him out of that, and then Cecere and Lenny drove Saperstein to The Barn in New Jersey, while "Mr. X" followed in his car. The witness's story of what he saw when he arrived at The Barn was proof enough of why he was testifying from behind a screen. When he entered The Barn, Saperstein was stretched out on the floor. A large photograph of Frank Sinatra smiled down from the wall, as the fallen Saperstein was stomped and punched by Red Cecere and Joe Polverino. Saperstein seemed at first to be dead; his face was purple, his tongue was hanging out, and he was covered with blood and spittle.

A thug named Jimmy Higgins was standing around watching the beating, decked out in a golf cap and spikes for an afternoon of sport. When he saw the stranger enter The Barn, he snatched a butcher knife off a table, slammed "Mr. X" against a wall, and pressed the knife against his throat. Higgins started asking Red and Indian Joe if he should kill him, but the golfer had trouble catching their attention. Saperstein was showing signs of life, and they were taking turns propping him up in a chair and punching him off onto the floor. Jimmy Higgins began to get impatient, complaining that if they were going to kill the two guys they should do it now because he had to play golf. This caught Cecere's attention and he said no, no — not that one, this one. So Higgins put the knife down, said, "See you," and sauntered out.

At that point DeCarlo arrived and flew into a fury. He shouted that beating Saperstein there could make trouble, that the place was all messed up and bloody and that it might even be bugged. DeCarlo ordered them to get Saperstein out of there, fast.

They hauled him out to a station wagon parked beside The Barn, where Cecere began to punch him again, but DeCarlo told him to stop, that it was time to talk. DeCarlo reviewed the debts owed by Saperstein to him, Cecere, to Polverino, and to another loan shark, Pete Landusco. Then DeCarlo pronounced his judgment; Saperstein would pay $5,000 vigorish each Thursday, and at the end of two months, he would pay off the entire debt, or he would be dead.

18

Saperstein began to plead that he could never raise more than $3,000 dollars a week, but DeCarlo cut him off: "Forget about it. Bring five or you're dead."

"Mr. X" told the grand jury that just a few days later he went to The Barn to plead with DeCarlo to reconsider, because Saperstein couldn't possibly raise so much money so fast. DeCarlo wouldn't hear of it, but Red Cecere had a chilling reaction. He said he hoped Saperstein couldn't find the money; Cecere would prefer to "take him down into my cellar for three or four days."

With that, the testimony of "Mr. X" was almost over. As the witness answered some final run-of-the-mill questions, Satz and Horowitz sat reading the grand jurors' silence with quiet satisfaction. The prosecutors had additional evidence to come that would stun them even more. In late November, Saperstein had written two letters to the FBI, naming DeCarlo, Cecere, and Polverino, and telling of the beating and of the threats that he would be killed and that his wife and son would be "maimed or killed if I do not pay." Saperstein wrote that he had phoned DeCarlo at the Harbor Island Spa in Florida to plead for more time, but that DeCarlo replied that "unless further monies was paid the threat would be carried out." By the time the letters reached the FBI Saperstein was dead — according to his death certificate, of a heart attack induced by gastric shock. His body was dug up and examined by the state medical examiner, Dr. Edwin Albano. He found in Saperstein's corpse "enough arsenic to kill a mule."

The prosecutors knew that all of this would be powerful evidence to the grand jury, and that they would be ready enough to vote for indictments. But murder and beatings were not federal crimes, and it was doubtful whether the story of Saperstein's letters, the arsenic, and his death could even be presented as evidence in a federal trial. However, a federal crime was clearly spelled out in the testimony of "Mr. X." After all those years of getting by with bullying the citizens of northern New Jersey with threats, beatings and murder because nobody would testify, at last somebody had; and DeCarlo, Cecere, Polverino, and Landusco were to be indicted on charges — of all things — of violating the new federal "truth in lending" law.

Satz made a closing speech. He told the grand jurors that "Mr. X" had done a worthy thing, an act of good citizenship; he had testified at the risk of great danger to himself, and the community owed him a debt of thanks. Then Satz and Horowitz herded the grand jurors out of the room, and onto another floor of the building. In the corridor outside the grand jury room, United States marshals checked to be certain that the area was empty.

Then someone gave a signal, and a lean, curly-haired young man in a conservative gray suit slipped out from behind the screen and dashed down the hall to the back stairway. The young man ducked through the exit door and hurried down the stairs two at a time until he passed the first turn. Then he continued down at a nonchalant pace. Just as the exit door closed above him, a deputy marshal called softly, "Goodbye, Mr. X."

A few minutes later, Gerald Zelmanowitz sat ashen behind the wheel of his Cadillac, telling himself over and over again, "Thank God, it's over." The testimony had been a more frightening experience than he had imagined. What if anybody found out, or even suspected? He shuddered as a phrase ran through his mind that was to return often in the succeeding years of his life: ". . . *take him down into my cellar for three or four days.*"

Gerry often said later that that was what pushed him over the line to become a witness — the brutality of the beating, the stupid cruelty of the loan shark's squeezing of Saperstein until he was incapable of making money to pay their vigorish. Gerry wanted to get out of that life, but his decision to testify before the grand jury was more complicated than just that.

Gerald Zelmanowitz had been a crook all his life, and a successful one — if such a career could be called that — until the summer of 1967. Actually, the chain of events traced back to July Fourth of 1965, when Gerry was spending the weekend at a New Jersey resort called Goldman's and met a woman at the pool. Her name was Lillian Balaban, and she had two teenage daughters and one of those marriages that had begun during World War II when she married a soldier at the age of fourteen, a marriage that quickly turned into an empty legal formalism soon after the war ended. She was several years older than Gerry, but an attractive, strong-minded blond, and before the weekend was over Gerry had decreed that she would get a divorce, that they would be married, and that he would move to New Jersey.

Louis Saperstein, a partner of Gerald Zelmanowitz in illegal stock transactions, was brutally beaten by their Mafia associates and subsequently poisoned with arsenic.

The move to Jersey was done mostly for the sake of keeping Lillian close to her parents, Joseph and Evelyn Ringel, with whom she and her daughters had lived for years. But Gerry also had reasons of his own. In recent years he had become an increasingly upwardly mobile crook, and this was the successful criminal's version of moving to the suburbs. He had begun as a run-of-the-mill Brooklyn thug — working as a teamster organizer, shaking down employers, running sleazy bars on Manhattan's West Side, dealing in stolen merchandise. Then subtle changes began to take place. It didn't happen exactly as Horatio Alger would have done it, but Gerry began to move up in the world, to better himself as a criminal. While his contemporaries on the lower fringe of the Brooklyn mob were still wearing white-on-white ties and pointed-toe shoes, Gerry was buying his clothes at Brooks Brothers and wearing gray pinstripes. Then Gerry, who had never completed a single course at Brooklyn's Abraham Lincoln High, began to read books. Gerry devoured books about money — stocks, bonds, commodities, finance. He read everything he could find about money, and he remembered it all. He became known as an accomplished "paper-hanger" — a specialist in fencing stolen and counterfeit securities. He also befriended a man named Fred Shapiro, who was hiding from the Internal Revenue Service because of his involvement with Harold Stone, senior partner of a Wall Street over-the-counter brokerage firm, in an ingenious and massive arbitrage operation. Gerry learned the technique well from Shapiro and Stone, and added a special twist — the profitable use of stolen and counterfeit securities obtained by organized crime. He became an expert at palming these off on Swiss banks as collateral to obtain credit for use in purchasing foreign stocks for arbitraging.

Then he began a process that is time-honored among ambitious young men of other callings — lawyers, insurance men, and politicians — who also suffer the handicap of being from the wrong side of the tracks. Gerry began to climb. He would spend his evenings out of Brooklyn, in Manhattan, at restaurants and cocktail parties, where he met a much higher class of mobster than he associated with during the day. By this time, Gerry had learned skills that were of interest to these men ("Sure, Mr. Colombo, I could show you how to open a Swiss bank account. . . ." "Let me tell you about my system of arbitrage,

Mr. Lansky. . . ."), and he began to make business contacts that would assist him to move up into the more sophisticated forms of white-collar crime.

Gerry developed a strong distaste for the life-style of small-time thuggery he had always lived — "I thought there were better things," he said later, "than hanging around eating spaghetti with a couple of idiots in Brooklyn" — and getting married to a New Jersey woman was a perfect time to make the break. He stopped doing business with the Brooklyn mob, to the extent that two of his old pals paid him a threatening visit in Jersey one day, just checking to see if there was anything ominous in his disappearance from the scene.

He became an instant mortgaged suburbanite. Gerry and Lillian bought a $200,000 house in Short Hills, an affluent community outside Newark, and spent $150,000 on the trappings: silk wallpaper, a Chagall painting, his-and-hers Cadillacs. Gerry was making big money, but it never seemed to be quite enough. He came under heavy pressure to swing more deals, to make bigger scores. He opened a business in Newark and called it Société de la Bourse, a term that meant stockbroker with a foreign twist, which fairly characterized his operation. This "investment" business became a front for a wide range of enterprises, most of which were illegal. The result was a life-style that was half overmortgaged suburbanite, half "Godfather." Gerry loved having a family and a comfortable home for the first time. He delighted in his warm home life with Lillian and her daughters, Shelley and Cynthia, who in turn loved the handsome, intense man their mother had married. But there were also strident phone calls in the night, sudden flights to Geneva, unexplained absences from town. The result was an affectionate, middle-class family life, punctuated with incongruous incidents of ugliness. One night Bobby Stricker, the boy who was engaged to marry Shelley, was spending the evening with the girls and Lillian when Gerry staggered into the house, rumpled and bloody. He excused himself to clean up, muttering something about a fight at the airport with an old associate from the Teamsters Union, who claimed Gerry owed some money from a deal involving the Amalgamated Bank. The family went on with their evening, trying to enjoy it as if nothing had happened.

Gerry said later that by 1967 he was sick of his life, tired of lying to his family, miserable over the uncertainty and the fear. He speculated that subconsciously he wanted out, that the stupid things he did were an inner effort to change his life. Whether it was that, or if it was merely the overreaching of a debt-ridden suburbanite, Zelmanowitz experienced a chain of disasters that shattered his precarious existence as a felony-prone family man. His first mishap came later in 1967, when he was indicted in the Supreme Court of the State of New York on conspiracy charges growing out of the embezzlement of some $57,000 by a minor official of the Amalgamated Bank of New York. It seemed that the bank employee had telephoned Zelmanowitz long-distance during the heat of the plot, so the toll records gave the police Gerry's name. With Gerry's background, the police had no difficulty in figuring out who was the brains behind the scheme. It had, indeed, been the "deal," the ill-gotten gains of which had precipitated the bloody fight at the airport. But still, the evidence against Gerry was mostly circumstantial, and it was a case he might well have beaten if it had ever gone to trial.

Things got considerably stickier in the spring of 1968, though, when Gerry was arrested in a Newark brokerage house, trying to peddle $300,000 worth of stolen Indiana Toll Road bonds that also turned out to be counterfeit. Actually, Gerry hadn't even known they were fake — he thought they were just stolen, and was furious to learn he'd been given bad goods to fence — but it turned out that their bogus heritage sidetracked the FBI from learning that they were part of a chain of stolen securities that led straight to the Vito Genovese Mafia family in New York. For the first time, Gerry had been arrested on a federal charge. He was released on bond and quickly resumed his life as a suburbanite, but the wheels of justice were turning and Gerry was in trouble.

Incredibly, in December of 1968, Gerry was arrested under almost identical circumstances in a Miami brokerage house. He was trying to sell $305,000 worth of stolen Gillette Corporation stock certificates, which were the leavings of a batch of $2 million that he had peddled to various brokerage houses on a swing to Atlanta, Kansas City, New Orleans, and, unluckily, Miami. This time, Gerry was in deep water. The FBI easily traced his path back to each of the prior swindles along the way, and each sale was a separate felony, carrying a possible prison sentence of up to five years. Worse yet, this caper had "Mafia" written all over it. The securities had been stolen from the Old Colony Trust of Boston. The FBI had previously identified those thefts with the Raymond Patriarca Mafia family that dominated organized crime in New England, and Zelmanowitz was known to be a "paperhanger" with links only to the New Jersey and New York mobs. It had to mean a high-level deal involving someone important enough in organized crime to arrange an accommodation between the two Mafia families.

So the Justice Department began to work on Gerry, to soften him up. Technically, he was a bail-bond jumper from the Newark charge when he was arrested again in Miami, so they stuck him in jail and sent two marshals to bring him back to Newark. To drive from Miami to New Jersey is an easy two- or three-day trip; the two marshals took a month, keeping Gerry in shackles and leg-irons during the day and in stinking small-town jails at night. By the time he reached New Jersey he had been considerably softened.

The FBI had sensed a revulsion in Gerry toward his life-style as a criminal. There was, for instance, almost a naïveté about his reaction to his arrests. He never made a serious effort to deny being guilty; he just seemed to feel that he was not all that bad and that somehow he could work things out. He was obviously different in dress, intelligence, and suburban life-style from the thugs who were believed to have stolen the securities, but he said nothing to suggest who they were or how he had come to be fencing their goods. Then somebody in the United States attorney's office noticed that Zelmanowitz and Louis Saperstein had done some deals together, and that led to a hunch: if Zelmanowitz wouldn't talk about who got him the bogus bonds, perhaps he would talk about the Saperstein case.

In early March they sent the FBI agents who were handling Gerry's paperhanging cases out to Gerry's home to arrest him again, this time in connection with one of the sales he had made on the way to Miami. It was an especially jarring experience for Lillian. Gerry had never said to her, "Look, I'm a crook — I break the law," but there was an unspoken awareness on her part that his various "deals" were all tinged, to a greater or lesser degree, with criminality. That implicit understanding became overt in the months before Gerry's first federal arrest, when Angelo DeCarlo visited Gerry several times at his house. In New Jersey, when Gyp DeCarlo began to drop around the house, a wife didn't have to ask what kind of work her husband was in.

So it was particularly traumatic when the FBI men came to the house for Gerry, because the background of events suggested that he was in serious trouble. But once inside the courthouse, the agents did not take Gerry directly to be booked on the bad-paper charge. Instead, they slipped him into a room where two agents engaged on the Saperstein case were waiting, a veteran officer named Frederick McMahon and his sidekick, Howard Rice. McMahon laid it out straight and quickly — he told Gerry about Saperstein's letters, about his subsequent death by poisoning, and about their belief that DeCarlo had had him killed. Gerry was staggered; he hadn't known about the letters or the circumstances of Saperstein's death. But he vividly remembered the violent afternoon at The Barn and Cecere's preference to forego the money if he could take Saperstein down into his cellar for a few days.

Gerry was torn between fear for himself and disgust toward the racketeers, and he gave McMahon an ambiguous answer. He said he knew something about it, but he also knew better than to spend too much time in that room with those agents. They let him out, and he quickly made bond on the securities charge and went home. McMahon was elated. To receive even an equivocal answer to a request to testify against Gyp DeCarlo was an opening of rare potential. He determined to pursue that opening to the limit.

In the next few days, McMahon and Rice paid a series of visits to Zelmanowitz in his home, always entering discreetly so that no one would suspect that Gerry was talking with the government. McMahon said later that he sensed in Zelmanowitz a feeling of obligation toward Saperstein and a desire to square accounts with DeCarlo, Cecere, and Polverino. The FBI man testified later that Zelmanowitz seemed to be groping for a way to set himself apart from the three thugs and what they had apparently done to Saperstein, and McMahon represented himself to Gerry as a confidant who could help him set things right. "He was a con man," McMahon said, "but he did have integrity; in the sense of a human relationship he did have integrity. In other words, I wouldn't go into a business dealing with him. But in the situation that we were in, I trusted him."

Once the groundwork of trust was laid, McMahon began to work on Gerry to make the break with his past by turning against DeCarlo. "Look, Gerry, you're a smart guy," he would say; "you don't have to live this way." Sometimes McMahon would bring along tapes of thuggish conversations the FBI had picked up from bugs around the country, and grisly pictures of corpses that had been found in the lime pits on the grounds of a New Jersey Mafia capo. McMahon would play the tapes and show the photographs, and he would tell Gerry that these were the kind of person he was protecting, that he was not that type of person, and that he could put that kind of life behind him. The arguments were apt, but the strategy was misdirected — for a time the pictures almost persuaded Gerry and his family that he would be insane to testify.

But Gerry also recalled his revulsion to leg-irons and southern jails, and he came to trust McMahon — as it turned out, perhaps too much. For during the agents' third visit, Zelmanowitz suddenly announced that he would do it, would testify behind a screen as "Mr. X." He didn't ask for protection or a deal, but McMahon pronounced, as expected, the magic words: that he would "bring his cooperation to the attention of the United States attorney." McMahon did not add a second element that most criminals would well have understood, but that Gerry didn't fully comprehend — that once he testified before the grand jury he was hooked. DeCarlo and the others would be indicted, but the government couldn't make a case against them at a trial without Gerry's testimony in open court. So if he refused to testify in court and went off to jail on the securities charges he would have accomplished nothing, and DeCarlo might suspect that he had talked and have him killed anyway. Thus, once "Mr. X" testified, the pressures were heavy on Gerry to trade his testimony in open court for the government's forgiveness of his past crimes.

But still Gerry and his family vacillated. They shuddered over those pictures of bodies in lime pits and imagined what would happen to all of them if Gerry testified. There were long, anguished family meetings, casting about for ways to spare Gerry the revenge of DeCarlo and also the pain of imprisonment. Then the prosecutors and FBI men began to discuss a possible way out; the Justice Department was developing a program to relocate witnesses far from the communities where they testified, someplace where they could live anonymously, so that the Mafia could never find them.

Until recent years, law enforcement had little use for a program to protect witnesses who testified against the Mafia, because few ever did. Whether it was *"omertà,"* the underworld's blood code of silence, or the fear that the racketeers generated, prosecutors rarely managed to get testimony from witnesses who really knew about the organized crime syndicate — that is, people who had been on the inside. Then in 1963 the silence was broken by the sensational Congressional testimony of the former Mafia hit man, Joseph Valachi. So devastating was Valachi's testimony — and the fact that he dared to give it — that the Justice Department kept him under round-the-clock protection by United States marshals until his death of a heart attack in 1971. Even though Valachi was in prison and had free room and board, the extra cost of his protection was calculated at hundreds of thousands of dollars, and law enforcement officials began to consider ways to protect witnesses without physically guarding them for every minute of the rest of their lives.

The need for a cheaper, simpler system of protection became more pressing after 1961 when Robert Kennedy became attorney general and began to mount the first really effective Justice Department effort against organized crime. The government began to experiment with ways to do this. Nothing was said publicly about these new techniques, until one day in 1963 when Kennedy was testifying before a Senate committee on organized crime and the illicit traffic in narcotics. Kennedy stressed the need to convince witnesses that if they came forward to testify they would be protected. Senator Edmund Muskie wondered how long the government could afford to protect them if they were not in prison like Valachi.

SENATOR MUSKIE: "How long can you give them protection unless you convict them of a crime that would insure a long sentence?"

ATTORNEY GENERAL KENNEDY: "How long can you give an individual protection who comes in and testifies?"

SENATOR MUSKIE: "Yes."

ATTORNEY GENERAL KENNEDY: "We have taken steps, Senator, to even move people out of the country.

"We have provided them positions and work in areas where nobody will really have any contact with them. We have arranged to move their families and have their names changed.

"I think that we have procedures now where, if an important individual comes forward and is willing to testify, that we can give him that kind of protection."

But Bobby Kennedy's Justice Department was busy with many things, and those procedures were employed only on an ad hoc basis, scrambling to deal with each situation as it arose. No regular procedures were worked out, no guidelines were written down, and the possibilities of witness protection spread throughout law enforcement agencies only by word of mouth.

Thus when United States attorneys Satz and Horowitz began to talk with Gerald Zelmanowitz about relocation in the spring of 1969, they began, as Bobby Kennedy had, with the possibility of moving the family to Europe. This suited Gerry perfectly. He was comfortable in Europe, and he had business connections there. Those connections were linked to the stock trading account in the New York brokerage firm of Hayden Stone that had been frozen by the IRS in 1968. Gerry had filed a suit charging that the IRS's $104,000 lien on that account was illegal, and demanding the release of the funds. After his arrest, the $104,000 became the keystone of his negotiations with the prosecutors; if the government would release the $104,000 and let him take his family to Paris, he would testify and would make no further claims upon the government for protection. Gerry's obsession with the $104,000 led some of the prosecutors to suspect that there was much more to it than that, that the money really belonged to Swiss banking interests, which had in response frozen much larger sums of Mafia money in accounts there. Thus the belief grew in Washington that Zelmanowitz still had a huge nest egg of Mafia cash nestled in some Swiss account — a feeling that was to shadow his life for many years.

For the present, though, Satz and Horowitz felt that Gerry's proposal was eminently reasonable, and they promised to do all they could to get Washington to release the $104,000. Meanwhile, the Newark prosecutors requested and received from Washington funds to send

Gerry, Lillian, and her parents and daughter Cynthia to Europe. Airline tickets to Paris were purchased, and Gerry began to brace himself for the ordeal of testimony.

What nobody in Newark realized then was the extent to which the Nixon administration was moving to establish a formal witness protection program. Once Attorney General John Mitchell's top aides put their minds to it, they quickly concluded that, politically, a get-tough-with-criminals administration could hardly begin by spending government funds to send former mobsters and their families to Europe. Relocating witnesses overseas was not to be part of the plan. It was instead strictly an alias program, a plan to give witnesses and their families new identities and to infiltrate them back into American society as obscure figures in communities far from the scenes of their crimes or testimonies.

Meanwhile, Gerald Zelmanowitz had passed the point of no return in Newark. In late June of 1969 he went to the United States attorney's office for a meeting with Satz and Horowitz. They reviewed their plans to relocate Gerry's family in Europe, and they pledged to do all they could to have the $104,000 released to him. Gerry was very impressed with the office, with its picture of President Nixon, Satz's appointment on the wall signed by President Kennedy, and all the other trappings of power. The United States attorney for the State of New Jersey was the highest official he had ever met, and to Gerry, Satz was the government. It was a situation that was to be repeated all too often after the alias program got formally under way, and it was to be the root of many of the problems to come. Politically naïve witnesses would accept commitments from and make agreements with Justice Department officials who seemed to represent a monolithic government. Due to the fragmented federal bureaucracy, such officials sometimes failed to make good on their promises. And occasionally they lost interest in a witness after obtaining his testimony and a conviction.

But to Gerry, David Satz was Uncle Sam, and the United States government was pledging to throw all of its protective might around Gerald Zelmanowitz and his family. He told them that he would do it — he would testify in open court.

Even after that, he refused to accept protection from the marshals.

Gerry wanted to be free to move about and operate, and he believed that he would be safe so long as he stayed publicly away from everyone associated with the prosecution. That assumption began to dissolve after DeCarlo, Cecere, Polverino, and Landusco were indicted in August. Gerry heard through the grapevine that DeCarlo had begun to mutter that perhaps "the Jew is a squealer." Horowitz tried to throw the defendants off the track by misleading their lawyers into believing that the government had no eyewitness, but he had to suspect that the defense lawyers were lying, too, when they seemed to believe it.

Cecere's lawyer posed a special problem, one that embarrassed the prosecutors, because he was a member of their legal brotherhood, and terrified Zelmanowitz for the same reason. His name was Michael Querques, and he was known around the Newark courthouse as a lawyer who turned up time after time representing men who were accused of offenses linked with organized crime. It is a part of the Anglo-American system of adversary justice and the legal profession's code of professional ethics that any defendant is entitled to an attorney, no matter how odious a character the defendant might be. Thus, a lawyer can receive the highest respect of his legal peers, even if he represents the blackest kind of scoundrel — once. That admiration begins to fade quickly when a lawyer turns up repeatedly in the cause of clients who appear to be systematically breaking the law. Then advocacy can cross the line into collusion, and thus the lawyer's code of ethics does not permit him to advise his clients before and during a conspiracy — only after. In Querques's case, the situation was made more delicate because he had been an assistant United States attorney in Newark for a time during the Eisenhower administration, and this gave him unusual contacts and entrée into the courthouse. One day Gerry was in the United States attorney's complex of offices when he suddenly looked up and saw Querques standing on the far side of the large room, chatting with a secretary. Gerry's mind reeled with fright. He had no doubts that if Querques saw him, he would tell his client — and that Cecere would know that Gerry's presence there could only mean that he had become a witness for the prosecution. Gerry quickly ducked into Horowitz's inner office, and Querques continued to chat, apparently having seen nothing. But Gerry could never be absolutely sure.

As the trial date approached, the defendants began to pressure Zelmanowitz to attend late night meetings in Querques's office, which was over an ice cream and pastry shop in West Orange. Zelmanowitz later told the court about his reaction: "There were five people involved in this. The fifth person is dead. I am the fourth person involved, and the other three are all friends. . . . Why in God's name do they want me up at the office late at night?"

The answer was obvious enough to Gerry, and he finally accepted the marshals' protection. At first they moved quietly into his home and remained out of sight, and Gerry stayed in touch with Querques but made excuses for not attending the nighttime meetings in his office. As Christmas and the January trial date approached, a team of marshals took Lillian and Cynthia on an extended tour of southern motels, and Gerry moved into a tightly guarded room in the courthouse. From then on, he would be under constant guard, until he emerged from the alias program as Paul Maris.

3...Witness

By January 6, 1970, the day he was to take the stand, Gerry had decided he was crazy to do this. As he sat in a small room behind the courtroom in the United States courthouse in Newark, guarded by four heavily armed marshals, he concluded that the government obviously thought it was dangerous as hell, because they were treating the people who came to Judge Thomas Shaw's courtroom as if they were hostile natives in an occupied land. Guards were everywhere, along the corridors, at every entrance, scanning the courtroom. All spectators had to walk through metal detectors on the way into the courtroom.

Special care was used in checking four surly men with scowling Sicilian features. They were the defendants — most notably Angelo DeCarlo, sixty-seven years old and white-haired but still erect, burly, mean-eyed; and Daniel Cecere, fifty years old, short and red-haired, with the lizardlike paleness of a nightclub operator, which he was. Markedly less defiant in demeanor were Peter Landusco, who had long been known as "Pete the Bull," but who at the age of sixty-four looked the part of a pudgy, balding grandfather; and Joseph Polverino, a greasily handsome muscleman called "Indian Joe," who resembled a piano mover with a mean streak. As it turned out, both Landusco and Polverino were to suffer timely illnesses in the following days. First, Polverino had to be hospitalized with a kidney ailment. Then Landusco's attorney complained that the disclosures of the case had caused his client "such anxiety and despair, I cannot effectively communicate with him." When the judge ordered psychiatric and medical tests to check this out, they revealed that Landusco had a diabetic condition that required immediate treatment. So both men were severed from the case and were never brought to trial.

The incident that caused Landusco such crippling anxiety took place just a few hours before Gerry was scheduled to testify — and if it upset the defendants, it terrified Zelmanowitz. It was the release by Judge Shaw of 1,200 pages of transcripts of what immediately became nationally famous as the "DeCarlo Tapes."

Indeed, the government had, as DeCarlo suspected, bugged The Barn. For four years, from 1961 to 1965, FBI agents had listened to conversations in DeCarlo's headquarters and had kept transcripts of what was said. DeCarlo's lawyer had suspected this, and had demanded that the Justice Department turn them over. The eavesdropping had been done without a warrant and was wholly illegal, and the defense wanted to make certain that nothing thus overheard was used against the defendants at the trial. DeCarlo's lawyer made it clear to Judge Shaw that he didn't want the conversations made public, but the judge — who wasn't called "Old Iron Fist" around the courthouse for nothing — stunned everybody by granting the defense the access to the transcripts it had demanded, and then by giving the same right to anyone else who wanted to see them.

There was a wild scramble by reporters to publish excerpts from the conversations, and reputations collapsed throughout New Jersey as the racketeers were quoted as swapping favors with police chiefs, prosecutors, judges, and political chieftains. On the tapes DeCarlo spoke warmly of Frank Sinatra as a friend and potential partner in a hotel-casino venture. So fondly were Newark Mayor Hugh Addonizio and Hudson County political boss John J. Kenny mentioned that both were ruined politically, but another promising public official, Representative Peter Rodino, was able to explain the approving things said about him and kept his career on the track.

But the part that stunned Zelmanowitz was the chilling proof of the murderous brutality of the men he was about to send to prison. In his candid conversations, DeCarlo, especially, made no attempt to conceal his true nature as a thug.

At one point, Harold "Kayo" Konigsberg, a sadistic mob enforcer, asked: "Will you tell me why everybody loves you so?"

"I'm a hoodlum," DeCarlo replied. "I don't want to be a legitimate guy. All these other racket guys who get a few bucks want to become legitimate."

Then there was the time when Anthony "Tony Boy" Boiardo reminisced, "How about the time we hit the little Jew?"

"As little as they are, they struggle," DeCarlo observed.

"The Boot hit him with a hammer," Tony Boy continued, referring to his father, Richie "The Boot" Boiardo. "The guy goes down and he

comes up. So I got a crowbar this big. . . . Eight shots in the head."
Tony Boy told how the little Jew spat and cursed at him to the end, and
that reminded one of them of the time when DeCarlo had told a victim,
"Let me hit you clean."

"That's right," DeCarlo recalled, nostalgically. "So the guy went for
it . . . we took the guy out in the woods, and I said, 'Now listen. . . .
You gotta go. Why not let me hit you right in the heart, and you
won't feel a thing?' He said, 'I'm innocent . . . but if you've gotta do
it . . .' So I hit him in the heart, and it went right through him."

Waiting to take the stand, Gerry could suddenly see himself in that
spot. "I'm going to be one of those things in the paper," he thought.
" 'Jewish Stockbroker Found Dead on Route 22 with Knife in
Throat.' " As he recalled it later: "I was soaking wet. My mouth tasted
awful. My head was hurting. I was shaking. My knees were just actually made of jelly. I was going to testify against a Mafia capo. What
else could I possibly do to be more suicidal to myself?"

But already it was too late to turn back. He could hear the voice of
United States Attorney Frederick Lacey making his opening speech to
the jury. The words were indistinct, but he knew they were asserting
that the government could prove its case because it had an eyewitness.
He could almost hear the gasps in the audience and see the fury at the
defense table as Lacey disclosed that the government's key witness
would be Gerald Zelmanowitz, "a man who has been moving in
excess of one million dollars in stocks and forged securities," a criminal but, "irrespective of that, he tells the truth."

And then suddenly the four marshals were escorting him into the
courtroom: "I go in before I know it. Everything is happening very
quickly. The Bible is stuck at me. My hand goes on it. My hand goes
up. Tell the truth. Oh yes, yes. In the witness chair I just can't speak. I
open my mouth for the first question and a croak comes out. I'm
trying not to look at anybody. They're asking me questions, and the
croaky squeaky voice is trying to answer. And then the thing is going
on in the background. Lawyers are talking, Judge is saying something,
uproar in the court, the defendants are all shuffling and people are
saying — my God, it's him."

Then there was an odd, awkward pause. It gave Gerry a few moments to settle down and realize what was happening. The defendant's

lawyers had objected that a pile of books and a lectern lamp in front of Judge Shaw obstructed their view of the witness. So there was time, as the bailiff prepared a better view for the defendants to glare their hatred across the courtroom, for Gerry to realize fully that he could never come back to his familiar world and his old friends after that day.

He later remembered managing a small feeling of relief: "At least I've got the government on my side. They're going to take care of me and help me get started again. I'm not going to be alone." But as he ran the events of recent weeks through his mind, Gerry thought ruefully that although he would not be alone, he would also not be in Paris.

In August, shortly after the indictment, the Nixon administration replaced Satz and Horowitz with Frederick Lacey as the new United States attorney, and Herbert J. Stern as his chief deputy. Lacey had been forced down the Nixon administration's throat by New Jersey's Republican Senator, Clifford Case. Case was something of an oddity in New Jersey politics, an office-holder with no underworld ties. He made it clear that he had picked Lacey as a man who would go in and root out some of the corruption that had flourished as public officials across New Jersey — most of them Democrats — had made their peace with powerful Mafia racketeers, while the Kennedy-Johnson Justice Department proved generally impotent to interfere. John Mitchell wasn't so sure that he wanted to unleash a loose cannon in the corridors of New Jersey officialdom, but Senator Case declared that he would block anybody else, and seven months into President Nixon's term it got so embarrassing that the administration accepted Lacey. He and Stern were an odd couple — Lacey the affable Irish bear, and Stern the fingernail-biting Jewish dynamo — but it immediately became plain that they intended to make waves.

With the trial date approaching in the DeCarlo case, Lacey had gone to Washington to make arrangements to carry out the deal with Gerry. He went to Will Wilson, the assistant attorney general in charge of the Criminal Division, who turned him down flat. The IRS had refused to release the $104,000, Wilson said, and the Justice Department had no power to make them do so. Lacey was also turned down on the relocation in Paris, even though the airline tickets had already been bought with Justice Department money. The reasons for this were vague, but Lacey knew that it would increase the feeling of betrayal on Gerry's part, because he believed that Washington was waffling on its promises to him out of distrust. Gerry sensed that the top officials in Washington thought he still had Mafia money stashed away in Switzerland, and that if he were permitted to leave the country he wouldn't come back to testify in future trials. For whatever reasons, Lacey had returned empty-handed from his visit with Will Wilson. (Wilson was soon to resign, amid disclosures that he had been accepting loans from a Texas banker who was involved in a stock manipulation scandal.) But Lacey was convinced that Zelmanowitz was an honest witness, and he was determined to arrange some way that the government could still obtain his testimony. "I liked him," Lacey said later, sitting in the chambers he now occupies as a United States district judge. "He's one of the brightest men I've ever met, and I felt that given an opportunity to go honest that he'd be the kind of fellow that if I had a securities operation I would want working for me." Lacey and Stern were quickly to become famous for their perseverance and success in prosecuting top members of the mob in New Jersey, and they began by persuading Gerry that he should testify, after all.

The keystone of their argument was that the Nixon administration had, as the rumors suggested, officially created a witness security program. Nothing had been said publicly about it, but when Lacey had gone through his orientation program in Washington with other new United States attorneys, they had been instructed how to use the new program. It was a carefully worked-out system, he told Gerry, for changing the identities of witnesses and relocating them in places where they would be safe. The full power of the government would be used to protect Gerry and assure him a new life.

Neither Lacey nor Zelmanowitz realized it at the time, but that juncture in their long negotiations represented a sensitive legal point, one that was increasingly to bedevil the alias program as the offering of new identities became a frequent element of plea bargaining in important federal cases. Gerry had hesitated, as criminal suspects often do, to take the irrevocable step of pleading guilty and testifying for the prosecution. At that point, he could still have chosen to stand trial on the securities cases and to leave the government stranded without a witness against the DeCarlo mob. If the final nudge that was to push him onto the witness stand was to be the offer of a new life, that offer raised an important legal issue concerning the defendants.

As a general rule of law, prosecutors are not permitted to offer inducements during the course of plea bargaining that could entice a suspect-turned-witness to slant his testimony against the defendants in order to gain better treatment for himself. For that reason, prosecutors are never supposed to offer guarantees of leniency when they bargain for guilty pleas involving future testimony. In practice, they often wink at this limitation by promising to "bring the witness's valuable cooperation to the attention of the sentencing judge" — who almost always plays the game by deciding to let the witness off easy. But offers of money are clearly over the line, and this has resulted in a Justice Department rule that in routine cases no witnesses are supposed to be paid more than the witness fee set by Congress: currently, $20 per day of testimony.

This raised a problem when the Justice Department began to relocate witnesses and support them and their families until the witnesses could complete their testimony and get their new lives in order: families couldn't live on $20 per day, but how much more could the government properly pay witnesses? After the Zelmanowitz experience, Deputy Attorney General Richard Kleindienst was to make a stab at resolving the problem by issuing an order limiting "subsistence" payments to $36 per day or $1,000 per month, on the theory that this would reduce the Justice Department's exposure to charges of using "bought" evidence. Later the government was to encounter chronic difficulties in adhering to Kleindienst's limits. Inflation and large families rendered the $36-per-day limit necessarily inoperative in many situations, and the Justice Department switched to a complicated system of stair-step payments geared to the United States Labor Department's regional cost-of-living figures and the size of the families involved. But that was only the start. The practice of hustling families out of their communities resulted in hardship sales of homes, cars, and furnishings, plus hurried purchases of similar items later at inflated prices. The government has frequently had to pick up the tab for this, sometimes paying more than $35,000 to a single witness.

Whether payments of this nature result in bought testimony is thorny enough, but it does not approach the complexity of the questions raised by the government's promises of new lives and good names. As transparent as some of the Justice Department's aliases have proved to be, when witnesses agree to testify most of them believe that they will receive in return a chance at a new life with a spotless background. Since many of the witnesses have criminal records and employment histories that would make a pirate blush, the promises of the alias program are an incalculable encouragement in persuading them to testify.

The courts have not yet come to grips with whether these offers of subsistence and new identities go too far, partly because the targets of their testimony frequently either don't know about the alias program or don't fully appreciate what it entails. One such case was to reach the Supreme Court in 1976, but it only served to illustrate how cloudy the plea bargaining problems are. It involved the forty-five-year jail sentence imposed on Ronald Calvert, a St. Louis man who was convicted of a mail fraud scheme that involved the murder of an inventor of a rotary automobile engine. The inventor had been insured for $2 million by Calvert and other plotters, three of whom later joined the witness protection program and testified against Calvert. It was not until after the trial that Calvert's attorney came to appreciate some of the issues raised by the subsistence payments to these witnesses, who had testified that no improper inducements had been offered for their testimony. One of the witnesses was Charles Hintz, who had a long history of seamy activities, including a conviction for transporting a female across a state line for immoral purposes and an arrest for child molestation. He has since been given a new identity by the government and has presumably been living in some community where his unsavory record is unknown. Calvert's lawyer never did question the propriety of the prosecution's offering Hintz a clean past in connection with his testimony, but the attorney did ask the Supreme Court to rule that the subsistence payments were improper inducements. Probably because this question hadn't been raised in the lower courts, on February 23, 1976, the Supreme Court declined to review the appeal — thus leaving for another time the decision as to whether the promises of the alias program are fair to victims of the resulting testimony.

In any event, the allure of a new life proved compelling to Gerald

39

Zelmanowitz. But he was determined not to go without his family. There were anguished, tearful family sessions, as Lillian, Cynthia, and Joe and Evelyn Ringel struggled toward a decision to abandon their relatives, friends and past lives and join Gerry in a new life, under a new identity. It was an especially wrenching experience for Lillian, who had always sought security in close family ties and deep community roots. Her own children had been delivered by the same doctor who had delivered her, and she had just assumed that they would all be there, in New Jersey, for him to deliver Shelley's and Cynthia's babies too. But in the end, Gerry's position made the answer inevitable. They would go together as a family. In November of 1969, he informed Lacey and Stern that he would testify. He would join the program.

Civics books teach that under the separation-of-powers structure of the Constitution, Congress creates new programs and the executive branch staffs them and carries them out. In practice, it's often not quite like that. An example: the Justice Department's witness relocation program.

The program had its origins in the experience and necessities of the Executive Branch. After Valachi, *omertà* began to crumble, and in the mid-1960s, law enforcement officials in the Justice Department, the IRS, and the Treasury Department helped a handful of witnesses to relocate under new names. The concept of a formal program began to take shape in the fading months of the Johnson administration, when the Justice Department began to experiment with what were called Strike Forces to fight organized crime. The technique was to pick an area that was rotten with crime and corruption and set up a separate anti-Mafia organization, bringing together the resources of the Justice Department, IRS, Treasury, Customs, and sometimes local police (but at first, not the FBI — J. Edgar Hoover was not a team player), with the single mission of penetrating and prosecuting the organized crime syndicate. As soon as the first Strike Force began to function in Buffalo in 1967, it became obvious that there would have to be heavy use of informers and that some coherent system would be needed to protect them after they testified.

The Justice Department virtually broke the mold with the first informant it selected for a Strike Force change of identity. He was Pasquale Calabrese, a brawling high-living young stud from Buffalo who gloried in pretty women, fast horses, and green money. It was an expensive style of life, which Calabrese had no talent to support, except as a stickup man. He did well with discount stores, dairies, and banks, but even Paddy Calabrese got in trouble when he held up the treasurer's office in Buffalo's city hall. He was arrested, tried, and convicted, and then from his cell he began to drop hints to the Buffalo underworld that they'd better do the "right thing" — that is, finance his appeal — or he'd talk. According to Calabrese, they countered with a plan to drive him "stir crazy" by forcing his pregnant wife, Rochelle, to pose naked in bed with one of his best friends. That did it. Calabrese, who wasn't noticeably afraid of anyone in Buffalo anyway, signed up to have his identity changed and then helped convict about a dozen local Mafia figures, including the ranking active Buffalo mafioso, Frederico Randaccio.

From there, Calabrese proceeded to give the first demonstration of why the type of person who is willing to testify against the Mafia is frequently not the best candidate to spend the rest of his life in quiet anonymity. He lasted three weeks in the job the Justice Department got him, as a $100-per-week repairman in an Ann Arbor, Michigan, ball-bearing factory. Since then he has had at least five different aliases, one as a swashbuckling private detective in Reno, Nevada, another as an FBI informer on gambling and prostitution activities along the Alaska pipeline, and he eventually involved the witness protection program in its first Supreme Court case — a matter to be discussed later.

The seeds of this interesting new governmental experiment had been planted, as so often happens, in the work of a presidential commission. As the problem of crime had become a growing political irritant, President Lyndon Johnson had created the President's Commission on Law Enforcement and Administration of Justice. He picked his former attorney general, Nicholas deB. Katzenbach, to run it, and Katzenbach brought in some of the young lawyers who had worked for Bobby Kennedy in his Mafia-fighting heyday. One of these was Henry Ruth, Jr., later to be Watergate Special Prosecutor, but then a specialist in combatting organized crime. The commission's final report on organized crime, written under Ruth's supervision and issued early in 1967, contained a cloudy recommendation that was later to be cited as the origin of the alias program.

It urged the federal government to establish residential facilities for the protection of witnesses (these quickly came to be known as "safe houses"), where they could be guarded for as long as they needed protection. Then the report added: "The Federal Government should establish regular procedures to help Federal and local witnesses who fear organized crime reprisal, to find jobs and places to live in other parts of the country, and to preserve their anonymity from organized crime groups." Ruth said later he had no thought of a program to create aliases — that when he approved the word *anonymity*, he thought it meant only that witnesses would be provided quarters in innocuous safe houses, where they could come and go without being spotted as government stool pigeons. But the staff attorney who actually wrote that part of the crime commission's report, G. Robert Blakey, insisted later than everybody involved understood that the commission had called for the creation of a program to give witnesses false identities.

Blakey, a former Notre Dame law professor who had also been one of the Hotspurs of the Organized Crime and Racketeering Section under Robert Kennedy, had a smoldering resentment over the failure of the nation's lawmakers to arm police and prosecutors with effective laws to fight crime, and he stuck around Washington after the crime commission disbanded to help write the commission's recommendations into law. Henry Ruth went off to New York to do law enforcement work in the field.

Thus the prestigious presidential crime commission came to be cited as the source of the idea to create a false identity program, although the commission had never confronted any of the hard questions that were certain to be raised by such a proposal. If the members of the commission did realize that they were giving their stamp of approval to the creation of an alias program, they apparently assumed that the hard questions would be publicly raised, debated, and resolved at some point before the suggestion became law. But in fact this never happened. At each succeeding step along the way, those who knew what was to be done and wanted to see it accomplished muddied up the proposal so that its essence would never become clear, and thus Congress would establish it without asking the probing questions that might have kept it from becoming a reality.

Nothing happened officially until January of 1969. Then Senator John McClellan of Arkansas introduced the bill that was to carry forward the law-and-order philosophy of the Nixon administration and its conservative southern allies. The bill was a massive piece of legislation called "The Organized Crime Control Act," and it had been drafted by a new aide on Senator McClellan's staff, the ubiquitous G. Robert Blakey. The bill had nine major chapters, including controversial provisions to strengthen the inquisitorial powers of grand juries, increase the penalties for habitual offenders, and reduce witnesses' protection against self-incrimination.

Nobody paid much attention to a chapter entitled "Title V: Protected Facilities for Housing Government Witnesses." All it did was to authorize expenditures of funds to build or rent "safe houses" where witnesses could be protected by United States marshals until it was safe for them to leave. Attorney General John Mitchell barely mentioned it when he gave his official blessing to the bill in testimony before Senator McClellan's subcommittee on Criminal Laws and Procedures in March of 1969. Nobody noticed when, a few weeks later, Mitchell sent McClellan a letter requesting that the "protected facilities" chapter be changed to permit the Justice Department also to spend funds "for the care and protection of such witnesses, to be used in whatever manner is deemed most useful under the special circumstances of each case." At the Justice Department's suggestion, this was done by simply inserting in the proposed law, after the clause that granted the attorney general the authority to construct protected housing facilities, the power to spend additional money "to otherwise provide for the health, safety and welfare of witnesses. . . ."

Thus Congress was not put on notice that the Justice Department intended to change any identities. The Organized Crime Control Bill came before the Senate for debate in January, while the DeCarlo trial was still going on but after Gerald Zelmanowitz had left the stand and had been whisked to Washington to begin learning his new identity. Yet not a word was mentioned in the debate about new identities. Senator McClellan simply remarked that the Justice Department said it had lost twenty-five witnesses to mob violence between 1961 and 1965, and that Title V would give the attorney general "broad powers" to provide "witness facilities" to protect them. The senators then brushed over the seemingly innocuous Title V and debated the more controversial chapters. On January 23, the Senate approved the Organized Crime Control Bill, 73 to 1 (Senator Lee Metcalf voted "no," without having said a word during the debate), and the alias program had moved halfway toward official approval. Five days later, the jury in Newark was to convict Gyp DeCarlo and Red Cecere.

The following May, Mitchell gave an equally sphinxlike performance in his testimony in the House of Representatives. He said only that Title V would give his department the authority "to provide housing and physical protection for witnesses and their families," and he submitted a written statement containing the guarded remark that the President's Crime Commission had suggested that witnesses be assisted in finding jobs and places to live in other areas of the country if necessary to achieve anonymity.

Congress never caught on. The Organized Crime Control Act became law on October 15, 1970, and the Justice Department took Title V as formal authorization to establish the alias program.

There were, to be sure, some technical problems that remained. No other nation in history, so far as is known, had ever found it necessary to create a government bureau to change the identities of citizens in order to induce them to testify against criminals. If word got out that the Justice Department was establishing such a program, then some potentially embarrassing questions might have been asked, and highly publicized. In theory, such questions are supposed to be raised by Congress at the eleventh hour, if not before, when funds are appropriated to operate the programs that Congress had previously authorized. But in practice, so many programs have been authorized that the members of the appropriations committees cannot look closely at them all — and the early appropriations for the alias program were granted on the basis of requests (which appeared in fine print) for additional witness fees that nobody on Capitol Hill questioned. In the first year of the program, the Justice Department asked for and got increased appropriations for witness protection merely because it said "costs were rising. . . ." The next year, Congress gave more money without being offered a reason. The next, more money yet was appropriated for what the fine print described as "security, documentation, transportation, relocation." It was not until March 12, 1974, that the fine print told Congress that "the Marshals Service is furnishing documentation for persons whose names are changed to protect them from organized crime. . . ." That was almost a year after the story of the alias program burst upon the front pages of the newspapers in the form of the adventures of a former witness named Gerald Zelmanowitz.

Meanwhile, after Congress passed the massive 1970 Omnibus Organized Crime Control Act, officials in the Justice Department got busy concocting the inevitable acronym as a name for the program, and the result was a gem of bureaucratic ingenuity: Project WISPER (Witness Intelligence Security Protection Enforcement and Regulation). But somehow WISPER didn't catch on, and neither did another name that was tried for a while, "Operation Silencer." And so the alias program became an oddity in the government, a program without an official name. Since it had not been approved as such by Congress or created by a published executive order, there was never an occasion to give the program a name that all officialdom would recognize as official — so government documents and usage ever since have variously referred to it as the Witness Security Program, the Witness Relocation Program, or the Witness Protection Program.

Yet no reference to changes of identity had been made during the congressional debates, and if anyone on Capitol Hill knew what was going to be done, he felt it prudent to keep it to himself. Thus there was never any debate on the legal and moral problems that might arise as the government undertook to wash away the past lives of hundreds of people — many of them hoodlums — and infiltrate them back into society under false names.

Thirty years before, it would have been inconceivable that the Justice Department could have created an $11-million-per-year program without telling Congress or the public its central purpose. Yet in many ways, the alias program represented a culmination of abuses within the executive branch that only reached their apex in the Nixon administration: excessive secrecy, deception, contempt for Congress, institutionalized lying, and bureaucratic arrogance.

It was not that the idea of an alias program was all bad, or even that it was necessarily a poor idea, on balance. It was rather that the witness protection program had become the ultimate federal program, the product of a number of governmental bad habits that had been developing for decades and that were not to be widely questioned until the anti-Washington backlash of the mid-1970s — habits that co-alesced, in the alias program, into an exotic example of government on a flyer.

What happened first was that a need had been perceived by the executive branch — the problem of dealing with organized crime — and it had been decided by the Kennedy administration that only a national effort by the federal government could do the job. Thus when the problem of witness protection surfaced, it was seen as a federal concern to be dealt with by the bureaucracy of the executive branch.

Characteristically, an innovative decision by a federal court nudged the process along. It came in 1969 from the United States Court of Appeals for the Fifth Circuit in New Orleans, a court that was well respected for its forward-reaching decisions dealing with the civil rights ferment of the 1960s. The case at issue involved Jessee Swanner, a moonshiner from the scrubby country along the Tennessee-Alabama border that is famous for its strong liquor and tough hillbillies. Swanner had agreed to testify against the kingpin of the area's makers of illegal corn whiskey, Ed McGlocklin — a man who was considered by some who knew him best to be the meanest man in Giles County, Tennessee.

Jessee Swanner moved to nearby Montgomery, Alabama, but soon he heard rumors that McGlocklin suspected that he was to be the government's prize witness in McGlocklin's upcoming trial. McGlocklin was quoted as saying that if he could find out where Swanner was, Swanner would never live to testify; Swanner was worried and told the government, which did nothing. The outcome was that, three days before Swanner's scheduled testimony, his house in Montgomery was dynamited and he and various members of his family were hurt. There was no evidence that McGlocklin was responsible — other than his reputation for violence — but the court of appeals held that the government had not done enough to protect Swanner and must pay him damages. So long as it was "more probable than not" that Swanner's home had been bombed because he was a Justice Department witness, the government was held to be liable because it had not taken steps to protect him.

Thus it was easy for officials in the Justice Department to conclude that what was required was a new Justice Department program. That this would create more jobs in the Justice Department and more authority and promotions for those already there was a matter that followed naturally. One of the unfortunate tendencies of bureaucratic government was quickly to assert itself; the provisions of the Organized Crime Control Bill that required an expansion of personnel were to be quickly implemented, while those that demanded more thought and ingenuity on the part of the people already there were to rest in comparative neglect. The Department of Justice was quickly to implement, in its fashion, Title V's mandate to provide "protected facilities." The Marshals' Service rapidly grew a new appendage, the Office of Witness Security, which eventually employed almost two hundred people to guard the witnesses and turn out the paperwork, both false and genuine, required by the alias program.

But another title of the Organized Crime Control Act, which had a far greater potentiality to affect organized crime, was virtually ignored. This chapter gave the government's crime fighters the legal authority to use powerful civil remedies that had been developed in the field of antitrust law, such as divestiture of assets, compelled production of records, and injunctive relief. But these were legal tools that were unfamiliar to most of the criminal lawyers who were assigned to fight the crime syndicate, and so the legal innovations rested in the United States Code virtually unused in the years following the enactment of the Organized Crime Control Law — while it gradually became apparent that no matter how vigorously the Justice Department pressed its orthodox prosecutions of organized crime figures, other men always took the places of any imprisoned leaders and the criminal rackets flourished.

But initially the prospect of obtaining more convictions through an alias program seemed a logical way to undermine the Mafia. If any thought was given to allowing local police units to provide the protection, or of requiring each witness to arrange for his or her own anonymity, the idea was rejected. It was also assumed that Congress lacked the expertise to hammer out the details of such a scheme, and that vague concerns of "security" made it desirable to handle the whole matter as secretly as possible. Well-meaning men in the government merely followed the assumptions of decades of governmental action: that the best way to deal with a new problem was quietly to create a new federal program.

The result was that Title V became law without a number of questions having been faced in Congress or the executive branch: did the Justice Department have the wit or resources to issue up to five hundred aliases per year — an average of almost two per working day — that would stand up? Was it fair to law-abiding citizens for the government to be issuing hundreds of hoodlums good names? Should the government admit that the only way it can protect its citizens is by changing their identities? Should it officially adopt a program dedicated solely to telling lies? Is the Mafia good enough at revenge to justify all this?

Meanwhile, Gerald Zelmanowitz was on the witness stand in New Jersey, contending with the problem of testifying in court. Herb Stern was conducting the government's direct examination, and he started slowly, trying to give Gerry a chance to get over some of his fear. At first there were repeated objections from the defense that he wasn't speaking loudly enough, but once he got past the part of pointing out the four defendants and identifying them as the men he was there to accuse, Gerry's natural assertiveness began to take hold. His voice came back and he told the same story he had whispered to the grand jury as "Mr. X."

For the first time publicly, he told of the last days of Louis Saperstein: the crushing vigorish, the brutal beating, the threats of death. The impact was devastating, but it was Gerry's performance under cross-examination that caused the *New York Times*'s reporter at the trial, Edith Evans Asbury, to pronounce Zelmanowitz the most brilliant witness she had ever seen.

Cecere's lawyer, Michael Querques, played right into Gerry's hands. Querques set out to destroy Zelmanowitz on cross-examination by demonstrating that he was such a rascal that nothing he said could be believed. The flaw in that approach was that the defendants could not get away with denying that they had been in a deal with Zelmanowitz and Saperstein, because too many records and eyewitnesses could bear witness that they had. Their defense had to be that the partnership had existed, but that it never took the felonious turn that the prosecution alleged. Thus, to the extent that Querques painted Zelmanowitz as a man who had spent his life committing crimes and hanging around with vicious thugs, he tended to reinforce the plausibility of the government's charge that exactly that had happened in this case.

Gerry quickly perceived this, and, as Querques bored in with incriminating questions, the witness replied with even more incriminating answers.

Was it true that Mr. Zelmanowitz hadn't filed an income tax return for years?

Of course it was true — the witness had never held a legitimate job and couldn't afford to say where he got his money: "I didn't file because I stole the money."

Hadn't the witness conned his father-in-law into making the down payment on his sumptuous home?

No need, since the witness had made more than a million dollars in various schemes since 1964.

As a matter of fact, Querques persisted, weren't the witness's home, furnishings, and Cadillac convertibles worth more than $350,000 in all?

"It could be more, Mr. Querques, could be more," Zelmanowitz purred.

What profit had the witness made on his illicit securities transactions?

"Spreading it among the five other thieves with me, we got approximately — oh, I would say about — my end, about sixty-seven, maybe eighty thousand, maybe a hundred thousand — I don't know, exactly."

The courtroom was transfixed. The prosecution, the judge, the spectators, and especially the jury sat in rapt fascination as the defense lawyer dug his client in deeper with every question, and the witness kicked in a little additional dirt with each answer. Querques saw what was happening and begged Judge Shaw to make Zelmanowitz stop volunteering more information about his past misdeeds than the questions required, but the devastating parry-and-thrust went on.

At one point, Querques seemed to have found a chink in Zelmanowitz's story. It happened when the attorney began to review the story of the witness's cross-country spree peddling stolen stocks, which ended with his arrest in Miami. Zelmanowitz conceded that he had been questioned by the FBI about that, but mentioned that he had told only about his own role in the scheme. Querques registered astonishment: the witness had named no other names? No, he had not. Five other men had given him two million dollars' worth of stolen securities to sell and he had not yet disclosed their names to the FBI? No, not yet. They are friends of the witness? Certainly.

Gerry shot a look at the prosecution table, as if to ask Lacey and Stern: "Is this man really going to ask me?" Gerry had held back from disclosing those five names even to the prosecutors. It was his ace in the hole, because one of the names was a well-known organized crime figure from New York whom the Justice Department would give much to convict — one whom Gerry didn't want to implicate without an ironclad commitment of full protection from the government. For the same reason, Gerry knew that Cecere's lawyer didn't really want the jury to hear the name of the notorious gangster Zelmanowitz did business with when he wasn't doing business with Cecere.

But by this time, Querques had piqued the curiosity of the judge and jury, and the lawyer himself seemed almost irresistibly drawn to ask the names that the witness had held back, even as he was telling the prosecutors everything else. The courtroom held its collective breath as the moth flitted closer to the candle. Where were the five men from? Two from New Jersey, one from Boston, two from New York. What were the names of the men from New Jersey? The names were a letdown to the courtroom audience: Joe Green and a "Mr. Silverman." The "man from Boston" was a Mafia chieftain whose name would have rocked a courtroom there, but meant little in New Jersey: Raymond Patriarca.

And the two from New York?

Gerry shot one last glance at Stern and Lacey and then let the big name drop:

"Mr. Fat Tony Salerno."

A murmur of recognition rippled across the courtroom and through the jury, and Herb Stern looked like a man who wanted to turn cartwheels. Anthony "Fat Tony" Salerno was a name that was notorious to tabloid readers in the New York area as a gangster with a vicious reputation, a capo in the Vito Genovese Mafia family who specialized in that most brutal of rackets, loansharking. Stern could be sure that the jurors got the message about the quality of thugs that Zelmanowitz was accustomed to doing business with, and the prosecutor now knew that there would be another sensational Mafia trial in that courthouse, with Gerald Zelmanowitz again in the witness chair. Querques quickly extracted from Zelmanowitz the fifth name — one that rang no bells of recognition, Gil Beckley — and then the lawyer quickly moved on to other questions. The name Salerno was never spoken again at that trial.

After that, it was all over but the legal maneuvering. The defense subpoenaed Lillian and Cynthia, apparently in hopes of prying out of them testimony to discredit Zelmanowitz, or to show that Saperstein had made a series of hysterical, threatening calls to their home in the days leading up to his death. The defense theory was that the bad blood could have been between Zelmanowitz and Saperstein, not the defendants and Saperstein, and that Gerry's testimony was an effort to dump his own guilt on them.

The marshals flew the women up from their motel hideout in North Carolina, and they got the same four-guard protection in the courtroom. But Lillian invoked the marital privilege of silence and refused to answer questions about her husband, and Cynthia knew nothing about the case. "Old Iron Fist" quickly dismissed them both.

The defendants' case was brief but, in a sense, very revealing. There were only two defense witnesses, and their testimony took less than an hour. One witness was a lawyer whose office adjoined Saperstein's. He said that Saperstein had attributed his facial injuries to an auto accident. He also quoted Saperstein as saying that he was depressed because he feared he had cancer — the implication being that he might have contemplated suicide.

This latter testimony took on a subtle significance when the second defense witness turned out to be the nurse at Saperstein's deathbed.

93274

When Saperstein was first brought to the hospital, his condition was diagnosed as acute indigestion. He spent the next eighteen hours in agony, and then, according to the nurse, in his final conscious moments he gasped: "Somebody put some silvery stuff in my food."

"Is this a joke?" the doctor asked.

"I will tell you the whole story in a minute," Saperstein whispered.

But he never did, and the doctor signed a death certificate giving gastric shock as the cause of death.

To the jury, it was puzzling, but to Gerry, it told an ironic truth. He had been there when Saperstein offered to take out insurance and throw himself out of the higher reaches of the New York Hilton. He had heard rumors that Saperstein was, in fact, heavily insured, with his family as beneficiaries. Saperstein was an old and sick man, hopelessly in debt and hounded by the DeCarlo mob. If he wrote a letter blaming them and then died of poisoning, his family would get the proceeds and his tormentors would get the blame.

To Gerry, the clincher was the testimony that Saperstein had suffered for hours in the hospital, while the doctors gave him useless medication for acute gastritis, and then waited until he was about to die before telling them that "somebody" had dusted his tuna fish sandwich with arsenic. It made sense only if that somebody was Saperstein. Gerry recalled that his outrage at Saperstein's apparent murder had been the shock that had pushed him into discussing the possibility of turning state's evidence in the first place. Now he believed what the FBI must have strongly suspected all along — that Saperstein had committed suicide.

Gerry mulled it over darkly for a while. He had been taken, conned, screwed — first by Saperstein, and then by the FBI. Gerry frowned over the memory of his outrage at Saperstein's "murder," and the part it had played in bringing him to the witness chair. Then he thought about Saperstein and his slippery ways, and Gerry chuckled; the joke was not really on him, it was on DeCarlo and Cecere, and Saperstein deserved that last laugh.

The closing arguments brought an odd indication of the defense's disarray. In an effort to justify Cecere's pounding of Saperstein, Querques argued: "If Saperstein stole fifty-five thousand dollars from you

and you found out about it . . . would you give him a punch? . . .
Certainly you would. That's what the law excuses. The law calls that
justifiable." The judge had to instruct the jurors to disregard Querques's strange reading of the law.

It took the jury four hours to convict DeCarlo and Cecere.

Judge Shaw sentenced each to twelve years in prison. Lacey and
Stern were elated. They had no way of knowing that, after only nineteen months of his sentence had been served, President Nixon would
mysteriously commute DeCarlo's sentence and let him out.

It later came to light that Nixon's act of clemency had come about in
an extraordinary way. DeCarlo had petitioned for release, claiming to
have cancer. Under normal procedures, his request would have been
routed through the prosecutor's office in Newark and through the
Criminal Division in Washington for their recommendations, before
being sent to the attorney general. But this time, the petition had been
bucked straight to Attorney General Richard Kleindienst, who approved it and shot it over to White House Special Counsel John W.
Dean, III. Dean quickly got President Nixon's signature on it — one
of only four acts of clemency the President granted all year — and
DeCarlo was out two days before Christmas of 1972. There were
rumors in the Washington gossip mill, which inevitably got into print,
that the clemency had been arranged by the singer whose smiling
picture graced the wall of The Barn, Frank Sinatra, through Sinatra's
good friend, Vice President Spiro Agnew. Some reports also said De-
Carlo had made a handsome contribution to President Nixon's reelec-
tion campaign. There were denials and no-comments all around, but
Special Watergate Prosecutor Archibald Cox was sufficiently intrigued
with the irregularity of events to conduct an investigation.

Nothing came of it, although one final irony came to light. DeCarlo
had been released despite the fact that he had never paid the $20,000
fine that came with his prison sentence. He had been warned that if he
did not pay by October 25, 1973, he would be brought back to prison.
DeCarlo died of cancer on October 20, still owing his debt to the
government.

But all that was bad news for the future. Gerry, having completed
his testimony, was caught up in a whirl of optimistic activity. The

On January 28, 1970, the testimony of Gerald Zelmanowitz led to the conviction of Daniel "Red" Cecere (above) and Angelo De-Carlo (below, right) in Newark Federal Court.

marshals bundled him into a car, and a heavily armed caravan of marshals headed south on the New Jersey Turnpike toward Washington. As Newark receded behind him, Gerry felt the fear and tension drain away. He was safe, and the full power of the United States government would be used to make it possible for him to start a new and better life.

4..............Officer and Gentleman

The Justice Department might have suspected it was getting into deep water with its new witness protection program one night in February of 1970, when Lillian Zelmanowitz announced that, come what may, her husband would not become a sergeant. There they were in the huge gray Justice Department fortress in Washington, only three floors down from the office of Attorney General John Mitchell, and the wife of one of the government's prize witnesses was close to throwing a tantrum.

It happened in a wing that is sealed off from the rest of the building because it houses the Intelligence unit of the Justice Department's Organized Crime and Racketeering Section. Mrs. Zelmanowitz and her husband were in the office of Gerald Shur, the chief of Intelligence and Special Services, who had just recently been put in charge of the alias program. Shur was a dumpy, jowly man in his late thirties, whose owlish horn-rimmed glasses and wide mouth created a faint impression of a very wise catfish. He was by instinct an open, candid man — so much so that even some of his legal adversaries wondered how Shur had been drawn to such an inherently devious program. The Zelmanowitz family was his first effort at relocation, and, out of an abundance of caution, he urged them always to come to the Justice Department at night. But with the darkness boring in from outside, Shur's office was dingy and bleak, and a chilly atmosphere settled in as Shur sat behind his desk, surrounded by photographs of his family and backed up by a needlepoint portrayal of the scales of justice on the wall, and preached sweet reason to the witness and his wife. But Zelmanowitz, the take-charge witness of the DeCarlo trial, sat passively as his wife rejected the government's fake identity papers that identified him as a retired sergeant in Army Intelligence. She declared firmly that she would never have married an enlisted man.

Shur had called in a veteran undercover expert from the Internal Revenue Service's Intelligence Division, Dante Bonomi, to handle details. He explained to Mrs. Zelmanowitz that the rank matched the fictitious background they had created for her husband as a former army cryptographer. Someone might notice, he argued, that an officer would hardly have operated a coding machine. Shur and Bonomi didn't raise the alternative of inventing a more exalted covert background for Zelmanowitz; their theory of identity changing was to keep as low a profile as possible in the new life, so they deliberately created mundane fake backgrounds that would not qualify the holder to land a very visible job.

But Lillian Zelmanowitz would not be moved. Her husband was not the sergeant type, and if the Justice Department had prepared papers making him one, why then, the department would have to type up new papers. Shur and Bonomi took a pair of scissors and shredded their carefully counterfeited identity papers into a wastebasket. Then they went back to the drawing board, suspecting that the government still had much to learn about its new witness relocation program.

It was the period when Congress was considering the Organized Crime Control Bill, and much could have been learned from the experiences of Gerald Zelmanowitz — if the Justice Department had been so inclined — because he turned out to be a relocation subject who was larger than life in ego, charm, intelligence — and, alas, conmanship. To an astonishing extent, the case of this one man proved to be a mirror of the entire program. In retrospect, it appears that almost all of the flaws and problems inherent in the program are typified in some form in the case of Gerald Zelmanowitz.

Problems arose as soon as Zelmanowitz arrived in Washington. The marshals checked him, his family, and a squad of bodyguards into a motel in the nation's capital, and the first night somebody stole all of the marshals' shotguns, ammunition, and walkie-talkies. For weeks, the thieves' wisecracks interrupted the radio communications of the United States Marshals' Service around Washington.

Difficulties soon arose over Zelmanowitz's tribe of in-laws. In this respect his situation duplicated that of the many witnesses who had Sicilian backgrounds and large families. In Buffalo, for instance, the Justice Department undertook to relocate a witness named Joseph Vito, who had agreed to testify against a reputed kingpin of the crime syndicate in Rochester, Russell Bufalino. Vito insisted on taking along about a dozen relatives. After the government created false identities for the whole family, Vito testified but Bufalino was acquitted. He is still at large and the Joseph Vito family is still in hiding.

The Justice Department, undeterred, indicted Bufalino again, this time on a new charge involving the theft of sixty color television sets from a warehouse. In this case the key witness was Jack Piskorowski, a small-time thief and con man whom the government relocated to Portland, Oregon. Eventually, Piskorowski established his own business in Portland, accused the Justice Department of blowing his cover when competitors sought information about him, and sued the government for $1,250,000 for allegedly failing to provide protection for his mother and father. Bufalino, as usual, was acquitted.

At first, Gerry's family included only Lillian and her parents, Joseph and Evelyn Ringel, and Lillian's younger daughter, Cynthia Balaban, aged nineteen. Her older daughter, Shelley Balaban, had married Bobby Stricker, and they were preparing to move to California. The Justice Department did not change their names, but it did move their furniture in a covert manner, so that their destination could be kept secret.

Unlike people in the military, or prisoners, for whom it had responsibility, the government quickly learned that when it undertook day-to-day responsibility for witnesses and their families, excruciating frustrations could ensue. Shur complained about one such incident in a memo about the Justice Department's efforts to find a suitable apartment for Gerry and his family in Washington:

"It should be noted that the acquisition of lodging is not an easy task when as many as six individuals must be satisfied. Representative of the problem is the one occasion when the witness selected an apartment, rental arrangements were made for the witness and separate quarters were secured for the Marshals. In addition, furniture was rented, only to have the witness's wife refuse to move in, because she could not ride in the elevators.

"It should be noted," Shur concluded ruefully, "that she was being moved from the ninth floor of a building with elevators."

Next arose what came to be known among harried Justice Department officials as "the Norman problem." Norman Yaguda was young, adventurous, a college freshman, and in love with Cindy Balaban. He began to shuttle down from New Jersey to see her, greatly to the distress of the government agents who were trying to change her identity. Gerald Shur took the lead in dealing with the Norman problem. He took a kindly, big-brother interest in their situation, and they liked him for his capacity to talk with them on a personal level. They told him how desperately they were in love, and Shur told them endearing stories about his love for his wife and the many joys of married life. Finally, they decided to simplify things by getting married.

It was an exciting cloak-and-dagger wedding, with the guests being met near the Washington airport by United States marshals in a bus and taken by a devious route to the Mayflower Hotel. Meanwhile, the bride and her mother were being driven by an equally circumspect route from their apartment hideout in Silver Spring, Maryland, to the Mayflower. The Marshals' Service, which in the capital city was staffed largely with black officials, outdid itself by finding a rabbi and laying on a wedding in the best East Coast Jewish tradition. The rabbi entered into the spirit of things by agreeing to sign a civil marriage certificate in the name of Roth, but he drew the line at issuing the religious certificate in any name but Yaguda, until their names were legally changed. At the ceremony and reception, the heavily armed marshals tried but failed to appear inconspicuous, giving the scene a Mafia-movie tingle of excitement that made the wedding a huge success.

The only sad notes were that Gerry had to stay away, for his own safety and for that of the guests, and that Cynthia's father, Seymour Balaban, did not catch the spirit of the evening. Balaban, a chemical company employee who still lived in New Jersey, was unhappy because he was not to be told his daughter's new name, or where she was to live. After that night, he could communicate with her only by writing to a mail drop operated by the Justice Department.

Shur tried to console Cindy's father about this, but it was an awkward task because the Justice Department actually had no control over whether she told him her new identity or not. Since she was an adult, she could have told anyone she wished, if she were willing to take the chance.

Such problems were far stickier in the case of young children who were relocated without their parent's consent, as Shur well knew, because of the government's experiences with Pasquale Calabrese. Three years before, on a warm Sunday morning in June, a Buffalo construction worker named Tom Leonhard had gone to the home of his former wife, Rochelle, for his weekly visit with their two young children. Leonhard found the place stripped of all personal belongings and the family vanished.

First he filed a panicky report with the local police, and when they proved uninterested, Leonhard made some discreet inquiries in the city's Italian community. Three weeks after his children's disappearance, the answer came back through the word-of-mouth grapevine — federal agents had taken the children and Rochelle away because her new husband, Paddy Calabrese, had agreed to testify for the Justice Department and the local mob had put a contract on his head.

As it turned out, that tip was only the beginning of years of frustration for Tom Leonhard. For almost two years, the Justice Department refused even to admit that it had anything to do with the disappearance of Leonhard's children. He made the rounds of the local offices of the FBI, the United States Marshals' Service, and the United States attorney, and the reaction was always the same: stony silence. But all the while, rumors and gossip were fleshing out the story. A team of United States marshals had appeared at Rochelle's house and had cleaned out the premises, taking her away with Leonhard's children, seven-year-old Michael and Karen, aged six. They had been moved to an air force base in Maine, where they lived as the Rossi family for four months, until Paddy Calabrese completed his testimony in Buffalo. Then they had all disappeared.

Tom Leonhard was a patriotic, my-country-right-or-wrong hard hat who came very slowly to the conclusion that he was being wronged by the federal government. He was a law-abiding man, who had been granted visitation rights to see his children each weekend by the courts of New York State, and he could not comprehend how the federal government could take his children away and refuse even to admit responsibility. Leonhard finally found a prosecutor in the anti–organized crime Strike Force who would listen to his complaints and forward Leonhard's letters to Rochelle, begging her to let him see the children. Finally, after a year of letter writing, a typewritten note came back from Rochelle:

"Tell Mr. Leonard [*sic*] that in no way shall I ever allow him to see them. They know of no other father than the father they have now. If Mr. Leonard [*sic*] is so concerned about the children he will know that this is best for them in these very important years of their life."

That ended Leonhard's hat-in-hand attitude toward the federal government. He was not a sophisticated man, but finally the issue had been clearly drawn: he was a law-abiding citizen who had a legal right to see his children, yet the federal government had given them to a criminal. Leonhard knew Calabrese to be a violent man who had once shot at Leonhard with a pistol and had cuffed the children around in fits of anger. Yet even after Leonhard was told that Calabrese intended to raise the children as his own in a shadowy, fugitive existence, the government still refused to admit that it had wronged Leonhard in any way.

Tom Leonhard scraped together all his savings and prepared to go to court.

First he won a decision from the local divorce court, giving him sole custody of the children. Then he demanded that the Justice Department honor the court order. The government refused, saying it had promisd to keep the Calabrese family's location a secret. Leonhard sued in United States District Court and lost all the way up to the Supreme Court. It was obvious that the courts had difficulty in coming to grips with this shadowy and danger-tinged new government program. On the one hand, there were hints from the government that Leonhard and his lawyer were somehow part of a plot to betray Calabrese to the underworld, and yet on the other, Leonhard was apparently being robbed of his children by the Justice Department without due process of law. In the end, United States Appeals Judge Irving Kaufman wrote an agonizing opinion conceding that it would take "the wisdom of Solomon" to know what to do, and concluding that since the officials of the Justice Department appeared to have acted "in good faith," the courts would not be permitted to second-guess the officials' "rational exercise of discretion." Thus, Judge Kaufman declared, Leonhard and the New York courts would be bound by the decision of the men who ran the alias program that leaving the children with Calabrese was in the children's best interest. (Rochelle was to charge later that Paddy Calabrese raped Leonhard's daughter not long after this.)

Leonhard's lawyer took the case to the Supreme Court, pleading that unless the justices intervened, "in all likelihood, Thomas Leonhard will never see his children again." The high court rejected his petition for review without comment.

The children grew up, thinking they were Calabrese's own, but changing names six times as the cover of their reckless "father" was blown, time after time. They assumed that every family changed names whenever they moved to a new city. But by 1975 Rochelle had had all she could take of the wild Paddy, and she left him and told the two children who their real father was. They subsequently visited Tom Leonhard from time to time, gradually coming to accept him as their father.

But Judge Kaufman's opinion for the Court of Appeals remained as a binding ruling — that the courts will not second-guess the Justice Department's decisions to relocate minors — and so the parents of children who have vanished into the alias program are usually advised by their attorneys that it would be futile to try to assert their rights in court. The result is to leave such parents without recourse, even when the facts suggest that they may have been terribly wronged.

This was the frustration that faced Weston Frank of Rochester, New York, when his two young sons disappeared with his former wife in the summer of 1975. After the usual weeks of anguish, confusion, and denials, Frank learned that the boys had been relocated, even though they had only a remote connection to a prosecution witness. It developed that Frank's former wife had married a man named Thomas Scalzo, who was the stepson of Joseph "Spike" Lanavero, who was awaiting trial for murder.

Spike Lanavero had agreed to testify against some of his former gangster associates, and the Justice Department relocated him to the Houston, Texas, area, along with Weston Frank's two young sons. Frank protested that the two boys were only the step-step-grandchildren of the government's witness, and that there was no real need for the Justice Department to take them from him, other than Spike Lanavero's reported insistence that he would testify only if his entire family were relocated with him. The Justice Department agreed to fly the boys back to Rochester every two months for as long as Lanavero was still in the program. But when his relocation period ended and he signed the government's release in the spring of 1976, the boys' visits to Rochester stopped. Weston Frank was left with no recourse but to protest that the Justice Department had taken his sons away and then had washed its hands of the whole affair.

The same kinds of frustrations have confronted Eugene Grossman, a Manhattan journalist-photographer whose children were swallowed up by the alias program in 1973. In that year Grossman's former wife took their two children, John, aged three, and Nancy, two, and went to live with a self-confessed swindler named Michael Hellerman. He became a government witness against Carmine Tramunti, who is sufficiently well known in New York as a "reputed Mafia figure" that Hellerman and Grossman's former wife and two children were relocated under false names.

A year passed before the Justice Department admitted that it knew anything about the children's disappearance. Then, after Grossman brought pressure to bear in Congress and in the press and offered to settle for occasional meetings with his children in neutral meeting places, the Justice Department replied that Grossman's former wife had dropped out of the program and that the government no longer knew where she and the children were. Faced with certain defeat if he took his case to court, because of the Leonhard precedent, the father could do no more than complain: "I don't see why the government is able to arrange for criminals to see their families and not do the same for me. Don't I have the same rights?"

The Justice Department's relocation brought no such wrenching change for Cindy and Norman Yaguda; they were newly married and things were strange and different anyway. To them, the visits to the restricted wing of the Justice Department, the armed guards, the false identity papers created the sense of watching a Mafia movie, except that they were in it. For a while, Norman had bad dreams about being caught by Mafia hit men, but in time that passed. But for months they always carried the small slips of paper bearing the special Justice

Department "panic number" they had been told to dial when danger seemed to threaten and guards were needed in a hurry.

There was even a lighthearted touch to their new names. At college Norman had been reading *Portnoy's Complaint*, and he was quite taken with the works of Philip Roth. He spoke to Shur about it, and found a receptive ear. Shur was pleased to give the newlyweds the names Cynthia and Norman Roth.

Their wedding trip was a cross-country jaunt in an old Chevrolet, toward Berkeley, where the Justice Department had promised to get them admitted to the university. In Oklahoma they picked up a young hitchhiker, so they tried out their new false identities for the first time: born and raised in Philadelphia, and now on their way out West. The young man replied with delight that he was from Philadelphia too, and what neighborhood did they come from? They stared at each other for a moment and then collapsed in laughter.

Once they got to California, nobody asked, and no one suspected that they were anybody but Cynthia and Norman Roth.

Bonomi had planned to resettle the youngsters in California, the Ringels in Philadelphia, and Gerry and Lillian in Texas. None would know where the others were, and all contacts would be made through the Justice Department's mail drop. Family reunions would be arranged by the Justice Department, at neutral meeting places. In their new lives, they would say they had no relatives — thus reducing the number of false answers that had to be remembered.

It was all in keeping with Bonomi's theory of simplicity in identity changing, and it undoubtedly worked well in his world of professional undercover IRS agents. But it often didn't satisfy the needs of people who wanted to assume normal lives. Later in the program, one relocated witness landed a good job in a resort hotel on one of the Great Lakes. Following instructions, he lied and told his employers he had no family. In fact, both of his parents died soon — within a few weeks of each other — and he had to slip away to handle their affairs. There were rumors among the hotel staff about a death in the family, and soon he was being pressed by a dubious management for reasons for his absence. It was a good job and he liked it, but to save his identity, he was forced to quit his job and move on.

Gerry balked at the proposal to break up his family. They were a close-knit group, and he had no taste for Texas. Over Bonomi's objections, Gerry insisted that they would all live together in San Francisco.

This proved to be a harbinger for the alias program. Many families have insisted on staying together, and most have wanted to move toward the sun. Thus there are said to be heavy concentrations of relocated families in California, Arizona, Texas, and Georgia. Most of them are from the East (more than twenty families are said to have been relocated from Buffalo alone), and they can be conspicuous when they congregate in a western community. Recently, witnesses have been told by the Marshals' Service that they cannot pick Atlanta, San Francisco, or San Diego for relocation — that so many witnesses have been hidden in those cities that they are considered full.

Bonomi and Shur advised the Zelmanowitz family members to select new names they could remember easily until using them became second nature. The trick was to keep the first name, so that if the person started to forget his name change in conversation, he could still get it right halfway through stating his name. For surnames, Bonomi recommended similar-sounding names, or names that had been in the family. They would be easily remembered and ethnically consistent.

Sometimes relocated witnesses have seemed to carry this principle to a dangerous extreme. One former witness, who is responsible for the convictions of more than thirty racketeers on the East Coast, is living in the Midwest with only his first and middle names switched. But the prime example is Herbert Itkin, the one-time FBI and CIA informant who vanished from New York in 1972 following the nationally publicized trial that led to the conviction of Tammany Hall leader Carmine DeSapio, James L. Marcus, city water commissioner under Mayor John V. Lindsay, and some heavy Mafia types. Itkin got a new identity through the alias program, but two years later his cover was blown by evidence produced in a civil suit in Los Angeles. It disclosed that Herbert Itkin had become an L.A. private investigator named Herbert Atkin.

Gerry's in-laws, Joseph and Evelyn Ringel, became Joseph and Evelyn Miller. Joseph was given a driver's license and Social Security card in his new name, but Bonomi gave Evelyn only a Social Security card in the name of Evelyn Miller. It was felt that she wouldn't need more, as she had a condition diagnosed as terminal cancer. She is still alive.

For Lillian it was more difficult. She had enjoyed her life as a well-to-do New Jersey suburbanite, and she had little enthusiasm for the charade of a new identity.

One day the marshals drove the family out from Washington into nearby Bowie, Maryland, to commit to memory the house that would be listed on Paul Maris's résumé as the residence where he once lived. The houses in Bowie tend to be modest and alike, and in this neighborhood, the home-owners had tried to create some individuality by painting them with pastel colors. It was an effort that observers from elsewhere frequently concluded had failed.

Lillian had the same reaction. When her "former home" was pointed out — it was small and pink — she sniffed that she "would never live in such a house." Lillian learned later that it was Shur's house.

Another time, the marshals drove Lillian and her parents to Philadelphia to view the neighborhood where they were supposed to have once lived. They were chagrined to learn that it had been a Negro slum for forty years.

Lillian at first was timid about using her new name around strangers, afraid she would slip. For a time she and her parents became almost reclusive, concerned that they couldn't carry off living a lie and that their pose would be so transparent that Gerry's life could be endangered. Later they became comfortable with their new identities, and Lillian thoroughly enjoyed the preferred treatment she received in San Francisco's better restaurants and dress shops as Mrs. Paul Maris. But even then, when the name Paul Maris meant glamour and success, she would occasionally slip and throw business meetings and cocktail parties into stunned confusion by turning to her husband in casual moments and referring to him as "Gerry."

It was Gerry who had persuaded the family to cross over to a new life, and it was he who made the easiest transition. He had never had a very strong sense of identity anyway. His Jewish immigrant heritage had been truncated when the ship carrying his mother from Russia to the United States was sidetracked by the outbreak of World War I, forcing her to spend her girlhood in Kobe, Japan. (Her stories of her experiences did, however, later help Paul Maris to flesh out his imaginary background as a former intelligence operative in Japan, who still owned electronics interests in Kobe.) She arrived in Brooklyn in her mid-twenties and never learned to speak or write English well enough to join the upward movement of the rest of her family. Instead she married a recently arrived Hungarian named Alexander Zelmanowitz. He became a house painter and died in a fall from a ladder when Gerry was barely old enough to remember him.

Later, Gerry learned that Alexander Zelmanowitz had had a second life. He had married a previous wife in Hungary, who eventually inherited all his property and left Gerry, his sister, and his mother to live in bitter poverty in the Brighton Beach area of Brooklyn, where his cousins were already moving up in the world.

It was not long before Gerry began to drop the surname Zelmano-witz — "too long, too ethnic" — and go by the name of Gerald Martin. This tendency to sever his roots was evident from the time Alexander Zelmanowitz died. Rebecca Zelmanowitz, Gerry's mother, was working long hours six days a week as a seamstress in Manhattan's garment district, and this gave Gerry the time and freedom to find his own identity from the polyglot selection offered by the Brooklyn of those days. He spent little time with the studious, earnest Jewish boys at P.S. 225, and, in fact, spent increasingly little time at P.S. 225. Hooky was more his game, and he played it often with Italian-American boys who were to end up later as small-time thugs on the fringes of the Brooklyn mob. He also began to emulate the gamblers and hustlers who demonstrated such enviable wealth around the pool halls and street corners where Gerry shined shoes.

By the time he was bumped up to Abraham Lincoln High, Gerry had become a clearly recognizable Brooklyn type — the young punk. He and his friends specialized in the kind of thievery that caused the most damage for the least return — they stole useful items to sell for junk. They would swipe automobiles. They would break open train batteries in freight yards and sell the lead and zinc strips to junk dealers. But their specialty was ripping the copper roofing strips from the tops of apartment houses and selling them for salvage; it was said that Gerry was responsible for more leaky roofs in Brooklyn in the early 1950s than Hurricane Ethel.

While Gerry was going through almost all the motions of becoming a Brooklyn tough, one quality was missing — violence. As the boys in his gang got bigger and more brazen about their criminality, some drifted naturally into physical violence, yet it was as if brutality and confrontation were an invisible line Gerry was unwilling to cross. Some of the others began to carry guns, and that he was ready to do, although he said later he had no intention of ever using one. But nevertheless he got caught carrying a pistol, when he was still in his teens. Thus when he was arrested at the age of fifteen for stealing a car, it seemed only a matter of time before he would achieve the final badge of thuggery, a hitch in reform school. His probation officer saw one last opportunity for Gerry, then a wayward and muscular sixteen-year-old, to break out of that mold. Some instinct prompted Gerry to see it too, and so he agreed to sign up with the Brooklyn Dodger Platoon of newly enlisted United States marines.

Private Zelmanowitz threw himself into his new identity as a "tough marine" with the same talent and excess that were to mark his later incarnations as international con artist and garment tycoon. Since his identity was always a pose, Gerry tended to overdo the flashy surface aspects and neglect the background work and conservation of gains that were fundamental traits of those who really lived the part. He became the Hollywood image of a marine — tall, muscular, and handsome enough to carry the flag in the honor platoon; drunk, pugnacious, and a devil with the women when on liberty. Inevitably, his *macho* sense of his role as a marine proved his undoing. One snowy night he was assigned the frigid — and, he thought, idiotic — task of standing guard over a locked shed. Gerry crawled into the cab of a truck and went to sleep. He was awakened by the hoots and cackles of the members of his platoon, who had been summoned outside by the lieutenant, who had discovered Gerry and walked away with his rifle. To Pfc. Zelmanowitz, this indignity was too much. He threw a punch at the lieutenant, and his marine phase ended prematurely, under other than honorable conditions. He returned as Gerald Martin to Brooklyn.

So when the time came to create a new identity for Gerry, he was more than happy to start from scratch. Bonomi thought that in Gerry's case, it would be safer to change his whole name. A hitch developed. During his marine phase, he had gone ashore one night and gotten a tattoo — his name, spelled "Jerry," high on his right arm. The Justice Department sent him to Bethesda Naval Hospital to have the tattoo removed, but the surgeon there said it would take several painful operations and even then, the name might not completely go away. Gerry decided not to try. Bonomi dealt with the situation by giving Gerry a middle initial: Paul J. Maris.

It was the first time the alias program dabbled with plastic surgery, and the record is cloudly as to whether it has done so since. Justice Department officials insist that they have never paid to have witnesses' faces altered by plastic surgery, although the witnesses are free to have it done themselves if they wish. But there have been a few indications that plastic surgery has been part of the program.

One hint came in April of 1974, when a witness calling himself "John Doe" filed suit in United States District Court in New York, seeking an injunction to force the Justice Department to live up to its alleged promises to relocate Doe. The plaintiff recited a litany of complaints against the alias program, claiming that as a narcotics informer he had been promised that if he were discovered he would be given a new identity — including plastic surgery to change his appearance. He added that he must have been discovered, because he had been shot at twice and stabbed three times and his house had been burned down; but the government had failed to come up with the new identity or new face. (As further evidence that the alias program was maturing as a government agency, it was accused of racial discrimination by Doe — he charged that it provided better witness fees, protection, and relocation benefits to white than to black informants.) The suit was dropped later when even John Doe's lawyer couldn't locate him.

Another incident involving plastic surgery came to light after Peter Diapoulas, the former bodyguard for New York mobster Joey Gallo, completed his relocation within the alias program. Diapoulas had been wounded when Gallo was gunned to death, and the trauma made him a willing witness for the government, but also a very cautious one. He had his face reshaped by plastic surgery — and later, when he agreed to be interviewed by Mike Wallace on CBS News's "60 Minutes" television program, it took all the artistry of the CBS makeup department to make him look like Peter Diapoulas again just for that one evening.

Gerry went the simpler route of most relocated witnesses. A change of hair style and color, a new mustache or beard, a habit of wearing sunshades is usually disguise enough to cover the new identity. Some witnesses say they've come face-to-face with old friends and classmates and have passed by without a blink of recognition.

It came to Gerry gradually that something was going wrong with his relocation. No span of time had been mentioned for the entire process, but he had assumed that one or two weeks would do. Weeks passed, and still his long sessions with Shur and Bonomi continued. The ostensible purpose of the meetings was to find out everything possible about Gerry and his family members in order to match their future identities with their actual backgrounds, and to relocate them in a place where they had no ties. But it soon became obvious that Shur and Bonomi were stretching the process out in hopes of extracting more evidence from Gerry.

A cat-and-mouse game ensued. Shur and Bonomi would explain that Gerry's documentation was almost ready, and Gerry would encourage them with a few more tidbits about his days as financial advisor to the mob. He told them of laundering Mafia money and of establishing secret Swiss bank accounts, and he dropped morsels of information about such figures as Joseph Colombo, Meyer Lansky, Tony Carillo, Anthony Salerno, Thomas Eboli, Michael Miranda, Angelo DeCarlo, Joseph Polverino, Daniel Cecere, and the others. Shur and Bonomi gobbled it up, and it was some weeks before they realized that they were only getting hors d'oeuvres from Zelmanowitz. The hard evidence he gave them tended to incriminate mafiosi who were old, or sick, or already in prison. No new cases were made against anyone as a result of these tantalizing sessions.

At one point when Bonomi was pressing especially hard for new evidence of wrongdoing, Gerry mentioned that he had been able to recall certain instances of bribery. Bonomi pressed him for details. Gerry bobbed and weaved. Bonomi kept after him. Finally, Gerry grinned and said he would tell all. During the height of his arbitrage activities, he said, he had regularly bribed two IRS agents. He could even remember the sums, he added — from $500 to $1,000 per week. And, he concluded, he had a clear memory of the IRS men's names, which he then told to Bonomi. Shur relayed the two agents' names to the IRS, but for the duration of his relocation, Gerry was never asked about them again.

After more than two months, Shur and Bonomi were prepared to give Gerry and his family their new identity papers and let them go, but a resentment had begun to develop that was increasingly to poison the Justice Department–Zelmanowitz relationship as time went on. Shur and Bonomi apparently remained convinced that Zelmanowitz still had access to large deposits of mob money in Switzerland, and that if his new identity permitted him to do so, he would return to his role as financial courier and advisor to Mafia chieftains. Zelmanowitz began to feel that the government was reneging on its promise to him, now that he had no more evidence to give.

The government's suspicions about Gerry arose from a fundamental flaw inherent in the alias program: the Justice Department was promising a new identity to a man it did not trust. In providing such a new identity, the Justice Department was torn between its obligations to the public and to the witness; thus the government was unable fully to protect the interests of either. This conflict was to taint, to a greater or lesser degree, each of the two thousand aliases the government was to create over the next six years.

On the surface, the United States appears to be the easiest country in the world in which to establish an alias. The reason is that the United States has not established an identity card system to keep up with its citizens. Unlike most of the countries of Europe, we have no requirement that a person routinely carry a specified item of identification, such as a passport or identity card. What this means is that the United States does not have what is known in government circles as a Standard Universal Identifier — a single numbered document that citizens can be required to produce to establish their identity. This is no accident or oversight, but a deliberate effort by the United States to perpetuate the frontier tradition of "go West, young man." It is an official recognition that there was good in the American tradition that a person could leave the mistakes of his past behind, move to a new place, take a new name, and start again. Thus Congress has resisted pressures to create a Standard Universal Identifier through the Social Security system. Over the years it has passed various laws declaring that citizens can refuse to disclose their Social Security numbers (except in situations where they are specifically required to do so by other laws) and cannot be denied such benefits as charge accounts, insurance policies, and credit cards for refusing to give their numbers.

Also, records of births and deaths are kept on a chaotic county-by-county basis, with little or no effort to cross-index deaths and births. This means that a person who wants a new identity can simply take one from somebody who has died. The fact of the recorded birth means that a certified birth certificate can be obtained — and with it, a passport, Social Security card, and any other identification — while the early death of the original owner of the name means that there will not be two adult persons claiming the same identity.

With the authority of the Justice Department at its command, it would appear at first glance that the alias program could easily construct identities that would be impregnable. Other agencies and arms of government cooperate by falsifying their records, so that the witness protection program doesn't even have to steal the identities of people who have died. On the federal level, the Social Security Administration and the Defense Department issue fake Social Security cards and military personnel documents. The Passport Office provides false passports. The FBI flags each witness's fingerprint card, so that if he gets arrested under his new name the government can step in quickly and see that he isn't thrown into a cellblock with gangsters who would kill him. Some state officials apparently have agreed to insert phony birth records and drivers' licenses in their files; witnesses who have surfaced report that Maryland and Rhode Island are exceptionally cooperative states. Witnesses' names are legally changed so that they can make contracts, sign documents, and swear under oath that they are the new persons, without legally telling a lie. This sometimes requires the cooperation of court officials to conceal the original name, and it is said that many such mysterious records are maintained in the courts surrounding Gerald Shur's home bailiwick of Bowie, Maryland. The alias program even provides false baptismal certificates for witnesses' children, if they were in fact baptized, and phony school records, but with their actual grades inserted.

But despite the government's apparent capacity to create foolproof aliases, in practice, it has often failed to do so. There are at least three reasons why. One is a policy decision by the Justice Department to go only halfway; another is the complexity of modern life, which makes it difficult for even the federal government to manipulate all the variables of a person's past; and the third is the government's own bureaucratic ineptitude. All three reasons were factors in the haunted life of Paul Maris, during the alias program's infancy.

Gerald Zelmanowitz had been promised a new identity, backed up by supporting documentation. The arrangement was never put into more concrete terms — precisely how many bogus documents would be furnished, and exactly what forms of backup documentation would be created to support the false identity papers. It was just assumed, as Herbert Stern put it later, that the government would provide "a new identity which would permit him to function without fear of exposure." But when the time came for Gerald Zelmanowitz to become Paul Maris, Shur and Bonomi gave him only a Social Security card, a driver's license, and an Army Reserve ID card. Lillian Maris was given only a Social Security card. Besides these documents, the family was given two other items of identification. One was a detailed chronological list of the events and places in the life of "Paul Maris" that were to be memorized. It reflected a compromise on the "sergeant" issue. It stated that Maris had indeed been an enlisted man and a cryptographer, but that he quickly earned an appointment to officer candidate school and began a meteoric rise as a commissioned officer.

The second item was much of the same information arranged in the form of a résumé that could be handed to prospective employers. Maris was to embellish it as his career progressed, but even at the outset, the résumé issued to him by the government was impressive:

PAUL J. MARIS

Thru 1957 — 8916 Laycock Avenue; Phila., Pa. 19153 (Phila. County)
1962 Nov. thru Jan. 1970 — 12613 Knowledge Lane, Bowie, Maryland.

WHITE MALE:
  DOB — 1/12/35 (Phila., Pa.)
  Ht. — 5'10".
  Wt. — Thru School 150 — gains (170–175).
  Hr. — Brwn.
  Eyes — Green.

9/49–6/53 — John Bertram High Sch. (Phila.).
9/53–6/55 — Baldwin Wallace — Berea, Ohio.
9/55–57   — Sound Enterprises, Inc., Cinn., Ohio & Lexington, Ky.

1–2/58 — Fort Dix New Jersey — U.S. Army, Fort Devens — Ayer, Mass. (A.S.A.).
Thru 62 — France (3 years).
Return — Fort Meade Maryland — 6 months. Fort Benning Georgia — Officers School (Columbus, Ga.).

Sound Enterprises, Inc. — OR Owner — ROBERT A. TURNER, P.O. Box 8257, Southland Station, Lexington, Ky. 40504.
Citizens Union National Bank, 201 W. Short St., Lexington, Ky. 40507 (Branch Bank).
Acct. No. 123–132–9.

Gerry believed, when he memorized his new life history and placed the résumé among his personal papers, that official records would show, for instance, that Paul Maris did graduate from John Bertram High School in Philadelphia. (Gerry did not dream that the government had gotten the name wrong — that the school's real name is John Bartram, not Bertram — and that he would be exposed immediately if he ever tried his new alias out on anybody from Philadelphia.) He also believed that records would show that Paul Maris did attend Baldwin Wallace College in Berea, Ohio, that he was discharged as a captain in the Army Security Agency, that he did maintain a solid account at the Citizens Union Bank in Lexington, Kentucky, and that he was born in Philadelphia on January 12, 1935. (Gerald Zelmanowitz had been born on that date in 1937, but somebody in the Justice Department decided that Maris should be a bit older because of his grown "children.")

The government did, in fact, intend to provide some backup for Paul Maris's résumé. Shur went to Berea and got a commitment from the president of Baldwin Wallace College, Alfred Bond, that the college would falsify its records to provide backgrounds for relocated witnesses and their children. But Bond insisted later that Paul Maris was not a name that was sent to the college to be inserted in the records. Apparently, the Justice Department simply slipped up and failed to send Maris's name to the college, for it is known that the academic backgrounds of others processed by the alias program have been laundered through the records of Baldwin Wallace College. Neither President Bond nor officials of the Justice Department will discuss the extent to which the new names of repentent former mafiosi may have been tagged onto Baldwin Wallace's alumni lists, but it seems possible that this tiny Ohio college could have developed — with Justice Department assistance — one of the largest Italian-American alumni groups in the Midwest.

The government may have believed that some elements of Maris's cover would survive a check, even without specific records on file to back them up. In selecting stages of a relocated witness's bogus background, Justice Department operatives often try to include claimed activities that simply cannot be verified. Many witnesses are told to claim backgrounds in military intelligence, and at least one has been instructed to say he worked for the Robert R. Mullen Company, a Washington, D.C., public relations firm that serves as a CIA front. When people try to check out these references, they are told that such information is never disclosed. The government also collects instances of institutions whose records have been destroyed — a high school in Ohio demolished by a tornado, a New Jersey school gutted by fire — and witnesses are told to give these schools as part of their past.

Gerald Shur said later that Bonomi had assured him that all of the records of Philadelphia's John Bertram (*sic*) High School had been destroyed by a fire in the late nineteen fifties, so that any inquiries about a student named Paul Maris would have run into a blank wall. When questions were asked later, officials at the school said they knew of no fire, that their records were intact, and that they included no student named Paul Maris.

The obvious difficulty with the government's alias technique is that, while a check of a witness's résumé might not make him out a fraud, it would not confirm him as a very solid citizen, either. But most witnesses are not told about these ambiguities in their cover, although they result largely from a policy decision by the Justice Department that witnesses should not be given foolproof aliases. The basis of this decision is murky, but Gerald Shur confirmed that the Justice Department does not intend to provide such heavy cover that a relocated witness could use his alias to harm an unsuspecting but reasonably careful American citizen. Thus the Justice Department says it never furnishes false credit references or other background documentation that could withstand the scrutiny of a retail credit check. There are other limitations designed to protect the public from venal witnesses, but these are more hazy.

There appears, for instance, to be a policy against falsifying FBI fingerprint records to conform with the false names. This means that witnesses can't get jobs that involve a check of their criminal records, because a routine fingerprint check with the FBI would disclose their original identity — and, usually, the fact that they have long criminal records.

But even this policy seems to have its exceptions. In 1975 the United States Commission on Wiretapping was holding a routine hearing into eavesdropping by private investigators, when such an instance came to light. The commission was questioning Jerris E. Bragan, a young man who had been part of a two-man private detective team in Alexandria, Virginia, until he was convicted of illegal wiretapping in 1972. He told the story of how he was schooled in the arts of electronic surveillance by his business partner — a savvy, slick young private detective named William R. Raymond.

It was not until later, Bragan testified, that he learned to his sorrow that William R. Raymond was really William R. Phillips, one of the most corrupt policemen turned up by the investigation of the New York Police Department by the Knapp Commission. Phillips had been caught extorting bribes from Manhattan's most famous madam, prostitute-author Xaviera Hollander, and had become an undercover informant for the Knapp Commission. His testimony helped convict a string of corrupt policemen and officials, but it also disclosed that Phillips had been involved up to his badge in bribery, prostitution, and even murder. Yet after all that, the Justice Department gave Phillips a new identity as William Raymond and put him in a position where he impressed young Bragan as just the man of the world to become his partner in a confidential new private detective agency that would do work only for attorneys. Bragan told the Commission on Wiretapping what happened when he took Raymond to get his private investigator's license:

MR. BRAGAN: "The procedures in Alexandria are supposed to be efficient. You are fingerprinted by the police department and the prints are sent through the FBI for clearance, and when they come back you are issued a license."

Q: "Was Mr. Phillips given clearance?"

MR. BRAGAN: "Yes, he was."

Q: "In other words, you had no idea that the man you were hiring as your partner was, indeed, not only a corrupt New York City police officer, but was under indictment for murder at the time in New York?"

MR. BRAGAN: "That is correct."

Q: "Has he since been convicted of murder?"

MR. BRAGAN: "Last fall he was convicted on both counts of murder and attempted murder and is serving two life sentences in Attica right now."

But Phillips avoided conviction in the wiretap case by the use of a ploy he had learned well in New York. He informed on his partner, Bragan, and in return, Phillips was let off.

There is no evidence that anybody in the government has ever thought through the implications of the Witness Protection Program's second major source of problems — the inherent difficulty of manipulating all of the variables that make up a person's identity in American society. In this sense, the officials who slipped the program through without hearings or debates in Congress were only creating future problems for themselves. They appear to have operated on the assumption that altering the names on a few identity cards and records accomplishes a change of a person's identity. In fact, it is often much more complex than that.

Because of the "go West" tradition of anonymity in the United States, a large number of Americans simply change their identities each year and disappear. Estimates of the actual numbers vary, because it is generally not illegal to drop out of one life and into another, so police departments make no effort to keep accurate statistics of missing persons. A half-century ago Captain John H. Ayers, chief of the New York City Missing Persons Bureau, announced his conclusion that a million Americans change their identities each year, and because nobody knows for certain anyway, this neat, round figure has tended to be repeated by others who have considered the matter since then. The actual number is probably considerably lower; the Social Security Administration receives about 200,000 inquiries each year from persons trying to trace someone who has disappeared (it sometimes passes the query on to the person who has absconded, but doesn't tell where he is, except in child nonsupport cases). Also, each year about a quarter of a million Social Security cards are issued to men over thirty — most of whom, for one reason or another, are apparently obtaining a new number under a new name.

But what this massive changing of names obscures is that the quality of the new identities is almost always dismal. Of the highly publicized and well-connected runaways in recent years who have later been found, almost all turned out to be considerably less well connected in their second identities. Professor Carl Holmberg, an internationally known cellulose chemist at Syracuse University who disappeared in 1955, was found seven years later grinding pigment in a paint factory. Thomas Buntin, a wealthy Nashville, Tennessee, insurance executive who disappeared and was declared legally dead, was located later clerking in a Texas store. William Henry Waldron, a Huntington, West Virginia, attorney, disappeared in 1950 and surfaced sixteen years later as a commercial fisherman in Florida who had been convicted of killing his wife in a family brawl. Norman Briggs, a Troy, New York, home builder who disappeared in an apparent boating accident and had been declared legally dead, turned up later as a cowboy in Wyoming.

The reality of identity in modern society seems to be that a person living under an alias is almost forced into a menial job, with a low-income life-style. If the person attempts to move up into middle-class American life, he encounters an intricate web of credit references, bank records, college degrees, medical histories, and insurance records — much of which is completely outside the government's control — all capable of exposing the lie of the second identity. People who discard their true identities to run away from an unhappy marriage, a detested career, or an overbearing family accept this as the price of their escape. But the alias program has never made this point to its witnesses. If anything, it has encouraged the misleading belief that with the federal government's sponsorship, a person can slip into a new identity as he would a modishly cut new suit and continue in the mainstream of American life as before.

In fact, Justice Department crimebusters often oversell the fresh-start idea, sometimes with almost religious fervor. One attorney, trying to persuade a reluctant witness that he would be rewarded with a safe and shining new life, exclaimed: "Just consider yourself reborn!" In many instances, the limitations of the new existence appear to have been obscured until after the witness has betrayed the underworld and there is no turning back. There is often a strong temptation for the FBI agent, narcotics officer, or assistant United States attorney, who desprately needs a witness's testimony to make an important case, to lean heavily on the "new life" promise of the alias program when he is trying to push a Mafia insider into turning state's evidence. Because the government does not officially make it clear how second-rate its false identities are, there was for several years no requirement that prospective witnesses be told about the limitations of the promised new existence.

This led to so many dashed hopes that in March of 1974 the Marshals' Service issued an order requiring an early meeting between each potential witness and a security specialist, who would explain to the witness "the degree of protection, subsistence, documentation, relocation and employment he can expect." The problem was that by the time that a meeting could be arranged between a government functionary and a frightened witness, the witness had often risked so much that the caveats of the bureaucrat came only as the first dash of cold water in the new life, rather than an advance warning of the hazards of that life.

This defect in the alias program has been magnified as the Justice Department has attempted to concentrate on white-collar offenses, which require testimony from middle-class witnesses. In routine cases of thuggery, the witness relocation program has found it easy enough to change the names of low-level gangsters and submerge them in menial jobs half a continent away. A few have been relocated without even changing their names. But the government has apparently never come to grips with the complications it creates when it offers a new life to a person with the kind of sophisticated background that has put him in a position to be an important witness concerning a white-collar crime.

Problems can be raised by supposedly simple matters, such as life insurance. When witnesses' names are legally changed, they face the choice of telling their insurance companies and risking having the new identity leak, or waiting until a death or other event creates a need to straighten things out with the insurers. A similar problem exists with Social Security benefits. Operating out of an office in Baltimore, the Social Security Administration assigns each relocated person a new number to go with the false name. This raises the possibility that the person will lose benefits earned under his old Social Security number, but the Justice Department says that it will deal with this on a case-by-case basis as the hidden witnesses die or retire — it will arrange in each case to have the benefits earned under both identities paid to the proper beneficiaries. Some witnesses claim, however, that the alias program's bureaucracy has been slow or unreliable in making such arrangements; one said he had to threaten to sue the government to obtain veteran's benefits he earned under his true identity. But the most persistent problem has been the one of credit.

Even though the Justice Department's policy is hazy, it does admittedly drag its feet on providing cover that would help relocated witnesses obtain credit cards, secure bank loans, open charge accounts, and survive retail credit investigations. Thus, in case after case, relocated witnesses have complained that they were taken from lives of white-collar comfort and were stranded in faraway communities where they were cut off from the lifeblood of middle-class living — credit.

Some relocated witnesses discover that their past is simply too valuable to sever completely. In Buffalo, a man named Angelo Monachino has testified in a score of cases and has been relocated elsewhere, under a new name. But Monachino was previously in the construction business with his brother, who has continued to build some of the structures that they began together. Periodically, one of these jobs gets in difficulty, and Angelo Monachino's expertise is needed. Then, Buffalo's citizens are treated to a rare public glimpse of the alias program — Angelo Monachino in a hard hat, supervising work on a construction job, as the company's security guards stand by with shotguns, eyeing the passing crowd.

The potential complications between the old life and the new seem almost limitless. One such unanticipated twist surfaced in the bizarre case of one of the alias program's most famous alumni, Frank Peroff. Under any circumstances, it would have been a challenge to conceal Peroff. He weighed 270 pounds and was a snappy dresser, had a lifelong penchant for larceny, and had provided a vicarious link between the Nixon administration and organized crime. The latter happened in 1974, when he testified before the Senate about an international drug and counterfeiting ring that he had infiltrated. Peroff swore that Robert Vesco, who had fled the country to avoid prosecution on charges of bribing former Nixon cabinet members John Mitchell and Maurice Stans, had also been involved in a scheme to smuggle heroin into the United States.

For some unexplained reason, Peroff was relocated in the Washington, D.C., area. Under his new name, he consulted a doctor about a lung condition. The problem was that Peroff had undergone a lung operation in a Washington hospital while he was still Frank Peroff, and his new physician needed X-rays taken at that time. In the course of obtaining those X-rays from the hospital, Peroff was forced to reveal some information about his new name and whereabouts. Then he neglected to pay the $600 fee submitted by the new doctor, who turned the matter over to a debt collection agency. Eventually Peroff filed a damage suit against the doctor and a government official for allegedly disclosing his cover name, and asked the court to order the Justice Department to provide him with around-the-clock protection.

The Justice Department has learned that an infinite number of everyday mishaps can shred a witness's cover. Such an incident was a traffic accident that occurred in Covington, Kentucky, in September of 1972. A black Lincoln with a lone occupant smashed into the car of Robert Stoffel, a taxi driver who was out for a spin with his wife in his private car. The car was demolished and Stoffel and his wife were injured, but the driver of the Lincoln left without making firm arrangements to pay the damages.

Stoffel suffered heavy medical expenses and lost his job because he had no car, and his attorney set about trying to determine if the man in the Lincoln had been insured. But coming to grips with the driver's identity proved as slippery as grasping at Jell-O. The address listed on state records when the man registered the Lincoln and obtained his license proved to be that of Steve Mellinger, a one-time star football player at the University of Kentucky and now a deputy United States marshal. The man had flashed a Maryland driver's license, but when officials in Annapolis were asked for background information to help track him down, they admitted that the license was a fake. They said they could tell no more because the man was a protected government witness.

By this time becoming frantic over his losses, Stoffel wrote the Justice Department, gave the name the man in the Lincoln had been using, and asked if he was indeed a government witness. All he wanted, Stoffel explained, was to find out if the Lincoln was covered by insurance. The reply came back in a letter from the United States Marshals' Office in Washington: no, the man was not then and never had been under the protection of the Marshals' Service.

All this piqued the interest of a reporter for the Cincinnati *Enquirer*, Gerald White, who began to touch base with reporters he knew who had investigated organized crime. Eventually he telephoned Joe Demma and Anthony Marro of *Newsday*, who immediately recognized the owner of the Lincoln by his description. He was Vincent Paradiso, a one-time errand boy and chauffeur for Long Island mobsters who were running heroin. Paradiso had turned state's evidence, and had convicted Vincent Papa, Angelo Loria, Sr., and two dozen other racketeers on charges of drug trafficking. Paradiso had then been hustled out of town by a team of marshals.

For a time, spokesmen in the Marshals' Service headquarters in Washington continued to deny any knowledge of the man in the Lincoln, but finally attorneys in the Justice Department confirmed that Paradiso was the man, and that he was under the protection of the United States marshals. He had long since been relocated elsewhere, but the Justice Department spokesmen said that the government would cooperate in helping Stoffel recover his damages. Yet when Stoffel finally brought suit, the government successfully disclaimed any responsibility, and Paradiso was never found. Mrs. Stoffel has since died, and her husband complains bitterly that the government should do a little something for him, since it has done so much for the former heroin pusher from Long Island.

On the most basic level, the alias program has failed its white-collar witnesses in the quality of the jobs it provides. Gerald Shur, in a burst of imagination, enlisted the United States Chamber of Commerce to help furnish jobs. Shur traveled around, speaking to businessmen's groups about the colorful new plan to strike back at white-collar crime and pleading for jobs for the mysterious persons who would have sacrificed their identities to testify against the Mafia. The businessmen have been intrigued, and have responded. About 150 corporations have pledged jobs on a no-questions-asked basis, and the Justice Department is quick to say that their cooperation has been a key to the operation of the program.

But even this cooperation has raised questions. Incidents have occurred that posed doubts as to whether there might be a conflict of interest in the phenomenon of the Justice Department going to corporations, hat in hand, for jobs for needy witnesses, while with the other hand, the same Justice Department is supposed to prosecute or sue many of the same corporations to enforce the laws of taxation, antitrust, and the environment. A colorful tip of this iceberg surfaced, in 1972, in the person of Pershing Gervais.

If ever a person were typecast as the Slick Cajun from the gaudy French Quarter of New Orleans, it was Pershing Gervais. Flashy, fast-talking and unabashedly a rascal, Gervais knew his way around the seamier side of New Orleans well enough to have been employed as an investigator at one time by Big Jim Garrison, freewheeling New Orleans district attorney. Gervais's role as an investigator had many facets: in 1971 he swore out a 107-page affidavit stating that he regularly collected money from the operators of pinball machines that were used for illegal gambling and that he distributed the money to various police officials and to Garrison, as bribes to guarantee that the forces of law and order would not crack down on this type of gambling. It appeared that Pershing Gervais had been a government informer for some time — he had been wired for sound during many of his financial transactions and he had recordings of his conversations with Garrison, high police officials, and gamblers concerning the payments.

Big Jim Garrison was indicted, along with the policemen and the gamblers, and the Justice Department thought it wise to get Pershing Gervais safely out of town until the time of the trial. Gerald Shur swung into action. He had Gervais's name legally changed to Paul Mason (Gervais got the inspiration for the name while watching television's Perry Mason and his trusty investigator, Paul Drake), and he arranged to have Gervais and his wife picked up by United States marshals and put on a flight to Canada, where they were to be relocated in the small town of Tsawwassen, about thirty-five miles from Vancouver.

But within a few months, "Paul Mason" appeared at the United States attorney's office in New Orleans, hinting that he was rethinking his testimony and protesting that he had been wronged. It seemed that when the team of United States marshals had swooped down on Pershing Gervais's house to whisk his family off to Canada, they hadn't been prepared to deal also with Mrs. Gervais's fourteen prize Yorkshire terrier dogs. The marshals promised to send the animals along after the family had been rushed to safety, but the officers proved inexperienced in dealing with show dogs, and the Yorkshires did not fare well: one killed another in a fight, and two litters of puppies were lost, and even after the federal government bought the dead Yorkshire for $1,500, Mrs. Gervais arrived in British Columbia in a decidedly sour mood. Things worsened when it turned out that everybody in the alias program thought that somebody else had arranged for lodgings for the family, and there was at first no place for them to stay. Then Paul Mason found that his job had fallen through. He said he had been promised a job as an industrial spy with an American oil company, which has never been identified. His job was to discover why the Canadian government had been giving preferential drilling rights to rival oil companies, but at the last minute the company's lawyers snuffed out the arrangement by pointing out that if Gervais testified against Garrison, it might be disclosed during cross-examination that he was currently spying on the Canadian government for a United States oil company.

But Gerald Shur had other resources. He got Paul Mason a job with General Motors of Canada, a job that Gervais later claimed was for the most part a fake. His title was Field Traffic Manager, and he got it after he and Shur had a cloak-and-dagger meeting in a Toronto hotel room with the president of GM of Canada, Ronald S. Winters. After this high-level debut, Paul Mason's career with General Motors was astonishingly obscure. He said his duties involved filling out some forms each week and mailing them to the factory, a chore that took about three hours of his time. For this he was paid $18,000 per year — more, he said, than other field traffic managers for GM, who really did whatever field traffic managers do.

Gerald Shur insists that "Mason" was given a regular job, requiring full time and effort, after the government simply asked for GM's co-operation with no hint of pressure. But if Pershing Gervais's version of his performance is substantially true, it raises questions as to what pressures, if any, the oil company and GM may have felt that per-suaded them to pay a handsome salary for whatever useful work a Cajun from Louisiana might perform in British Columbia. In the end, GM allegedly got almost nothing for its wages in the way of work. So unless these corporations (nobody will say if there have been other similar instances) acted out of pure patriotism, the question remains whether the Justice Department has incurred some subtle debts in the process.

A more obvious problem with the alias program's appeals to the business community has been that the jobs offered have, for the most part, been distinctly modest. Predictably, most of them have been far removed from the company till. And that has meant, generally, menial jobs at low pay.

When former attorney Herbert Itkin arrived in California after his decade of intrigue as an informer for the CIA, FBI, and Justice De-partment, the government's best offers seemed to be a job as a truck driver or one as a bartender. Edmund Graifer, a college graduate who married into a New York Mafia family and later squealed on forty members of the clan, was relocated in Virginia Beach with his wife and two children. He complained later that the government arranged a job as an unsalaried salesman, something he had never done before. But when he tried to make a business deal, he claimed that his lack of a past created a blank wall: "What do you tell a businessman you want to work with? I'm So-and-So and for thirty-two years my life is a blank? I never worked for anyone?" Government officials grumble about wit-nesses who expect to take a new identity and then start out in the executive suite, but they also concede that the government can rarely furnish relocated witnesses anything beyond menial jobs.

Another chronic problem was underscored by the experience of Allen Magid, a former manufacturer of children's apparel in Brooklyn, who fell prey to Mafia loan sharks, agreed to testify against them, and was relocated to the San Francisco area. Magid got a job as a sales manager in a department store, and seemed to be working his way up the corporate ladder when his job was interrupted by repeated trips to New York to testify. During one trial a judge mistakenly permitted Magid's cover to be disclosed, so that he had to be relocated. Magid has charged that the Justice Department did not provide the background documentation that would permit him to get a decent job again. The government has replied that he has not cooperated, that he has run up debts, and that he was never promised a foolproof background. Magid last turned up in Phoenix, where he was selling merchandise door-to-door and blaming his misfortunes on the alias program.

The Witness Relocation Program's most visible white-collar failure has been the case of Marvin Nadborn, the one-time manager of a Brooklyn car agency, who has now become a sort of snitcher's Flying Dutchman — doomed, he says, by the lack of a job to traveling from city to city, sniffing out the rottenest rackets he can find, and then informing on the criminals for the fees the government and the insurance companies will pay. Nadborn got into the alias program in the way many witnesses have, by becoming involved as an outsider in organized crime activities and then by agreeing to testify against those on the inside. What set him apart was his remarkable knack for involving himself in crime. It was born of a weakness for gambling, which got him into debt and the hands of Brooklyn's loan sharks, but it proved to be a more primal quality than just bad luck and bad judgment. Nadborn attracted crime. He had an instinct, like a well-witcher's attraction to subterranean water, which drew him to crime in situations where others might never have known it was there to find. For a time, this provided a bonanza for the Justice Department.

When the government's crimebusters first found him, in the late 1960s, Nadborn, the debt-ridden car dealer, was selling stolen cars for the mob and paying ruinous vigorish to loan sharks. In exchange for leniency and relocation, Nadborn agreed to testify against the car thieves and the loan sharks. But that was only the start. He also exposed a bank vice president who received kickbacks for approving loans to bankroll loan shark operations and helped the Secret Service catch a band of counterfeiters with $500,000 in phony ten-dollar bills. When two of the counterfeiters appeared later in Nadborn's kitchen with a pistol and a threat to kill him for being a suspected snitch, Nadborn talked them into letting him join them in the disposal of some drugs they had hijacked from Kennedy Airport. Then he saw to it that they got arrested with the drugs.

At that point, the Nadborn family was clearly ripe for relocation, and the Justice Department whisked them out of Brooklyn, off to a city a continent away. At one point, Nadborn claims, he found a job paying $42,000 a year as general manager of a Volkswagen agency — but when he asked the Justice Department to tell the employer he was a relocated witness and not a criminal, there was only an embarrassed silence. The job went to someone else, and Nadborn became the tar-baby of the alias program. He had a wife and three children (two of them in college) and a home with a swimming pool, but no past to qualify him for a job to sustain his style of life. When he was relocated, Nadborn had signed the usual release required by Justice Department regulations, which "forever releases the United States Government, or its agents, from any further responsibility for protection or any disbursement of government funds. . . ."

The Justice Department's releases are more or less jokingly called "death warrants" by witnesses because the story has spread, mistakenly, that it is no longer a federal offense to murder them, once they have formally terminated their status as Justice Department witnesses. But almost everyone concerned realized that the releases were empty gestures, and in 1976 the Marshals' Service stopped using them. As a practical matter — and a moral one, as well — the government can never wash its hands of people who have risked their lives to testify at the Justice Department's request. This was illustrated by a quiet exchange of court papers in Miami's federal court late in 1975. A man named Emilio Garcia filed suit, saying that he had testified for the government against some three hundred drug pushers and that he had been taken into the Witness Protection Program, but had subsequently been dropped. He claimed that attempts had been made on his life, and accused the government of, among other things, cruel and unusual punishment. The Justice Department quickly filed a reply, implying that Garcia had been guilty of indiscretions that fully justified his severance from the program, but then declaring that the government had decided to take him back.

The fact is that the men who run the alias program would not risk having the blood of any witness or family member on their consciences, and they also know that if a witness is ever abandoned by the government and then killed, the relocation program will die with him. So despite the releases, whenever a relocated witness telephones the special Justice Department "panic number," with the word that a cover has been blown and the family is huddled in terror, heavily armed government guards appear quickly and rush the witness and his family away, to begin the whole process again in another place.

In Nadborn's case, the government has managed to make the best of his continued dependence. Because of his affinity for crime, he has been able to operate as an itinerant, free-lance fink. He wanders into a crime-ridden city, noses around a bit, and in due time presents the authorities with an opportunity to catch some criminals in the process of committing a major crime. They do, and he collects informer's fees from the Drug Enforcement Agency or FBI, witness fees from the Justice Department, and sometimes insurance rewards for recovered goods. Federal officials confirm his claim that he has accounted for important arrests across the country involving heroin, cocaine, stolen and counterfeit securities, stolen airline tickets, and bookmaking rings. Nadborn claims he can make $30,000 at it in a good year, but he says it's a miserable life of cold fear and bad motels, and he blames the men who run the alias program. "They just don't care. They leave you there, out in the cold, like an animal. I don't want their money. . . . I just want a job, a chance to get my life straightened out."

In addition to the government's self-imposed limitations on the quality of aliases, and the inherent difficulties of changing identities in a data-laden society, the alias program has suffered from bureaucratic bungling and ineptitude by the men who run the show. Most of the citizens who enter the program tend to start out viewing all high public officials as skilled professionals, as the best that can be had for the jobs they do. But, in fact, the Justice Department is peopled mostly by lawyers — square, narrowly trained technicians who have no education in creating false identities, and who are certainly less cunning in such black arts than the gangsters they are attempting to deceive. When Gerald Shur first came to Newark to interview Gerald Zelmanowitz, he brought with him an impressive-looking personnel form and mentioned casually that it was a CIA document, used to elicit all possible information about potential agents. The implication was that the most clandestine agencies of the government were in on the new program — but in fact, all the CIA did for Zelmanowitz was just to furnish that one form.

Some attorneys in some of the task forces have proved ingenious in helping with the aliases. One lawyer assisted a particularly effective witness by somehow obtaining in his new name an actual military discharge, complete with a string of medals that made him — on paper — one of the most highly decorated heroes of World War II: Distinguished Service Medal, Navy Cross, Silver Star, and Purple Heart. Actually, the witness did not serve in World War II. But he is now a businessman, and he takes such pride in his "war record" that visitors to his office are confronted with his many medals on the wall, framed and mounted on blue velvet. That witness' alias has withstood one of the United States' most stringent tests of acceptability. During an election campaign he briefly met President Gerald Ford, and in the process became friendly with a White House aide. After that, for as long as Ford was President, the witness periodically visited his friend in the Executive Office Building adjacent to the White House, flashing his credentials at White House police, who never suspected he was an impostor created by the Justice Department.

But the day-to-day operation of the witness protection program, including most of the work done on false identities, is done by the United States Marshals' Service. The marshals are basically the process-serving and prisoner-guarding arm of the federal government, with no previous undercover function that might have given them expertise in creating false identities. Moreover, the marshals are the bottom of the barrel in the Justice Department's personnel hierarchy. Unlike the FBI, they have no rigid standards for employment. Many of them are former city cops or sheriff's deputies who happened to have enough political clout to land a job with the federal government. As a result, the Marshals' Service is not renowned for its industry and ingenuity, and few people familiar with the federal government would select the Marshals' Service if given a choice of federal agencies to whom they would entrust their lives.

There appears to be a further, more subtle, problem in the insensitivity of some officials of the Marshals' Service to the problems that relocated families face. Government personnel who have worked with witnesses say that dealing with their unreasonable demands, irresponsible actions, and spendthrift habits can require the patience of Job — a quality frequently found lacking in the upper echelons of the Marshals' Service, where retired military officers have often found jobs.

In 1971 Gerald Shur received a furious letter from one of the prosecutors in the Baltimore Strike Force, Joseph Kiel, complaining about the "arrogant, peevish and offensive" treatment of a relocated witness by Reis Kash, who was then the official in the U.S. Marshals' Service in charge of the witness relocation program. Kiel charged that Kash, a retired army warrant officer, was a "myopic bureaucrat, who is totally unskilled in interpersonal relations," and that his "inept and crude handling" of the witness had prompted the man to threaten to refuse to testify in a series of upcoming trials. Kiel's letter, classified "strike force confidential," alleged that Kash had refused to provide subsistence payments and documents that had been promised by the government, apparently because the witness had a large nest egg of his own, which Kash assumed to have been obtained through shady activities. According to the letter, Kash told the witness that "any documents obtained have been obtained out of the goodness of my heart," and that the best way for the witness to settle the dispute would be to "blow the country." After further rounds of letters and charges, a mediator within the Justice Department ruled that the government did owe most of the money claimed by the witness.

In another letter-writing incident, a different Marshals' Service official was accused of insensitivity and callousness. He had been quoted in *People* magazine as calling witnesses "wise guys" who often expect more than they deserve from the government and who make him appreciate his weekends spent with "nice people" on the golf course. A subsequent issue of the magazine carried a letter from an unidentified woman witness, pleading the cause of hidden witnesses who are dependent and economically handicapped because they have testified for the government. "I don't expect the taxpayers to take care of me all my life," she wrote, "but my husband paid $70,000 a year in taxes when he was alive, and I am responsible for convictions in 40 cases (on charges of drug abuse and conspiracy). Witnesses are not 'wise guys' . . . we are not just pieces of dirt."

The government won't say who in the Marshals' Service conceived the practice of simply grinding out consecutive new Social Security numbers for witnesses. But several witnesses who went through the program at various times report that they were given sequential Social Security numbers with other members of their families. One witness claims to have rejected the cards on the spot, and to have obtained his own Social Security credentials, with nonsequential numbers.

What relocated witnesses complain about most is run-of-the-mill bureaucratic fumbling and procrastination that might normally be shrugged off as part of the cost of doing business with the government — but which are excruciating when the victim's identity and safety are at stake. Most complaints are about delays in receiving documents, subsistence payments, and job assistance. Witnesses have been packed off to faraway cities, only to be stranded for weeks before their papers and checks started to arrive. Sometimes the documents were palpably false. One witness received a Xerox copy of a birth certificate, obviously altered. Another enrolled his children in school, using the false background he had been taught. The Marshals' Service had promised to recycle his children's school records through a Maryland public school, using their new names but the grades they had actually earned in school in New York. The records were many weeks in coming, and the witness resorted to elaborate lies about his children's performance in the Maryland public schools, in order to pacify the principal of the new school. Finally the records arrived — and punctured the witness's fine-spun story with a clear notation that one child's grades were from a New York school.

One bungle jeopardized the cooperation of one of the most productive informants the Justice Department has ever had, a legendary undercover operative named Herman Goldfarb. Goldfarb is a short, paunchy, balding one-time insurance broker from Brooklyn and Long Island, who once served a year and a half in prison for grand larceny. A nonstop talker who likes to tell people he has an I.Q. of 159 and reads 2,205 words a minute, Goldfarb emerged from prison in 1961 insisting that he was innocent (he had pleaded guilty) and badgering the FBI to let him join their side by infiltrating organized crime. In return, he asked only two things: a review of the record in his case, and a loan to put him back in the insurance business. Seven years later, Goldfarb had "made" 198 cases for the government, including a string of indictments he engineered by operating a phony trucking company while he gathered evidence against gangsters who were fleecing businessmen in Manhattan's tough garment district. (While he was at it, Goldfarb made a profit with the trucking company.)

When it was over, Goldfarb was given a new identity and relocated in another city and was told that the Justice Department would help him get a $200,000 loan from the Small Business Administration. There is little agreement about what happened next, except that Goldfarb didn't get the loan. His story is that the Justice Department was supposed to tip off the SBA that he was a relocated government witness and should be excused from the requirement to state on his loan application all his prior identities. Justice Department officials said they waited for him to apply formally, but that they finally did put in a word for him with the SBA. SBA officials say Goldfarb kept assuring them that the Justice Department would vouch for him, but it never did, so they disapproved the loan.

Feeling betrayed, Goldfarb complained to the Senate Permanent Investigations Subcommittee and threatened to sue the government. Worse yet for the Justice Department, there was an implied threat to stop testifying, and Goldfarb was still commuting frequently to New York to appear before grand juries. Explaining that the problem with the first application had been a "bureaucratic" one, the Justice Department quietly arranged for Goldfarb to get his loan.

Nobody on the outside knows how many other blunders have been brushed under the Justice Department's rug, but the persistent difficulties of the alias program have raised questions as to whether any government agency, however efficient, could successfully cope with the life-and-death problems of so many people. Officials said the program was relocating witnesses at the rate of about five hundred per year in 1976, which would mean that almost two thousand of them, plus their families, would be scattered across the country under false identities by the end of that year. Most of them haven't been heard from since they took their government aliases, and many law enforcement officials say that the program has been a strong plus in the government's fight against organized crime and, had it been efficiently run, could have put the crime syndicate to rout.

But occasionally a situation comes to light in which the alias program has so devastated a witness and his family that it creates doubts as to whether the government should ever involve itself so deeply in the lives of its citizens. Such was the case of Richard J. Blake, Sr.

On August 14, 1974, William J. DePugh, a special inspector for the Internal Revenue Service, submitted a report to his superiors on the Blake case. It told the following story.

Prior to 1969, Blake was a partner in a small tree-trimming business in Des Plaines, Illinois, which specialized in servicing suburban city governments in the Chicago area. Blake discovered that in order to trim trees for the municipal governments around Chicago he was expected to pay kickbacks to city officials. Blake and his partner didn't like it, but paying the kickbacks was the only way to stay in business, so they paid. Two years later, a routine audit by the IRS disclosed these illegal payments, and Blake and his partner were handed a gentle ultimatum by the IRS — become confidential informants against the corrupt officials or face charges themselves. They agreed to act as confidential sources for the IRS, but in 1972 the government betrayed them by subpoenaing them as witnesses against the corrupt officials before a federal grand jury. This blew their cover with the bribe-takers, and so terrified Blake's partner that he spent nine months in jail for contempt before he finally agreed to accept relocation and testify.

Blake finally made the same deal with the Justice Department — he would testify, in exchange for the government's promise to relocate him and his family, provide them with new identities, and give them enough money to establish a new home and business. Blake testified, and then began a nightmare of government bungling, indifference, and stupidity.

First, the Justice Department did nothing. There was no protection, no money, and there were no new identity papers. Yet somebody remembered; another witness in the case was shot and killed. On the advice of the IRS agents, Blake took his family to Bozeman, Montana, and tried to relocate himself at his own expense. While he was gone, the IRS slapped a tax lien on his house. He lost his business and his house, and when he failed to find a place to live in Montana, the Justice Department paid him two months' subsistence and sent the family to Spokane, Washington. There the government provided him with a driver's license and Social Security card in his new name, but no money and no help in finding a job. He passed the test to obtain a state real estate broker's license, but the Justice Department refused to certify his fingerprints under his alias, and the license was denied. Blake, his wife, and his five children rented a house, but the government failed to ship his furniture; the family spent Christmas of 1973 sleeping on the floor in the empty house, and soon after that the three older children said they couldn't take it anymore and left to join their mother, who had been divorced from Blake several years before.

Shortly after Christmas, with Blake, his wife, and the two remaining children destitute and beginning to suffer from cold and hunger, the government gave him a check for $1,000 — on the condition that he sign the "death warrant." He signed.

The final disaster came when Blake slipped back to Chicago in the spring of 1974 in an effort to recover funds from the sale of his home that had been placed in escrow, and to secure copies of the school records of one of his children. He encountered one of the former officials whom he had mentioned in grand jury testimony, former State Senator Walter P. Hoffelder, and Hoffelder had him arrested on charges of intimidation. The charge was a misdemeanor, but bond was set at $100,000, and the affair had come full circle — Blake, the innocent party and reluctant witness to a kickback scheme, spent two months in the Cook County jail before he was finally acquitted of "intimidation," and the men whom he accused have not yet been brought to trial.

In his report to his superiors, IRS inspector DePugh summed up the Blake case with rare candor:

"It would be very hard to convince anyone that the Blake family situation could be used by the Government as an example of how they take care of people who cooperate. To betray the confidentiality status of a person against his will; to let him build up expectations of a new life under the official auspices of the U.S. Government; to let him wander undirected across the country in search of a new life; to let him expend his own funds on the Government's business; and then to have him sign an instrument releasing the Government from its responsibility when he is desperate is not something the public or other possible witnesses for the Government would put much faith in."

On DePugh's recommendation, the government accepted Blake back into the alias program, and he has again disappeared from the Chicago scene.

Gerald Zelmanowitz was unaware of the warning signals about the witness relocation program on the crisp day in March of 1970, when he and his family made their last visit to the stern halls of the Justice Department. They received their new identity documents and parting advice from Shur and Bonomi, and, as they stepped outside into the clear, cold afternoon, Paul Maris felt the burdens of the guilt and worries of the old life begin to lift from his spirit.

Later that day, Paul and Lillian Maris and Joseph and Evelyn Miller boarded a jet at Baltimore's Friendship Airport, nonstop to San Francisco. It was the first time in months that Maris had gone anywhere without bodyguards. As the plane lifted off toward California, he experienced a great feeling of well-being. He had been given an absolution that thousands, perhaps millions, of people had secretly yearned to have — a chance to wash away all the scars of youth and, with the wisdom of midlife, to start again with a clean slate. He told himself that he had learned all of the harsh lessons and he would make none of the same mistakes. Paul Maris would be a better man than Gerry Zelmanowitz had been.

5...........................Tycoon

Paul Maris's elation at being safe and anonymous in California faded fast. He, Lillian, and the Millers rented a small furnished apartment, but then they became self-confined prisoners within its vanilla walls. They were frightened and without friends, so they spent day after day and night after night facing each other across the cramped living room and talking of their severed pasts.

It would not have been in Paul Maris's nature to stagnate in self-pity for very long but, in any event, he was forced out of the apartment at the end of the first month by poverty. The first of the month came, but with it no government check. When he had agreed to become a government witness, the Justice Department had promised to pay subsistence for one year, or until it got him a job. After he got to San Francisco, nobody from the government contacted him about the job. He didn't give it much thought because he preferred to get his own job, but later it occurred to him that there might be something ominous about the Justice Department's silence.

That feeling grew as the check became longer overdue. He had been promised $36 per day, and the checks had come regularly from the time his family had been hustled away from their home in Short Hills until he left Washington as Paul Maris. When he got to San Francisco he still had five months of his year's subsistence coming. But weeks passed, and no money came. Maris began to phone Washington, but Shur was either unavailable or evasive. The landlord was beginning to press for his rent, and Maris, edgy over the family's dwindling balance, launched into a frenzied job-hunting effort. Out went fifty copies of his new résumé, resulting in about thirty job interviews. Maris fought to choke back the stirrings of panic when he failed to receive a single job offer. For the first time, he fully realized how confining his cover as a cryptographer was. Nobody in San Francisco needed a cryptographer, yet he couldn't tell prospective employers about the experiences that had given him exceptional expertise in such fields as securities analysis, banking, stocks and bonds sales, and securities trading.

Then he thought he had found a line of work where scrambling and results would be rewarded without concern for the person's background; he would sell real estate. Maris took a course in real estate, studied for the real estate brokers' exam, and drove with Lillian one day to a meeting hall in the San Fernando Valley to take the test. It was not until he presented himself to be tested that he discovered that, for him, there was a catch. They wanted to take his fingerprints. Maris stalled and stammered around, made excuses, and then slipped away from his proposed career as a real estate salesman.

His calls to Washington became more strident, demanding his money and pleading for a job. He complained to United States Attorney Lacey in Newark, who was furious with Washington for waffling on the deal Lacey had made. Lacey recalled how impressed he had been with his witness's skills with stocks and salesmanship, so he called a friend at Merrill, Lynch, Pierce, Fenner and Smith. He leveled with him about Maris, and the friend said yes, they could probably find a place for a man such as Paul Maris as a stockbroker. But the Justice Department balked. It was against regulations to falsify the fingerprint check required by law for stockbrokers, Lacey was told, and to report on Paul Maris's fingerprints truthfully would blow his cover. With Paul Maris's career with Merrill, Lynch squelched at the outset, Lacey had no recourse but to protest to Washington that "the relocation program was such that it wasn't going to work if you didn't have a man able to pay his rent and feed himself."

Maris was saying the same thing — and more — in increasingly frantic calls to Washington, some of them late at night to Shur's home. Then he began to get the message. Nobody would say it directly, but gradually he realized he was encountering the same old problem: they were cutting off his subsistence because they were convinced that he didn't need or deserve it, suspecting he still had access to hidden Mafia money.

At about that time the landlord served them with an eviction notice, and Maris was stunned by the realization of his position. He had been tricked and betrayed by the government, he felt, and he was isolated and powerless to fight back. What could he do, sue them? He could not go back to being Gerald Zelmanowitz, yet Paul Maris was an economic cripple, doomed to menial jobs and a marginal existence for the rest of his life.

Maris decided to fight. He got a handful of applications for credit cards, and filled them out in the name of "Captain Paul J. Maris," a serviceman stationed in San Francisco. Most were ignored, but Diners Club sent Maris a credit card, and he was on his way. Maris used the card to buy an airplane ticket to Washington, where, he had decided, the only way to get his due was to go to the Justice Department and take his case to the man at the top.

To most persons, that would have meant crashing into the office of the attorney general, John Mitchell, where Maris could well have got himself locked away as a dangerous kook. But to Paul Maris, the man effectively at the top of the legal world was the official in operational control of the Criminal Division, Henry Petersen. So on a warm spring morning in 1970, an obviously agitated young man barged into Petersen's outer office and announced: "I want the money you promised me — not a penny more, not a penny less. You've got to kill me because I'm staying here until you take me out and murder me, but I want my money and I won't leave until I get it!"

It was a dramatic and moving performance. Unfortunately, Petersen was not in. His two secretaries were visibly impressed, but it would all have been wasted, but for an assistant in a nearby office who heard the commotion and stuck his head in to see what was going on. The attorney soothed the agitated visitor with sweet reason, assuring him that his cause seemed just and that surely, if he would just go back to California, the logic of his position would carry the day. Maneuvering him toward the door, the lawyer told Maris that he had made his point, that the matter would be looked into, and that no further demonstrations in the Justice Department would be necessary. Maris should go home; he would hear from the government.

Maris found himself standing on the sidewalk outside the Justice Department, feeling foolish — partly because of what he had done, and partly because he had left without even getting the attorney's name. But there was nothing more he could do. He realized that he felt more at home, more secure, struggling in San Francisco as Paul Maris, than in the ambiguous world of Washington and the Justice Department.

Again relying upon his Diners Club card, he flew meekly back to San Francisco.

A few days later Maris was called to the United States attorney's office in San Francisco and given a check for slightly more than five thousand dollars. Maris was almost happy to sign the obligatory "death warrant," which "forever releases the United States Government, or its agents, from any further responsibility for protection. . . ."

Formally ending his relationship with the Justice Department was less traumatic than it might have seemed, because so many things the government was supposed to have done failed to happen after the family went west. One was the admission of Norman and Cynthia into the University of California at Berkeley. The Vietnam war was still on then, college draft deferments were golden, and colleges were packed. There was a one-year waiting list for admission to the University of California at Berkeley, and the Justice Department had agreed to use its clout to get them in right away. But once the couple got to California, only Norman heard from the Justice Department. He received from Baldwin Wallace College a transcript, giving Norman Roth credit for the same course credits and grades that Norman Yaguda had earned at New York University. He was also granted admission to Berkeley, as promised. But nothing happened concerning Cindy. As September approached and still no acceptance, Maris called for help to the Newark corporate attorney, Thomas Campion. Campion said he'd make a few calls to friends on the West Coast, and, after sitting out the first semester, Cindy was admitted to Berkeley.

Meanwhile, Norman found himself in danger of being drafted and prosecuted for draft evasion at the same time. When the Justice Department transformed Norman Yaguda into Norman Roth, he had been told that his precious 2-S draft deferment would be transferred to the new name. But several months after Norman got to California, he received a nervous call from his father in New Jersey, saying that agents of the FBI were looking for Norman Yaguda because he had dropped out of N.Y.U., had lost his student deferment, and was now evading the draft. On the other hand, Norman Roth was prime draft bait, as he had never received a 2-S deferment.

Maris took direct action. He marched Norman into the Berkeley draft board, flashed his credentials, introduced himself as "Captain Paul Maris of the Army Security Agency," and identified Norman as one of his undercover operatives. Maris said he was there to get the young man's draft deferment. Norman was quickly given assurances and a form to fill out. In a few weeks, he received his permanent deferment in the mail.

When Maris signed the release with the government, it seemed as if a magic hand had flipped the "go" switch in his life. Gone was the rage and the self-pity, the distracting and time-consuming arguments with bureaucrats, the crippling notion that his fortunes centered upon Washington. With the government check he paid his bills, bought some new suits, and felt ready to take on San Francisco. Maris realized that when that five thousand dollars was gone, he had to be prepared to take care of his family alone.

It was at about that time that he landed a job with the Equitable Life Insurance Company. At that point it seemed just a timely break, but later, Maris realized that the Equitable job was the cornerstone of his new career. It was the connection that afforded him respectability for the first time in his life, a good job with a prestigious company that gave Paul Maris a legitimate background from which he could move anywhere in business that his talents would take him. It was also the first manifestation of an odd public myopia that was to surface time and time again to bolster his identity at critical points in his second life — the fact that people tended not to see flaws in his story, so long as it was in their interest to take him for the person he claimed to be. Once he acquired the first glimmer of success with Equitable, this trait was to gain him rapid acceptance in the business, political, and philanthropic life of San Francisco. But in the rise of his good fortune, Maris himself failed to see the reverse side of this phenomenon; that his identity would be subjected to the most piercing scrutiny, if he ever stood in anybody's way.

The opportunity at Equitable sprang from Maris's impressive performance on a test. They had given him a routine battery of aptitude tests for insurance salesmen, and he shattered the norms for the kind of intelligence, aggressiveness, and ingenuity that sold insurance. Company officials wanted very much to hire this hard-charging, newly retired army officer. Maris's references were thin, but that was accepted as a product of his intelligence background. The references he gave were also rather odd for a military man: Glen Robinson, an official in the United States Marshals' Office in San Francisco, and two civilian officials in Washington, Dante Bonomi and Gerald Shur. Phone calls were placed to Robinson and Bonomi, but both were unavailable. But Equitable's sales executives were eager to put this promising new salesman on the street, so they went ahead, assuming that the references could be tidied up later. Somehow this never got done, but after a few days it didn't make any difference. Paul Maris had already demonstrated that he was one of the hottest insurance salesmen on the Equitable team.

Equitable found Paul Maris to be a man who read corporate profit-and-loss statements with the same ease and zest that many men scanned the sports pages' box scores, and so the company put him to work selling group health policies to businesses. They handed him a computer printout of one hundred companies that were big enough to need group insurance for their employees yet were not affiliated with larger corporations that would already have coverage. It was an alphabetical list, and Maris began to knock on doors and pour out charm and persuasion. He began to sell policies, working his way down the alphabet.

Before long, Maris found himself at the *d*'s, and that brought him to the Alvin Duskin Company. Its owner and namesake was a young, balding, slightly disheveled man who had inherited a tradition of fabric manufacturing from his father, a garment business old-timer who had specialized for years in knitting cotton material for women's clothes. But young Alvin had larger ambitions and a more creative flair, and he had expanded the business into a company that not only knitted fabrics but also designed, manufactured, and sold women's apparel.

Alvin Duskin was happy to have Maris review the company's books, and Maris immediately saw why. A quick survey of the records convinced him that the Alvin Duskin Company was in need of any help it could get. It was virtually bankrupt. As Maris added it up the firm owed $1.3 million in accounts payable, it had less than $60,000 for the current month, and it had lost more than $800,000 in the prior fiscal

*In October, 1970, Alvin Duskin brought Paul Maris into the San Fran-
cisco knitwear firm his father had founded. Barely a year later Maris was
president and Duskin was out.*

year. He explained to Duskin that he didn't need any insurance: "You're broke, bankrupt, dead."

Duskin was impressed with the knowledge and self-assurance of his new acquaintance, and indeed Duskin did have very little to lose. He invited Maris to join the company and try to keep it from going under. The Maris family assembled in the apartment living room to consider Duskin's offer. They had no illusions about the chances of success, but there was a compelling logic to the situation. Nobody but a Paul Maris would consider such a proposition. But for him, it was a long-shot chance to make up for his late start in life — and if it failed, he could always go back to selling insurance.

Paul and Joe Miller pooled their funds, and together they came up with $5,000. It bought 50 percent of the insolvent Duskin Corporation.

Maris came aboard in October of 1970, first as an unpaid financial advisor, and later in the fall, as the salaried treasurer of the company. Alvin Duskin's decision to take this charismatic stranger into his company provided another example of the tendency of people who wanted to believe in Maris to see him as he claimed to be. Duskin, by then, was clutching at any straws he could reach, and Maris represented a chance to pull things back together. Still, before he made Maris an officer in the company, Duskin hesitated on principle to take in someone whom he knew so little about. He mentioned this one day to a cousin who sometimes advised him, and asked if perhaps they shouldn't check Paul Maris's background out. The cousin said no, Maris had worked for Equitable Life, and big insurance companies undoubtedly bonded such employees. His background would have been thoroughly checked out then, the cousin said. Duskin was relieved by this, and was anxious to go ahead, so he never questioned Maris's background again.

Paul Maris threw himself into a frenetic campaign to keep the Duskin Company afloat and, at the same time, to pump up its deflated sales. It was the kind of free-style rescue operation that required all his qualities of energy and persuasion, and he turned them on, full blast. Maris first made a swing around the country, persuading the company's suppliers to continue shipping yarn and its customers to wait for swinging new styles that were on the way. He hired a new sales force, opened salesrooms across the country, and expanded the company's production force. When Maris came, the payroll had slumped to about 80 employees, and the salesmen hadn't been paid in weeks. He persuaded them that better times were on the way, and began to build the staff up toward the peak of 350 that it was soon to reach.

Meanwhile, they were pinched for credit, and Maris neatly bailed them out. Duskin had applied for a loan from the United California Bank, but the Duskin Company was too shaky to rate an unsecured loan. The bank demanded collateral. Paul Maris announced grandly that he, personally, would guarantee the note. He did, backing it up with a statement of his substantial holdings in Japanese electronics interests, plus his handsome Washington home. Maris listed a fashionable address on Massachusetts Avenue, in the heart of the capital's stately "Embassy Row." It was a mansion that Maris had admired during his stay in Washington, and since he estimated it to be worth about the same as his equity in his home back in New Jersey, he saw nothing amiss in giving this address as his own. The bank, impressed, approved the note.

Over the next six months, the Alvin Duskin Company began to come to life. Sales perked up, the company began to make deliveries on time, and its credit began to jell. But Maris knew they had somehow to secure a large transfusion of outside capital in order to afford the promotional and advertising effort required to make the company grow. He began to cast about for financial backing and, in April of 1971, he discovered the Creative Capital Corporation of New York. Creative Capital was a high-risk venture-capital firm controlled by the "Parsons Group" in Detroit, a high-rolling banking and investment conglomerate that parlayed the bull market of the sixties into almost a billion dollars on paper before collapsing in the business slump of the early seventies.

But when Paul Maris found Creative Capital it was looking for a place to put its money, and Maris set about persuading its board chairman and chief executive officer, Milton Stewart, that the Alvin Duskin Company was just the place. After generous doses of enthusiasm and persuasion by Maris, Stewart concluded that in the Duskin Company he had discovered a diamond in the rough. Alvin Duskin was a gifted dress designer but a scattershot businessman. Paul Maris had a dazzling business head and an obvious gift for promotion and sales. So Stewart came up with a plan: Duskin would concentrate on design.

Maris would be made a vice president in charge of marketing and sales. Creative Capital would loan the Duskin Company $400,000 and take a majority interest in its stock, and within two to five years, the company would be in the black.

Duskin and Maris leaped at the offer — or, more literally, they flew quickly to New York to sign the papers. It was a triumphant occasion for them, and afterward Duskin proposed a free-wheeling evening on the town in celebration. But Maris insisted on flying back to San Francisco immediately, that evening. He did not want to spend the night in New York. Duskin said it was crazy to fly back to the Coast the same day. Eventually Maris gave in, but he would agree to no more than a quiet dinner and then straight to his hotel room. Somehow the incident took the glow off the occasion; it was out of character for the gregarious Maris to crawl into his shell that way, and for Duskin it cast a tiny shadow over what they had accomplished that day.

In the following months the company began to boom, but the activity centered increasingly on Paul Maris — and away from Alvin Duskin. Duskin didn't really object to this, because he was developing an overriding interest in politics. When Maris first met him, Duskin was just tasting his first heady draft of winning politics in the form of the anti-high-rise referendum. Duskin had first become involved in environmental issues when he enlisted in citizens' efforts to preserve Alcatraz Island for the public and to block a plan to pipe water from the mountains to Los Angeles. Then when the high-rise issue developed, Duskin took the lead in the campaign by environmentalists to limit the heights of new buildings. When the campaign succeeded in placing an anti–high-rise proposition on the ballot (it was later voted down), Duskin was given approving recognition in the press for having led the charge. From that point, his appetite for politics swelled, and his zest for the garment business dwindled.

Thus it caused little surprise or bitterness when, late in 1971, Milton Stewart announced that he had decided to remove Duskin as president of the company and replace him with Paul Maris. Duskin was bored with business, anyway, and he was itching to run for mayor of San Francisco. So he sold his stock to Creative Capital and went cheerfully off to launch his political career with a race for supervisor of San

Francisco. Unfortunately for him, thirty-two other hopefuls also ran, and Duskin got lost in the pack, thus becoming one of the youngest political has-beens in northern California.

It seemed then that Alvin Duskin had been the pigeon of the affair, and Paul Maris the falcon, but later it developed that much of this incident, too, was not as it appeared to be. Much later Maris would claim that Creative Capital had tried to enrich itself through the ouster of Duskin, at the expense of the Duskin Corporation. He said Duskin's departure, or escape, depending on the viewpoint, left the Duskin Corporation with the burden of $1.3 million in back debts — plus $600,000 in notes Duskin and his father had personally guaranteed, plus $150,000 for Duskin's share of stock — all of which were turned over to Creative Capital to pay.

Duskin later agreed that Maris was not the villain; he blamed Milton Stewart and the government. Maris was a promotional wizard, Duskin would say later, "an incredibly charismatic man who unfortunately knew nothing about dress design or manufacture." To Duskin, Stewart's blindness to this was a version of the familiar myopia that surrounded Paul Maris. Stewart believed he could stage a dazzling financial coup by bankrolling Maris, and so he failed, in Duskin's view, to protect the company from Maris's excesses.

Duskin saw a fine irony in this, because the Creative Capital Corporation was a small business investment company, whose venture capital was supplied in part by the federal government's Small Business Administration. Thus, if Creative Capital had been bilked by Paul Maris to the point that the SBA was forced to absorb part of the loss, it would have been a case of the SBA being robbed by its sister agency, the Justice Department — and the SBA would never have known.

Duskin's outrage was directed mostly at the Justice Department. It was "basically immoral," he believed, for the government to use duplicity to place a law-abiding citizen at the mercy of a Mafia wolf in sheep's clothing. Duskin placed the blame on the concept of the alias program. "It is outrageous," he said later, "for the government to operate a program that creates false backgrounds for criminals and then turns them loose on law-abiding people." (Duskin felt so strongly about this that he took his complaint to the high-powered Washington

107

attorney Edward Bennett Williams and said he wanted to sue the government. After Williams pointed out the novelty of Duskin's claim and Williams's $50,000 retainer fee, Duskin abandoned the idea.)

In January of 1972, it was announced that the name of the Alvin Duskin Company would be changed to the Paul Maris Company. The usual ad was prepared for the trade newspapers to show the fashion world what the new chief of the company looked like. But Paul Maris declined to have his picture taken, just as he had not wanted the company to bear his name in the first place. But this time he was adamant, citing his government "undercover work." He was the boss, so Carlson/Leibowitz, Inc., a Los Angeles advertising agency, came up with an ad showing a large picture of a telephone bearing the name-plate "PAUL MARIS CO." The caption read:

On January 10th, the Alvin Duskin Co. officially becomes The Paul Maris Co., wearing the name of the man who has been the company's decisive force in bringing you the country's most distinctive Junior knits. If you have any questions, today, January 10th, is the day to call and talk. Mr. Maris believes in a direct line . . . and communication.

It was typical of Maris that even this eccentricity paid off. This ad was just mysterious and distinctive enough to be more memorable than a picture would have been. The same was true of the gushing coverage that Maris received in the trade press and the San Francisco dailies. Maris explained that he couldn't permit his picture to be published until he received his discharge from the army intelligence reserves (he had promoted himself to colonel, with duty in the State Department and Atomic Energy Commission), and this added only a titillating flavor to the articles about the mysterious fashion tycoon.

Maris proved to have a magic promotional touch. He believed that the key to success in the highly competitive women's apparel business was recognition of the company's label, and "Paul Maris" quickly became one of the hottest labels in the business. From the company's ad agencies' point of view, Maris was in many ways the dream client. To most businessmen, controversial ad themes were poison. Maris not only encouraged his admen's daring themes, he contributed some of his own.

The Maris line featured casual knitted tops and long, clinging styles aimed at the young market, and Maris set out to persuade the younger set that being with it required knits as well as jeans and granny dresses. He was in the business, ultimately, of selling sex appeal, and one magazine ad for the Paul Maris Company stated his pitch succinctly. It was a large, close, picture of the crotch of a young girl clad in tight denims. The message was spelled out in large bold letters: "IT TAKES PAUL MARIS TO GET ME OUT OF MY JEANS."

The Maris Company called on Carlson/Leibowitz again for a more sophisticated ad campaign to associate Paul Maris clothes with the young life-style. The result was a series of four "life-style" ads, run alternately in *Glamour* and *Mademoiselle* magazines, which were unlike anything the fashion world had seen thus far.

The first two-page spread pictured a girl, clad in Paul Maris's latest frock, at home with her male roommate. Her message was modern. They were living out-of-wedlock and loving it, but it was the new morality, not immorality: "We do not have affairs nor are we adulterers."

The second ad portrayed a young girl — also slinkily done up in a Paul Maris creation — allegedly responding to the message of the first ad, posing with her fiancé and announcing that they had decided to wait: "I could never live with a man before marriage. I just couldn't."

The third showed a Maris-clad young woman cuddling a child and justifying her decision to be divorced: "Oh, God, I do not believe in divorce. But neither do I believe in marriage without love."

The fourth ad was a softer pitch, showing a black woman in her Paul Maris knits, lamenting that human relations are not yet what they ought to be. Each ad was capped with the motto: "If Nobody's Talking About It, But Us, Then Let Us Talk About It."

A flood of letters poured into the magazines. The "we are not adulterers" ad was the prime target, generating indignant protests from those who thought it was advocating sin, and approval from others who said advertising was finally telling it like it was. At *Mademoiselle* more mail came in in response to that one ad than from any advertisement or editorial the magazine had ever published. Whatever the reaction, it was pure gold for the Paul Maris label. Sales boomed in dress shops across the country; women knew about Paul Maris.

Randy Skinner and John Avdeeff are students at Glendale College, California. Because her clothes must express her body and her mood, Randy's choice: the Sideflash day nighter knit. We now call it the "Randy" knit. 3200

Number One in a Series

Randy Skinner and John Avdeeff

"We do not have affairs nor are we adulterers"

Is anybody out there listening to me, really? I mean sometimes I feel like we have to recognize everybody else's reality but nobody recognizes ours. John and I are living together before marriage because we want to know and learn to love each other.

I don't believe marriage is something you use to get to know one another. It is for enjoying what you've found out about each other. I wish marriage could be a celebration of the fact that you've found you do enjoy living with each other.

My parents had a life style that worked for them. But I don't see it working for us. Is cleaning and cooking and raising children a fair exchange for someone using his intelligence to make you comfortable? I don't think so. And raising children should be done together, not more so by one parent.

We want to work together for what we believe in, to live together, to be together. And this is the way we start.

Money isn't that important to John and I. Maybe this is all very nice and idealistic. And when I get older and money hungry and cynical, I'll read this and laugh. No, wait. I'll never laugh at it.

I'll just feel sad if I don't live up to it.

If Nobody's Talking About It, But Us, Then Let Us Talk About It.

PAUL MARIS CO.
510 THIRD STREET, SAN FRANCISCO, CALIFORNIA 94107

Glossy magazine ads for the Paul Maris Company, matching its president's unorthodox and innovative ways, were executed by Carlson/Leibowitz, Inc., of Los Angeles.

The Maris gift for promoting the company name took many forms. When he turned the tables on the French designers by showing his fashions in Paris, there were articles — some approving, some appalled — in newspapers across the country. Each American company also had an annual in-house style show for buyers and fashion writers, and the competition to get them to attend was fierce. In 1972, the trade press received from the Maris Company round-trip plane tickets to San Francisco, together with invitations to a "country fair" at Paul Maris's estate in the Sonoma foothills north of the city. There, they were treated to drinks, music, swimming, and a generous display of the forthcoming Paul Maris fashion line. The news reports of this were all approving.

Another annual ritual of the women's fashion industry is a gathering in Texas for a showing of upcoming fashions at the Dallas apparel mart. There, the most fertile minds in the industry compete with each other to capture the attention of the buyers, who will select their stores' lines for the coming year. One year, Paul Maris topped all his firm's rivals, hands down. Whenever the buyers emerged from the apparel mart, they were confronted by a sign five stories high, on the building across the street. It read: PAUL MARIS COMPANY.

For all of his flair for publicizing his name and his company, Maris himself was rarely seen about San Francisco. He did not cultivate the cocktail-and-dinner-party circuit, and he never showed up at public events where he might become the center of attention. The colorful Paul Maris of the newspaper columns was in fact a homebody, a man who spent his evenings at work or with his family and his weekends in the country. It was not that Maris was antisocial — he was always given a good table and effusive treatment at the few select restaurants that he patronized — but just that he was an uncommonly private public figure. So subtle was this phenomenon that nobody noticed it, until he was gone.

As gregarious and as close as Maris was with his employees, none of them suspected that he was anybody except who he claimed to be. It was not that they had not noticed Lillian's tendency to call him "Gerry," or had not considered the implausibility of some of his stories of past undercover intrigues. "Hell, nobody believed all that CIA stuff," one of his sales managers said later; "but nobody thought anything about it either — everybody tells war stories." Also, for all of his urbane charm and sophisticated bearing, Maris was subject to occasional glaring lapses of stye. He usually gave the impression of being extremely well informed about any subject he discussed. Nobody seemed to notice that Maris dominated most discussions, and thus they usually centered on subjects that he knew all about — business and money. But even here, with Maris holding forth with an obvious mastery of the vocabulary and theory of his subject, he would occasionally drop into his flow of conversation a "youse guys" or "I could have went," which might have jolted his listener into wonderment, except that by then Maris had moved the conversation blithely on to other ideas and more persuasive arguments. Even when such remarks were delivered with a distinctive trace of Brooklyn, nobody seemed to question that they were uttered by a college graduate from Philadelphia.

The reason was that Paul Maris was a believable person. His expensive taste in clothes and furnishings meshed comfortably with his go-for-broke approach to business. "My ego is too big to fit into the seats back in tourist," he once explained, when somebody questioned his expensive habit of always going first class. He had a style and ego that were natural to him and beneficial to the business he was in, and they suited the role he had assumed so well that no one — not even Kat Walker — imagined that he was not exactly who he appeared to be.

Maris had a gift for motivating his workers and making them feel involved in the company's success. He was an outgoing man who radiated charm and energy, and he took a one-big-happy-family approach toward the business that worked because he believed in it himself. He knew everybody in the plant, and he joked and horseplayed with them with an easy familiarity and sense of fun. Once when Maris was meeting with a group of buyers in the company boardroom, he gave a signal and the company tap dance class, with Kat Walker in the lead, did a tap routine through the room. Maris's relationship with the plant's workers included an unusual rapport with the stolid Oriental women who spent the long, tedious hours at the cutting boards and sewing machines. Because of the language barrier the banter did not usually extend to them, but they sensed — accurately, it turned out — that Paul Maris understood what the life of a seamstress was like.

The sum total was that Maris ran a happy shop. Visitors invariably remarked about the atmosphere of headlong, dedicated activity by everyone in sight. It was an invaluable quality for an operation that had much to overcome. It was no secret that the company was tottering so near the financial precipice that Maris often had to delay ordering needed yarn until he had landed a big new order for clothes. Factory old-timers also shook their heads over some of his blind spots about the trade. He would get carried away with enthusiasm for so many styles that the Paul Maris Company frequently offered a wider variety of articles than its factory could turn out. He would go all out for a new wrinkle, such as triple-stitched seams, although the Maris plant lacked the triple-stitch sewing machines to keep pace when orders for the new style poured in. He would sometimes be overly influenced by his wife's taste, so that Paul Maris clothes occasionally projected a hint of matronly East Coast suburbia. But for the most part, Maris had the respect and loyalty of the people who made up the company, and to a significant degree he would enjoy this trust for as long as he was Paul Maris, and even beyond.

Maris also played the more orthodox role of the community-minded business executive. He put into effect a vigorous program to hire blacks, women, former drug addicts, and — perhaps not surprisingly — ex-convicts. American Indians were then much in vogue with doers of good works, and Maris caught the spirit. He brought Indian women from the inland reservations to San Francisco for training at the sewing machines. He sent Indian men to Thunderbird University in Arizona to learn management. And he was negotiating with the United States Bureau of Indian Affairs for financing to establish an all-Indian branch of his plant at Uplake, California, when Creative Capital stepped in and quashed the idea on the grounds that the company was spreading itself too thin.

Outside the company, Maris agreed to serve one year as chairman of the United Jewish Appeal's campaign in the garment industry, but he shied away from activities in the community at large. He turned down Alvin Duskin's request that he manage his campaign for supervisor, and he said no when he was approached to join the Bay Area finance committee for George McGovern's 1972 presidential campaign. When the word of the suggested McGovern connection drifted back through the Justice Department grapevine to Washington, some of the men in the know hooted at the thought. "I could see the headlines," one of them said later: "George McGovern wakes up one morning after a hard night's speech about Watergate and reads on the front page that his California campaign is being run by Gerry Zelmanowitz." But for the most part, officials in the Justice Department didn't think the rise of Paul Maris was very amusing. Deputies in the Marshals' Office in San Francisco who were in on the story would marvel over each fawning article in the local press, and at least one official in Washington admitted sitting in his office and gnashing his teeth over a story in the *Wall Street Journal* about the new wunderkind of the West Coast garment industry.

One reason for some government officials' annoyance at Maris's prosperity was that they considered it proof that their suspicions had been right — that he must still be plugged into Mafia money or he could not possibly have made such a rapid comeback. But more than that, there was a rising concern that Maris's growing prominence posed a threat, to himself and also to their program. It had never been contemplated that relocated witnesses would become flamboyant public figures, people to be talked about and scrutinized. As Herbert Stern put it, "Nobody promised Mr. Zelmanowitz that he would go hence from New Jersey and become a czar of the dress world." But that was what was happening, and there was much discomfort in Washington over the prospect. There was an uneasy feeling that the alias program had unleashed a loose cannon in California, and its firepower seemed to be growing every day.

Regardless of apprehension elsewhere, Paul Maris had never been happier in his life. For the first time, he was a person he admired. As a young tough, then as a carousing marine, and finally as a Mafia stockbroker, Gerald Zelmanowitz always tried to prove himself, but the results had given him no pride. He always suspected that he had fallen into those roles out of fear that if he did try to make it in the straight world, he would not be good enough.

But Paul Maris was a person one could respect, and he reveled in being who he was. He loved the hard work, the long hours, the satisfaction of building a legitimate business, the camaraderie with his colleagues, the respect of people who were themselves respectable.

He began to change in subtle ways. For the first time he had a wide circle of friends, and he began to communicate his feelings to them to an extent that he never had before. He began to unwind, without the fear of possible arrest constantly looming over his shoulder. It became a pleasure to go about a city where he was treated with respect and without the constant fear of the law, or worse.

In some ways he was still a victim of his tendency to overplay his role. As the father figure of the Maris Company, he tended to become overly paternalistic, paying wages and commissions that squeezed profits and bestowing fringe benefits that the struggling comapny could ill afford. In his zest for good works he spread his efforts too thin, saddling his company with programs that it was not solid enough to manage or sustain.

Paradoxically, he changed most toward those who knew who he was — his family, and especially, Lillian. As a full-time professional criminal he had been isolated even from them, telling them little about his activities and passing only the most superficial remarks about his activities within the family circle. But Paul Maris delighted in coming home at night and regaling Joe, Evelyn, and Lillian with the details of what great things he had accomplished that day. For the first time he found himself sharing his successes and disappointments with his family, and he gloried in the approval and respect he received in return. For years, Lillian and her parents had tried to pump him up with assurances that he was brilliant, that he could accomplish anything — claims that he himself never quite believed. Now, he began to believe them himself, and they spent long hours talking about the smallest details of what he was doing or trying to do.

Paul's transformation made the greatest difference with Lillian. She saw him becoming at last the exceptional person she had always believed he could be, and she delighted in it. In public, she sometimes overdid it, assuming a pose of superiority for him and her that cast her in the role of the grande dame of the Maris Company and chilled the easy give-and-take that he enjoyed with his staff. Mrs. Maris was not popular with the workers at the Paul Maris Company, and the animosity between her and Kat Walker was total and open. But at home, her pride in Gerry — she never called him Paul in private, except in gentle mocking of his own self-esteem — brought them closer than they had been in years. He would often come home late to find a note that

Lillian had written before she went to sleep, telling how proud she was that he finally had the opportunity to do the things she had wanted him to do, to be the kind of husband she wanted to have; how happy it made her to see him finally fulfilling his destiny. They both knew it was corny, and they loved it.

For the man known as Paul Maris, it was the most satisfying time of his life. He later said that he inwardly *became* Paul Maris, that he came to think of himself as Maris and assumed that that was the persona he was destined to have: "The only home I ever had, the roots I ever made, the only commitment to community, to family, to society, were as Paul Maris. I liked him a lot better than Zelmanowitz. He was a nice guy."

Gerald Zelmanowitz did not imagine at that time that his commitment to being Paul Maris could be a trap, that he might make decisions and do things in his determination to remain Maris that would risk everything he had gained. The flaw was that no matter how much it pleased him to be Paul Maris, in reality he was someone else, and yet he was unprepared to face that reality when it came.

6..........................Overreacher

When Paul Maris settled in California he made a decision to change his basic style of life. He would not commit any more crimes. To most people, that would be considered a modest personal goal, but to him, it represented a fundamental change of life. He had never, in his adult life, held a job that did not involve systematic lawbreaking. That had been true of his union activities, his after-hours bars, his overseas investment operations and his securities trading. Because he had no legal income, he had not filed an income tax return in years.

His reincarnation as Paul Maris gave him an opportunity to break that pattern, and he resolved at the outset to do it. He realized that there were some less-than-altruistic reasons for this spasm of virtue; he was on probation in the East and in bad odor with some well-placed individuals in Washington, and he believed that if he were to be caught so much as jaywalking, some people in the Justice Department would leap at the chance to put him in prison with some of the men who had been sent there by means of his testimony. So complete was Maris's conversion to lawfulness that he even began to pay his federal income taxes.

But there was more than self-preservation to Maris's determination to go straight. He viewed his clean slate as a boon not to be wasted — an attitude not characteristic of all of the alumni of the witness relocation program. The Justice Department's official position is that it makes no effort to keep track of "terminated" witnesses once they have signed the final release, and there have been allegations that some have used their government aliases as covers for bigger and slicker skullduggery. Such changes are difficult to document because the government is so closemouthed about the program. But incidents have come to light to suggest that some witnesses, after a stab at working for a living and some disappointments at the hands of the bureaucracy, have simply reverted to type and gone back to committing crimes.

Such was the case with a convicted New York safecracker named George Elias. After he agreed to testify against some of his Mafia associates, the government created a new identity for him as George E. Hammond, and in 1973 relocated him to the warm climes of San Jose, California. Noting that their charge had extensive experience with break-ins and safes, the Justice Department assisted him in obtaining a loan from the Small Business Administration to establish an enterprise called the Consolidated Lock and Alarm Company. A burglary wave ensued in the San Jose area, and eventually George Elias Hammond pleaded guilty to six counts of first-degree burglary and related felonies.

A similar case of backsliding occurred with Joseph Barboza, who had once lived the sweet life as a highly paid hit man for the New England Mafia. Twenty-seven lucrative murders later, he testified for the government against some of his former employers, and the alias program sent him to San Francisco as one Joseph Bently. But Barboza didn't last at the job the government got him in a restaurant, and before long state officers arrested and later convicted Barboza for what for him was an old habit — murder.

Another backslider was Louis Bombacino, a one-time Chicago hoodlum who testified against some of that city's top gangsters in 1970 and then was relocated under the name of Joseph Nardi in Tempe, Arizona. The FBI got him a job as a floor sweeper with the Arizona Public Service Company. When his employers finally fired him two years later, it was learned that he was not only doing a brisk business selling expensive irrigation equipment belonging to the APS, but he was also a central figure in a thriving new gambling and prostitution ring that sprang up in Tempe. The city council became so concerned about the sudden surge of Mafia activity in their community that it voted to apply to the Justice Department's Law Enforcement Assistance Administration for a $250,000 grant to create a new organized crime investigating unit in the police department. In 1976 the Justice Department's activities in Tempe came full circle, as the Justice Department granted the request in the form of a grant to set up such a unit for the entire county area that includes Tempe.

Another dubious gift to the Southwest from the alias program was James Berry, a Gary, Indiana, man who had testified in a narcotics case involving a Black Mafia group called "The Family." He was relocated as Ronald Turner to Fort Worth, Texas, where he shortly became active in the hijacking of trucks. Turner proved to be the kind of crook who would cheat even his partners in crime, and in 1974 some of them kidnapped him at gunpoint and took him for a fatal ride.

The full extent of such felonious escapades by relocated witnesses is impossible to pry out of the Justice Department, but an unnamed staff attorney was probably guilty of only slight overstatement when he was quoted by *Newsweek* magazine in 1976: "Over the last several months, we have seen these individuals being arrested almost daily." Gerald Shur admits that about 10 percent of his relocated witnesses get arrested under their G.I. identities.

But events have shown that secreting former felons in unsuspecting communities can raise serious questions for the Justice Department, even when the hidden witnesses are not convicted later of committing crimes.

One such embarrassment occurred in 1975, when the *Miami Herald* published an article hinting broadly that a relocated witness had been responsible for the disappearance of an elderly businesswoman and her bank account under circumstances that suggested foul play. The witness was a convicted stock swindler originally named Michael Raymond, who in 1971 had bared his felonious past in testimony before the Senate Permanent Investigations Subcommittee and had subsequently been given the new identity of Michael Burnett by the Justice Department. According to the article, in 1975 a sixty-six-year-old former Fort Lauderdale newspaper columnist and public relations representative named Adelaide Stiles began dating a man named Mike Burnett, who was later identified by four of her friends from photographs as the witness Michael Raymond. The article said that Adelaide Stiles was last seen on July 21, 1975, climbing into a car with the man known as Mike Burnett — en route, she had told friends, for the Florida Keys, Nassau, and Europe. It was later discovered that she had checked into a Miami motel on July 21, and on the same day had withdrawn all but a few dollars of her checking and savings accounts — exchanging part of the money for a $6,000 cashier's check, which later turned up endorsed by a corporation said to be wholly owned by Burnett. When her worried friends contacted Burnett later about her disappearance, he said they had had a spat and that he had left her at the motel on July 21.

The Fort Lauderdale police considered Burnett their prime suspect, but he had left a trail of false telephone numbers and addresses, and they never managed to locate him for questioning. At about the same time, the police in West Palm Beach were also trying to find Burnett for questioning about the similar disappearance of a local accountant named Max Bouchard, who had done business with Burnett, vanished, and never been heard from again. Neither police department had suspected that Burnett was a relocated witness, and thus had no reason to ask the U.S. Marshals' Service to locate Burnett for them. A year later, Adelaide Stiles and Max Bouchard had still not been seen nor heard from, "Michael Burnett" was still a member of the posh Miami Bankers Club, where he passed himself off as an international financier, and Gerald Shur said that he and the Marshals' Service had never been told that their witness Michael Raymond was being sought by local police anywhere.

A similar embarrassment was avoided by the Justice Department when it violated its own rules to conceal the fact that it had relocated a confessed multiple murderer as a student on a college campus. The man was Ira Pecznick, a one-time Mafia holdup man in Newark, who testified against the Campisi crime family in 1974. In the course of his testimony, Pecznick left no doubt that he was a very tough item himself. He admitted that he had helped the Campisi mob commit five murders — most of them assassinations of rival gangsters, but one involving an innocent witness who had the misfortune of seeing Pecznick and the Campisis commit a robbery. There was also a sixth victim, who had been unlucky enough to select the baby-faced Pecznick as the butt of some boastful showing off in a Newark tavern, and whom Pecznick shot in the head. The man survived, and after a chat with Pecznick, decided not to press criminal charges. Despite his scarlet past, Pecznick was a boyish-looking twenty-nine-year-old in 1975 when he was pardoned by the governor of New Jersey and was relocated to another state by the Justice Department, and he used his new identity to do what many young men do at that age — he enrolled in college. All went well until the student was arrested on a minor charge, and his fingerprints were sent to the FBI in Washington. Then the government was confronted with the prospect of disclosing that it had placed a man with a record of hair-trigger violence and murder where he could mingle with the unsuspecting students of a college. The FBI instead reported back that the arrested college man was who he said he was, with no mention of the criminal and killer, Ira Pecznick. Because he was accused of only a misdemeanor and had a spotless police record, the baby-faced young student was given a suspended sentence, and nobody — except the Justice Department — knew the truth.

A more common shortcoming among relocated witnesses seems to be using their government cover to run up debts, and then vanishing without paying. The alias program learned of this hazard with its first witness, Paddy Calabrese. He changed his name and his community six times, and each time left a gaggle of angry creditors. Sometimes they knew enough about his background to send his bills to the Justice Department, but there is no indication that any of them were acknowledged.

The problem, as Calabrese so amply demonstrated, was that Mafia insiders tend to have rich tastes and poor work habits. He was never able to live on the wages he earned after his relocation, and one Justice Department attorney has been quoted as saying that the bills he left in his wake pyramided into the thousands of dollars. Justice Department officials say that the unpaid debt syndrome is their greatest problem, and concede that they have been unable to solve it. On the one hand, the government is powerless to actually make the hidden witnesses pay; the Marshals' Service repeatedly threatens to blow the cover of those who persist in running up debts, but officials admit that they never would actually betray the identity of a witness over debts. On the other hand, the government does not accept responsibility to pay the debts, and no creditors appear to have been successful in collecting from the government in court. So the Justice Department is left in the unhappy situation of creating situations it is powerless to control, and the taxpayers are left supporting a government program that preys upon some members of the public.

The alias program's secrecy prevents the dimensions of the debt problem from being known, but one case that has come to light illustrated how persistent the problem can be. It involved Paul Parness, another refugee from the Buffalo rackets, who cut his teeth as a government witness by testifying against his own brother, and then joined the ranks of relocated witnesses who testified against — but failed to convict — the durable Rochester underworld figure, Russell Bufalino.

The Justice Department gave Parness a new name and relocated him and his family first in Tulsa. With the aid of a letter of recommendation from the Marshals' Service, he was quickly over his head in debt, and he slipped off to Minneapolis. A tribe of Oklahoma merchants began to clamor for his whereabouts, but the Justice Department couldn't tell without blowing his new cover. But by that time, Parness had plundered the merchants of Minneapolis for — among other items — a motorboat, motorcycle, pickup truck, minibike, riding lawn mower, diamond ring, and Cadillac. But Parness was still needed to testify in future trials, so that even after he had welshed on the bills for most of those items, the government relocated him to North Carolina, where he was well on his way to becoming the most affluent truck driver on the eastern seaboard when the Justice Department finally froze his credit by throwing him in prison. Parness had stepped over the line by committing a crime in the process of running up debts; he had fraudulently registered the Cadillac in North Carolina in violation of a federal law against such interstate chicanery. Justice Department officials say they are quick to indict witnesses who commit crimes in the course of running up debts, and Parness was one of several they have prosecuted. In October of 1971 he was given a four-year sentence for interstate fraud.

Paul Parness's insolvent ways would never have become known outside the alias program except that another branch of the federal government had become concerned about certain people who fail to pay their obligations. The Department of Health, Education and Welfare, struggling against rising welfare costs caused by parents who fail to pay child support, began denying welfare payments to dependent children unless all legal steps had been taken to make their fathers contribute to their support. Parness's wife divorced him while he was in prison and obtained a decree ordering him to pay child support — an order that he ignored after he was released from prison and relocated again by the alias program. Thus his case became a matter of public record as an unprecedented clash among three agencies in government. On one side, HEW and the office of the district attorney of Los Angeles County demanded to know Parness's location so that he could be forced to pay child support. On the other, the Department of Justice refused to comply on the ground that, as the United States Marshals' Service explained in a letter to the California D.A., it "would contravene the policies underlying the Witness Protection Program." The case bogged down in legal wrangling, and Parness has continued on his indebted way.

Whether the U.S. government has a legal duty to reimburse unsuspecting citizens who are cheated by relocated witnesses is a question that is being tested in the courts, through the case of a compulsive swindler whom the Justice Department relocated from Chicago to San Diego. In Chicago he was known as Joseph Stein, and he gained an international reputation as a swindler after a string of arrests and, ultimately, a conviction in a 1972 mail fraud case in which nineteen men were charged with cheating more than seventy hospitals, colleges and convalescent homes of more than $1 million.

After some time in jail, Stein offered to testify for the prosecution in a relatively minor case involving the alleged corruption of a probation officer by the Mafia, and in exchange the government agreed to relocate him to San Diego as Joseph Stone. There is no evidence that Stone hesitated a moment after reaching San Diego before resuming his old occupation as a swindler. He purchased an impressive home, declared himself to be an investment counselor with a Ph.D. in finance and economics, and began to spread charm and financial advice among the horse-riding, golf-playing set in San Diego. In the course of time, Stone was indicted on charges of cheating the director of La Jolla's prestigious Scripps Research Institute out of $55,000 in a bank investment scheme, and of swindling a San Diego pathologist out of $11,500 that was supposed to have been invested in a Mexican tungsten mine.

Before he could be put in prison again, Joseph Stein/Stone died. But the pathologist who had been stung in the tungsten mine caper had also been burned in another bogus enterprise of Stone's, and this proved to be a more serious matter. The pathologist, Dr. Lawrence Steinberg, was a trustee for a pension fund operated by San Diego area pathologists, and he and the medical group had loaned Stone $59,000. When Stone died, bankrupt, only $7,500 of this had been repaid.

Dr. Steinberg then became the first person to sue the United States for damages resulting from being swindled by a relocated witness. He accused the Justice Department of placing Stone in a position in which he could win the confidence of the pathologists, although the government knew that Stone had been a habitual swindler. According to the suit, Stone had begun to live well and cultivate unsuspecting investors as soon as he hit San Diego.

The Steinberg suit was expected to take years to work its way up from the U.S. district court in San Diego to the higher courts, where it could establish the government's liability, if any, for the misdeeds of the criminals that it conceals among the population.

Government spokesmen say officially that many relocated witnesses have taken advantage of their new identities to break lifetime habits of chicanery and crime. If these statements are accurate, the witness relocation program may be the most effective idea in criminal rehabilitation since they stopped lopping off convicts' ears. Justice Department officials won't name names, but they have been quoted in various articles about the program as saying that one witness has become a $40,000-per-year salesman; another, with a criminal record stretching back to Prohibition days, is a success in real estate; another has a high executive position with a department store chain; another has made such a mark in his new hometown that a group of businessmen has urged him to run for office; and one is said to have become a millionaire. Gerald Shur tells a more ambiguous anecdote to sum up the witnesses' work record. One employer phoned Shur to report that the witness he had sent him had reverted to his old criminal habits. "The police are coming over to pick up your boy," he said, "but I want you to send me another one."

Despite the Justice Department's public expressions of confidence, on April 16, 1974, Gerald Shur issued a confidential order to the personnel of the witness protection program to begin keeping closer tabs on relocated witnesses. "The FBI has requested that we keep them advised of the witnesses' current name or alias and address," Shur declared, and he instructed the Marshals' Service to report "any intelligence from the field regarding a witness (i.e., possible illegal activities . . .), any reports concerning abuses of the program by witnesses . . . [and] reports of witnesses who violate the law after relocation."

Paul Maris's own decision not to commit any more crimes was unambiguous and firm, but beyond that, he seemed to harbor no pretentions toward becoming a straight arrow of the corporate world. His determination to stay out of jail left considerable moral elbowroom to use in the rough-and-tumble of the garment trade, and Maris applied to his business career some of the same sharp practices and cutting of ethical corners that had been his working norm in professional racketeering. In the women's apparel business, nobody seemed to notice. In fact, Maris's ethical reflexes seemed well attuned to the world of corporate business — he adapted smoothly to some of the more slippery practices of this precarious new trade.

The garment business often suffers from problems of cash flow, and Maris quickly became a virtuoso of some of the tricks of the trade to bring in cash in times of need. There was often a sense of pell-mell disorganization about the Maris Company's operations, and he developed a reputation for overbilling customers, or sending bills for orders that were not requested, or for shipments that were not yet due. The mere fact of sending the bills generated credit with the factoring company that handled the Maris Company's accounts receivable, and Maris could immediately draw on this credit in the form of cash. When the customers wrote the factor later explaining that they didn't order that much, or that the shipment had never arrived, or that some other mistake had been made, it was all chalked up to chaos in the ever-churning Maris account, and charged against future Maris business. Occasionally, Maris was also known to persuade some city's dominant store to promote heavily a popular Paul Maris line, and then later he would dump loads of the same styles into a competing store at lower prices. When cash was tight, he also proved a master of the "your check is in the mail" stall, and some of the advertising executives who worked on the innovative Maris ads say they have not been paid to this day. But at the time, this modified Mafia-stockbroker style of operation apparently did not stand out as remarkable in the corporate world. After he became well known in the West Coast apparel business, Maris was given the unofficial stamp of approval of being selected to head the

United Jewish Appeal among his peers in the clothing industry. His solicitation campaign quickly went over the top.

Given the catch-as-catch-can nature of the garment industry, Maris's freewheeling style seemed to represent a spark of genius, and Creative Capital at first thought it had struck gold. In the fall of 1971, an international meeting of entrepreneurs interested in the growing new field of high-risk venture capital was held at the University of Toronto. One of the featured speakers was Milton Stewart, who gave a detailed lecture on how to turn a profit by investing in struggling companies. The talk was recorded and distributed as part of a Time, Inc., tape-cassette seminar on venture capital, and thus Stewart was reminded — repeatedly — in later years that he had chosen as his example of the dream businessman a rising young San Francisco clothing manufacturer named Paul Maris.

In the taped lecture, Stewart's presentation was clinical and dry until he reached the subject of Maris, when Stewart became almost lyrical. Paul Maris, Stewart exclaimed, "has all of the earmarks of the classic entrepreneur, the guy I spend my life looking for! He's the only man in the United States I have ever met who made a capital gain out of his military service [laughter]. He is literally a brilliant administrator, hardworking as a guy can be. . . ." Stewart went on to praise Maris's virtuoso performance in keeping the Duskin Company afloat. It was a speech that he would often later regret.

As it turned out, Maris's Achilles' heel as a businessman was his virtuosity. Gerry Zelmanowitz exhibited a lifelong pattern of adopting the most flamboyant — and as Paul Maris, the most ultimately self-destructive — behavior that he thought suitable to the role he was playing. When he became the hotshot young chief executive of the company, he proceeded to perform as he imagined such a swinging person would. The result was great for the company's image, good for sales, and questionable for the long-term statement of profit and loss.

Maris built a handsome executive suite of offices on the fourth floor of the nondescript old factory building and staffed it with good-looking women and well-educated men. It was a time when some of the brightest graduates of the Harvard Business School were opting for small companies instead of the big-corporate treadmill, and Maris paid well enough to hire some of the best. The emphasis on executive staff could be traced in the buildup of desks. Under Duskin, there had been six desks in the plant; when the Maris furniture was later sold for debts, there were more than two dozen desks.

The most striking adornment of the executive suite arrived after Maris had departed. It was a huge stuffed blue marlin, which Maris had apparently caught and — at enormous expense to the company — had mounted as an impressive symbol of conquest to grace the Paul Maris Company's wall.

Then there were the leased cars. With his Rolls-Royce and Mercedes setting the style, other cars leased by Maris executives included three other Mercedeses, a Ferrari, an Aston-Martin, a Datsun sports model, a Chevrolet station wagon, and a panel truck. A ground-floor corner of the Maris plant had been leased to the state for an unemployment office, and there used to be a joke in the neighborhood that the sleek Maris Company cars parked nearby gave the unemployment office a bad name. Maris insisted that his staff's rich taste in cars was harmless — that each executive was given $200 per month to rent a car and could add more and get a fancier model if he wished. Creative Capital claimed that the company paid more than the going rate for the rented cars, and when the company records proved inadequate to settle the issue, neither side could prove its case.

A clearer example of a Maris boondoggle was the company's computer. Most garment houses in those days were highly personal operations, run by a few old-timers on intuition and feel. Maris believed this was old-fashioned and inadequate; that a company could anticipate trends and function more efficiently based on analyses of past sales, shipments, purchases, and production. So he rented and installed in the Maris plant a computer — not a terminal linked to a computer, but a whole computer — to track the company's business and handle routine bookkeeping. As it turned out, Maris was a visionary in this; computer use is now increasing in the women's apparel industry. But his error was in being too much the visionary. His computer would have been feasible for a business with five times the volume, but for the struggling Maris corporation, it was more vision than the company could afford.

Most employees of the Maris Company defended Paul on his controversial expenditures. He was trying new ideas, striking out in new directions, and for the most part it seemed to be working; the company was suddenly on the business map in a big way, and production and sales were booming. But on the issue of nepotism, Maris had no defenders but himself. He always said that he believed in nepotism, that it made sense to hire relatives, who would work hard for modest pay and, most of all, whom you could trust. And on this point, he more than practiced what he preached. Lillian Maris took over as public relations director. Her father, Joe Miller, was chief purchasing agent. Then there was Cynthia Roth in the advertising department, her husband, Norman, pushing a broom, between classes; Lillian's other son-in-law, Bobby Stricker, was selling goods on commission; her cousin, Jerry Marantz, was in the knitting department; his wife was behind the counter in the factory store; Joe Miller's brother was in the purchasing department; his brother's wife was in the shipping department; and a couple of relatives named Eddie and Edith Brosnik were in clerical jobs. But despite Maris's belief that this was sound business, ultimately it worked to his disadvantage. Creative Capital grew uneasy over the growing horde of in-laws on the payroll, the other employees grumbled about favoritism, and there was an undercurrent of puzzlement as to how a family from Philadelphia could have so many relatives from New Jersey.

The most controversial of Maris's extravagances was the "Old Fashioned Country Fair" at his Sonoma retreat. Milton Stewart and Creative Capital were in an awkward position to complain about it, because the board of directors, which they controlled, had approved in advance the idea of throwing a combination cocktail party–sales convention–fashion show at Maris's place. Moreover, the event was a smashing success. The country fair motif created a colorful, relaxed setting, complete with game booths, strolling vendors, live music, contests, popcorn, cotton candy, and all the trimmings. The buyers and fashion writers were in a relaxed mood by the time the style show began, and they oohed and ahhed as the models paraded across the lawn in the distinctive Paul Maris knit fashions — long dresses, pantsuits, sports outfits. The guests boarded the charter buses for San Francisco in a happy, affirmative mood. The new Maris line was well launched.

It was a typical Maris coup, and it carried a characteristic Maris cost overrun. Total tab: $37,000. Milton Stewart was jarred by the cost, but also by what he considered to be Maris's use of the occasion to make improvements on his estate at the company's expense. There had been landscaping, wiring, lighting, and even the purchase of thirty-five captain's chairs for the occasion. Maintenance workers from the plant had done gardening, cleaning, painting, and other tidying up around the Maris place. It was an ambiguous situation — all arguably done in the cause of making the style show a success, but also a festering point between Maris and his suffering financial backers.

There was also a little incident that aggravated the sense of uneasiness among Maris's backers. During the preparations for the country fair, a maintenance man from the factory was working at the Sonoma estate, and inside the ranch-style house he noticed a curious thing. He saw a recent high-school yearbook from South Orange, New Jersey. Leafing through it, he spotted the face of Cynthia Roth, smiling from one of the photographs. But the name under the picture was Cynthia Balaban, and the book said she had graduated from the school in New Jersey, not Philadelphia, as everyone had been told. The maintenance man replaced the yearbook, barely able to wait to get back to the Maris factory among his friends. The story was too good to keep, and it was not long before it reached the ears of Milton Stewart.

It was at about that time that Creative Capital called on the services of Proudfoot Reports. For an investigative agency, it was a venerable and respected institution; more than seventy years on the New York scene, it was a landmark of discreet investigative service. If there was anything amiss with Paul Maris, Creative Capital could assume that Proudfoot would find it out.

The full story of what happened after that has since been obscured by legal proceedings, with the company that emerged from the wreckage of the Creative Capital Corporation, called the Clarion Capital Corporation, suing Proudfoot Reports for $7.5 million for alleged negligence, and with Proudfoot maintaining an embarrassed silence. But Maris was not reluctant to tell his side of the story to close friends, and his version suggested that, with no idea of the thin ice he was on, he skated easily across the situation on the strength of Maris charm and Maris luck.

One day Maris was at work behind his huge mahogany desk when a call came from New York. The voice on the other end identified itself as that of John Collins, an investigator for Proudfoot Reports. He had been assigned to run a routine check on Maris, Collins said, and he wanted to get some facts and references to use as a starting point. Confident of his cover and secure in his masquerade, Maris launched smoothly into a rendition of his phony background. The story pleased him so much that he pushed back his paperwork, propped his feet up on the desk and spun out the tale of his college training in engineering, his early work in cryptography, his interest in electronics that led to investments in a Japanese electronics manufacturing firm and two American FM radio stations, his service as an officer in the Army Security Agency. . . .

At this point, according to Maris's recollection, Collins's impersonal attitude seemed to melt. He said he had a son who had been in the ASA; perhaps he and Maris had met. Perhaps so, Maris replied, but the agency was large and much of his work had been of a highly clandestine nature. Sometimes he did not operate under his true name. Where was his son stationed now? Collins explained that his son was no longer in the agency; his son was dead. Maris said he was sorry, but Collins seemed to want to talk on about the ASA and Maris's life in it, so Maris talked on for the better part of an hour, telling of assignments in the ASA, of scenes and experiences in that beautiful Japanese city, Kobe, of the *esprit* of the men in the agency. And yes, Maris added, perhaps he had crossed paths with Collins's son.

Gradually, Maris began to weave in details of his business background, explaining ambiguities in his résumé, telling of business successes and profits, dropping names of satisfied customers and creditors. When the conversation was over, Maris asked if he could do anything else to help Collins with his task, and the investigator said no, he had enjoyed talking with Maris, that it had been a great help.

Maris hung up, chuckling to himself that he'd made Shur and Bonomi's work easy; that Collins wouldn't be likely to dig too critically into Maris's government-issue background. If Maris had suspected the true situation — that most of the background facts he had given Collins would not stand up under the most cursory checking — he would have been petrified rather than amused. But a couple of weeks passed and Maris sensed an easing of tensions with Milton

Stewart. He knew then that the Proudfoot report had been received, and that his alias had stood up. That experience reinforced Maris's belief in the strength of his cover, a mistaken confidence that was later to bring him much grief. For what he did not know was that he had passed muster on the strength of his own fast talk and good luck — and that the Proudfoot incident, if anything, actually demonstrated that his alias would not stand up at all under careful scrutiny.

The first page of Proudfoot's report to Creative Capital consisted of a string of statements about Maris, which, except for his name, address, and marital status, were uniformly false and contrary to official records:

> Paul Maris, the subject of your recent inquiry, was born in Philadelphia, Pennsylvania on January 12, 1935.
> Maris is married to Lillian, nee Miller and the couple have two children, namely: Cindy, age 19 and Shelley, age 20.
> Subject attended and graduated from John Bertram High School, Philadelphia, Pennsylvania in 1953. From 1953 to 1957 subject attended Baldwin Wallace College, Berea, Ohio. The Registrar's Office of that educational institution verified that subject was awarded a Bachelor of Science degree in 1957.
> Approximately March 1958 subject began his service in the United States Army and was assigned to Fort Dix, New Jersey. . . .

After mention of Maris's training as a cryptographer and some duty in New Jersey and Paris, the report continued:

"He returned to Fort Meade, Maryland and in 1963 was chosen to attend Officer Candidate School at Fort Benning, Georgia. . . . Later in 1963 subject was assigned to the Military District of Washington (MDW) and was promoted to First Lieutenant. He attained the rank of Captain in 1964 and the rank of Major in 1965."

Later, officials were to marvel over which was most incredible: that a person could go from Officer Candidate School to Major in two years, or that he could persuade a detective over the telephone that he had done it. The report went on:

"Subsequently, subject received a voluntary release to the United States Department of State. In 1970 he was separated from service and as a civilian analyst was associated with the work of the United States Atomic Energy Commission."

The report then quoted six unnamed businessmen's opinions of Paul Maris. They were uniformly glowing; Maris had "turned the company around," he was "possessed of a high degree of integrity and business acumen" and was "much admired by those with whom he has business relationships." The thread that ran through these interviews was that none of the businessmen had dealt with Maris for more than two years, and all were pleased that his company's record of timely payment of bills had improved during that time. It was a perfect example of Maris's capacity to lift himself by his bootstraps — Creative Capital was being reassured that it had entrusted its money to a man with a record of paying his bills, yet that record had been established with money he had obtained from Creative Capital.

The only named source who reported on Maris's life prior to two years before was Thomas Campion, the attorney from Newark. Campion was quoted as saying that he considered Maris to be "an individual of high personal integrity" and that he knew others who "held the subject in equally high esteem." These unnamed others were apparently Campion's former law partner, prosecutor Frederick Lacey, and individuals "who knew Maris in the Washington, D.C. locale": that is, Bonomi and Shur.

Campion confirmed later that he did verify that he knew Paul Maris and that he held him in high esteem. The corporate attorney had been requested several years before to donate his services to assist a young government witness, Gerald Zelmanowitz, who had some legal difficulties, in disposing of his home, after he was relocated under a new identity. Campion had been bowled over by the raw genius of the dropout from Brooklyn, whom the attorney remembered years later as "probably the most remarkable and brilliant human being I've ever met." So when the man from Proudfoot phoned and asked if Campion knew and admired a man named Maris, the lawyer gave a literally true, but fundamentally misleading, reply: "Yes." Was this an ethical way for a lawyer to reply to an investigator's query? Campion insisted later that he had made up his mind to protect Maris's cover if he could, but not to tell a lie. He said that to his great relief, Collins's questions allowed him to accomplish both: "He just didn't ask the right questions."

No other known source recalls having been contacted by Proudfoot, and Clarion Capital alleged in its suit that the great majority of the statements in the report were "simply taken from Maris himself by the defendants and set forth as true." Proudfoot's president, Patrick Murphy, has refused to comment, or to tell where John Collins — no longer a Proudfoot investigator — can be found.

Maris had met the first major test of his existence and had passed. His identity had gained the seal of approval of a prestigious Madison Avenue investigative agency, and if he had known the full story, he might have coasted on that certification for the rest of his life. But it had come so easily that he did not suspect it was all a product of good luck and what his associates had come to call admiringly "the Paul Maris snow job." He did not know it, but the Proudfoot report had set him up to become the final victim of the government's duplicity. The government had created a facade of lies to give him this chance for a second life — and then, as an ultimate deception, had misled even him as to how far its lies would extend.

Things went smoothly for the Maris Company in the weeks following the receipt of the Proudfoot report. Then in the fall of 1972, Maris began to spend days at a time out of town. He had always traveled a lot, dashing around the country while operating the company out of his hip pocket and out of telephone booths. But this was a little different. There was a regularity about these absences from San Francisco, and he always seemed to go east. Each morning at nine, California time, Kat Walker's phone would ring and the familiar voice would be there: "Hello, Kat, this is Paul." They would discuss the schedule for the day, and the voice would make decisions and give instructions to be passed along to the staff. But no matter what crises were breaking, or how badly his personal touch might be needed, he did not break the routine. There was the one call each morning at nine, his instructions for the day with no call-back number to reach him in case of trouble, and then silence until the next morning.

Then in late October, Maris appeared back at the Paul Maris Company, bright and chipper and with no mention of his absences. Nobody pressed him for an explanation, and the incidents were soon forgotten.

134

But an astute observer of the nation's press might have noticed a coincidence between Maris's last, long absence and the duration of the trial of a group of Mafia figures in Newark, New Jersey, on charges of forgery, counterfeiting, and transportation across state lines of almost $2 million in stolen bonds and securities. The observer might also have noted that the daily noontime break in the trial in New Jersey fell precisely at nine in the morning, San Francisco time. And then the astute observer would have realized the significance of the fact that the star prosecution witness was a self-admitted professional criminal named Gerald Martin Zelmanowitz.

The case of *The United States* v. *Anthony Salerno, et al.,* was, like most trials, only a partial, and even a distorted, reenactment of the events that brought the defendants before the bar of justice. As in all trials, the story told to the jury was limited by the breadth of the charges, the rules of evidence, the availability of witnesses, the failure of memories, and the credibility of the parties. And thus what was said in the courtroom provided only a revealing slice of the full story of what had happened.

It had begun in 1967, when Zelmanowitz became friendly with two men, Gilbert Beckley, a gambler known in the rackets as "the book-makers' bookmaker" because he specialized in taking layoff bets from overloaded bookies, and Joseph Green, who operated numbers lotteries. Beckley's luck had lately been sour, and he proposed a joint venture. He and Green had contacts through the rackets that could put them in touch with gangsters in New England who were experienced at stealing securities but who had too many rough edges to be good at peddling them. Rumor had it that these thugs had $4 million in hot stocks on their hands, all stolen from the First Bank of Boston and the Old Colony Trust of Boston, and yet the thieves were cash-poor. Beckley, Green, and Zelmanowitz made a deal. They would purchase the securities for a fraction of their market value, sell them at a huge profit, and pocket the difference.

But the old saw about the existence of honor among thieves does not apply automatically when New Jersey gamblers do business with racketeers from Boston. Before such a deal can be consummated, strangers must meet and hold incriminating conversations; large amounts of cash must change hands in neutral meeting places; assurances must be given that the goods to be fenced are not the subject of strenuous law enforcement heat. Some guarantee is needed that neither party will be betrayed to the police, held up at gunpoint, sold bogus goods, or otherwise cheated, gulled, or ripped off. That was where Anthony "Fat Tony" Salerno came in.

It had long been traditional for the parties to such a transaction to obtain an assurance of regularity — if not total honesty — by the intervention of some figure who was regarded with such respect, or terror, in Mafia circles that he could guarantee the deal. For this he was paid 6 percent. It was high, but for "protection," as it was accurately called, it was considered a necessary cost of doing business. In this case, Beckley and Green went to neutral ground, Manhattan, and secured the services of a man named Salerno. Whether or not Zelmanowitz had been acquainted with Salerno before was never established, but even if he had known no more than the average newspaper reader in New York, he would have associated the name Fat Tony Salerno with violence, loansharking, bookmaking, and the Mafia.

The three partners began a series of delicate negotiations, first meeting in bars and restaurants with Salerno, and later with Salerno and a short, fat man from Boston named Angelo Rossi and a father-and-son combination from New York, William and Howard Silverman. There were seven or eight meetings in all, culminating in two "closings," presided over by Salerno. In one, the Zelmanowitz group passed over $60,000 in cash and the Silvermans delivered about $305,000 in Indiana Toll Road bonds. In the second closing, the Zelmanowitz partnership delivered $20,000 in greenbacks as a deposit, and Rossi handed over about $2 million in stocks that Zelmanowitz was to sell on consignment. Zemlanowitz had been uneasy about dealing with Rossi, who impressed him as a most unprofessional crook. But Rossi assured them that the stocks were clean, that they were blank stock certificates that had been stolen from the bank's transfer agent without his knowledge, so that they were still listed as being in the vault and wouldn't be on any brokerage house's roster of stolen securities.

As Rossi spoke, Salerno nodded sternly. Zelmanowitz attached great significance to those nods. It was a period in his life when he saw himself as a rising figure in the sophisticated side of organized crime, when he was cultivating men who were mentioned in the newspapers as

Mafia overlords, and was dropping notorious Italian-American names. But Zelmanowitz, as always, tended to overplay his role. As events were soon to demonstrate, he was taking the Mafia too seriously.

As Zelmanowitz saw Salerno's function, he was the "rabbi" of the arrangement. Salerno's approving nods meant to Zelmanowitz that he was giving the transaction his blessing — and that if either side did not perform as promised, that party would pay the terrible price of having sullied Salerno's standing under the ancient Mafia code of honor.

In fact, Salerno was just sitting there nodding, and collecting 6 percent.

Zelmanowitz first took the Indiana Toll Road bonds to a Newark brokerage house, Edwards and Hanley. He had used all his skills as an international securities paperhanger to make the transaction as persuasive as possible, including flights to London to have some forged transfer documents notarized. But it turned out that not only was the certificate of prior ownership phony, so were the bonds themselves. A clerk in the brokerage house showed the bonds to a man who had previously been an agent of the Secret Service, and he smelled counterfeiting. So when Zelmanowitz returned to Edwards and Hanley, the FBI was waiting, and that was when he suffered his first federal arrest. The fact that he was then free on bond following his New York arrest for embezzlement did not faze him, but the prospect of federal prosecution did.

Shaken and furious, Zelmanowitz returned to Manhattan as soon as he made bond, and reported to Salerno that his guarantee had been betrayed. At first, Salerno reacted just as Gerry assumed such matters would be handled. He called Howard Silverman in and ordered him to bring his father to a meeting or he would "break his legs."

They met at the Longchamps restaurant on lower Broadway, and Salerno sat them down, positioning himself in the center seat of judgment. Zelmanowitz spilled out the story of betrayal; the Silvermans had assured Salerno that the securities were clean and instead had delivered tainted goods.

Zelmanowitz was astonished by the Silvermans' lack of fear. They explained calmly that they had obtained the bonds from an associate of Salerno's from Connecticut; that if the bonds were counterfeit, that man was the person Salerno should bring to account. Zelmanowitz was stunned by Salerno's calm reaction. Gerry had not really expected Salerno to kill the Silvermans right there in Longchamps, but he had considered it unthinkable to give the guarantees that they had to a capo in Manhattan, and then just shrug it off later as someone else's mistake. But Salerno just grunted that he could get Gerry's money back. There were no outburst of Sicilian anger, no threats of retribution, no reference to the Mafia code of honor. They left Longchamps, and Zelmanowitz never heard from Salerno about the Silverman deal again.

That left Zelmanowitz under indictment and under financial pressure. But he was again out on bond, and he began to make the rounds of brokerage houses again, this time selling the stocks he had obtained from Rossi. Gerry was one of the best paperhangers in the business, and things were smooth until he reached Miami, where he ran into betrayal again. Rossi had pledged that the stocks had been stolen without leaving a trace, but what he hadn't mentioned was that someone had skimmed off $13,000 worth of Gillette Company stocks before Rossi passed the remainder to Zelmanowitz. The batch of stocks had been fenced quickly, so that by the time Zelmanowitz reached Miami with the rest, it had been discovered that the whole bundle of Gillette securities had been stolen. Again, Gerry was caught red-handed.

After the federal agents returned him to Newark, in their own sweet time, and Gerry once again made bail, he confronted Rossi. This time, he had no illusions that Salerno would square things, and anyway it was too late for any measure of vengeance to help Zelmanowitz. But Gerry was astounded at Rossi's reaction when he confronted the little round man with the calamity his flawed merchandise had caused.

"Well, what the hell, you're man enough to do two or three years," Rossi said; "you can do it standing on your head." Gerry's mind boggled with anger and amazement. Now that Salerno's guarantee had vanished, and Rossi's broken promises had delivered him to the FBI, they were expecting him to follow the code, to be a "stand-up guy"! At that time, shortly after his manacled thirty-day tour of southern jails, Gerry was just beginning to consider the possibility of testifying. As time went on, the memory of Rossi's remark did more and more to persuade him that he should

Not long afterward, Gerry did testify at the DeCarlo trial, dropping

Fat Tony Salerno's name like a bombshell. Then strange things happened. Gil Beckley and Joe Green vanished. Nobody was sure why, but everyone knew that they had been killed. In time, Paul Maris informed the Justice Department that he had received a message from Fat Tony Salerno. Maris reported that agents claiming to represent Salerno had approached Zelmanowitz's sister in New York, saying that wherever Gerry was, they had $250,000 for him if he would fail to identify Salerno. As the trial approached, the prosecutors found themselves in an uncomfortable situation. Gerry's sister denied that any such approach had happened. Maris said he reported the incident to keep the record straight, but that of course he would not consider such an offer. But then he began to express doubts as to whether he could identify the man he had known as Salerno.

On October 11, 1972, the trial began on a note reminiscent of the DeCarlo case, with Salerno and Rossi glaring balefully at Zelmanowitz, and the Silvermans appearing subdued and resigned. Zelmanowitz claimed later that he had also had doubts as to whether he could identify Rossi after so many years. But as he took the witness stand, he glanced over at Rossi and the fat man drew his finger across his throat.

"I almost laughed out loud," Zelmanowitz recalled. "A little, fat, round man, a hundred pounds overweight, trying to frighten me. Those words rang in my ears — '*You can do two or three years, standing on your head*' — and I said to myself: 'Mister Rossi, you can do two or three years too, you son-of-a-bitch.'" He testified about Rossi's actions in loving detail, and when it was all over, Rossi got four years.

But when the prosecutor came to the point of calling upon Zelmanowitz to identify Fat Tony Salerno, the trial was thrown into confusion:

PROSECUTOR: "Mr. Zelmanowitz, Count I of the indictment in this case charges that you together with the defendants Anthony Salerno, Angelo Rossi, Jr., Howard Silverman and William Silverman . . ."

ZELMANOWITZ: "May I speak to Mr. Langway [the prosecutor] a moment, please?"

JUDGE: "No, you may not, sir. The question has not been asked."

ZELMANOWITZ: "It's not in regard to the question, your honor. I would like to go to the men's room if I may."

That was the end of the case for Fat Tony Salerno. There was a thirty-minute conference between Zelmanowitz and Herb Stern, during which Zelmanowitz said he wasn't sure that he could identify the Anthony Salerno in the courtroom as the same Anthony Salerno who had been the rabbi of his ill-fated deal in New York. Then Stern returned to the courtroom, and speaking through clenched teeth, dropped the charges against Salerno.

The trial resumed without him, and Zelmanowitz was asked:

PROSECUTOR: "When you indicated the defendant Anthony Salerno as the Anthony Salerno referred to in the indictment did you see that man sitting in the courtroom?"

ZELMANOWITZ: "The man you pointed to?"

PROSECUTOR: "Yes."

ZELMANOWITZ: "Yes."

PROSECUTOR: "Is that the Anthony Salerno with whom you conspired under the charges in this indictment?"

ZELMANOWITZ: "It is not."

It was a maddening experience for the prosecutors. There were a number of Anthony Salernos in New York, but only one Anthony "Fat Tony" Salerno who was known as a kingpin of organized crime, and they had indicted that Fat Tony Salerno. Yet their star witness said they seemed to have indicted the wrong Salerno. Justice Department officials still mutter "perjury" when the incident is mentioned, but they admit they have no evidence to contradict Zelmanowitz's story that he just could not identify that man.

In the aftermath of the reported contact of Zelmanowitz's sister by Salerno's agents and Gerry's subsequent loss of memory, it was notable that both the prosecutors and his friends sized up the incident in the same light. Their reasoning was that it is one thing to testify against a thuggish racketeer like Gyp DeCarlo in New Jersey but quite another to affront the Vito Genovese Family of New York by giving testimony against one of its captains. Zelmanowitz was well acquainted with the power and brutality of that organization and, by the time of his testimony, had begun to have second thoughts about the efficiency of the alias program. Afterward both Gerald Shur and a close associate of Zelmanowitz's used almost identical words in explaining his failure

Gerald Zelmanowitz failed to identify Anthony "Fat Tony" Salerno (between detectives, above) *when Salerno was brought to trial in federal court in Newark in October, 1972.*

of memory about Salerno: "Gerry made his peace with the New York Mafia."

It was Zelmanowitz's last scheduled appearance as a government witness, and later Stern brought him before the judge for his own sentencing. It was one of those rituals that the law requires, but one that is all form and no substance. The form was that Zelmanowitz had pleaded guilty to eight felony counts carrying a maximum total prison sentence of forty years. The substance was that he had agreed to testify at the risk of his own life, and it was unthinkable that he would now be sent to prison with the men he had convicted, or their friends. Stern reminded the judge of Zelmanowitz's service in testifying against De-Carlo; that he had been responsible for "putting away one of the most vile criminals in our society." The judge gave Zelmanowitz the obligatory lecture, speaking in chatty, unemotional tones but characterizing him as "totally amoral . . . a man who would steal or not as the opportunity presented itself." Then he gave Zelmanowitz a three-year suspended sentence and let him go.

Back in San Francisco, Paul Maris resumed a life that seemed significantly different from the judge's assessment of Gerald Zelmanowitz. Paul Maris apparently did not steal, as the judge concluded Zelmanowitz would have, for there was later testimony to indicate that Maris did not, although he obviously had the opportunity. The testimony came in connection with the lawsuit for damages filed by Creative Capital as part of the legal action brought to oust Maris on the day of the Good Friday Massacre. That suit did allege misappropriation of funds, but it was based on the worst suspicions of Maris's backers before they got access to the company's books and records.

Afterward, when Milton Stewart's deposition was taken, he accused Maris of arrogance, overspending, and the use of company funds and property for questionable personal expenses and home improvements. Under oath, he did not accuse Maris of stealing or any other crime.

Paul Maris was not a compulsive criminal, as Gerald Zelmanowitz had been, but neither was he yet a successful businessman, as he saw himself to be. He still occasionally fell victim to his own self-image, and in December he overplayed his role as the flamboyant business whiz, in a move that would end his post-Proudfoot honeymoon with

Creative Capital. It was a situation in which Maris had a good idea and might have pulled off one of his famous coups, but his effort boomeranged because he did not use the discretion that a genuine businessman, with no self-image to flatter, would have displayed in such a matter.

The incident began with the announcement by a New York company, Interstate Stores, Inc., that it had decided to close about half of a chain of discount stores that it owned called the White Front stores, including all eleven of the White Front stores in the San Francisco area. Interstate had been losing money on the White Front chain, and because it had a winner in its thriving chain of toy discount stores, Toys-R-Us, the decision had been made to cut its losses by closing the White Front stores that were operating in the red. This gave Maris the idea that he might bootstrap himself into ownership of the White Front retail operation without risking his own capital. The key was that White Front leased its store buildings and sublet much of the space inside to concessionaires. Maris planned to take over the leases, to purchase White Front's inventory at rock-bottom prices, paying by a loan on the inventory itself, resell most of the stock to the concessionaires and persuade the retail unions to reduce their wage demands so that the whole operation could do business at a profit.

Maris threw himself into it with his usual enthusiasm, and he made impressive early progress. He lined up a bank loan adequate to cover the cost of the inventory. He negotiated sales of this inventory at a profit to the concessionaires. He made headway in persuading the retail clerks' union that, with a thousand jobs at stake if the stores closed, they should cooperate in an effort to reduce operating expenses.

It was a long-shot operation, but Maris was within striking distance of success when he pulled a major blunder. He called in the press and announced that he was negotiating with Interstate to buy all eleven of the White Front stores in northern California, and that they hoped "to have an announcement by next week." His purpose was to soften up the unions by dangling the possibility of saving those thousand jobs and to let potential concessionaires know they could buy into the White Front system. He may also have been carried away with his own image of Paul Maris as the financial wizard who saved sinking enterprises at the eleventh hour. But whatever the motive, it placed him far out on a limb, because Interstate Stores greeted the announcement with a stony silence. Maris was spared public embarrassment only because the press in San Francisco printed his optimistic announcement and didn't check with Interstate. But the deal fell through because some of the owners of the store buildings wouldn't approve Maris's takeover of their leases, and the White Front stores closed as scheduled in January of 1973.

From a business point of view, Maris's plan had been imaginative and well worth the effort, the kind of low-risk venture that entrepreneurs attempt all the time — and assume will fail most of the time. But Rule Number One of such operations is to say nothing until the deal is done, or at least until the other parties are willing to agree that it is a live possibility. When Maris went public alone and wound up looking foolish, he tarnished his golden boy image with the money men at Creative Capital. They began to worry more and to take a closer look at the profit-and-loss statements of the Paul Maris Company.

By the spring of 1973, the Paul Maris Company's sales had zoomed to more than $8 million per year, but expenses had risen faster. Creative Capital found itself with $2 million invested in a company that could not seem to make a profit. Milton Stewart wanted to keep Paul Maris in charge of sales and promotion, but to give someone else control of outlays. That would involve moving Maris to New York, and this Maris vehemently refused to consider.

Stewart was puzzled, but the losses were such that he began to plan for Good Friday.

It was at about that time that Maris discovered that he was being watched. He probably would not have noticed it, except that it happened on a chilly, depressing night in the spring of 1973, not long after the word had come that Gyp DeCarlo had been released from Atlanta Penitentiary. The news reports said DeCarlo was released because he was dying of cancer — he had been reportedly dying of cancer for years — and Maris assumed that he would stick close to home in New Jersey and would be closely watched by the FBI. But Maris knew that if DeCarlo wanted to kill him he would send someone else, and that once he was given access to his hidden money and his gangster friends, all the FBI surveillance in the world wouldn't shield him from De-Carlo's revenge if Maris could be found.

Maris was walking his dog in the park across from the apartment that night, and the thoughts of DeCarlo and the moans of the foghorns from the Bay had put him in a dark and suspicious mood. Thus he noticed, as he circled the park, two men seated in a green Corvette with Oregon license plates. There was something familiar about it, something that teased his memory. He noticed that the car was parked facing his apartment building, far enough away so that the men could see the front entrance, the side garage exit, and the lighted window of his apartment. He made a point of walking past the Corvette, and Maris felt the hackles of his neck tingle as the men fell silent as he walked by.

Maris suddenly realized why the car with the Oregon plates looked familiar — he had seen it in front of his building when he walked the dog the night before. He also recognized one of the men. He had been there the previous night, too.

Maris fought back the waves of panic, groping for an innocent explanation. The man he recognized might live in the neighborhood; this could be his usual car pool ride home from work, topped off with a quiet chat before parting. Maris told himself that it made sense, that his suspicions were just a recurrence of the paranoia of his early days in San Francisco. In those days he had not been accustomed to walking about unprotected except for his government alias, and he spent much of his time mentally whistling past graveyards. Situations that would later be accepted as commonplace set his defenses jangling. A car would remain in his rear view mirror too long. A man seated alone in a restaurant would appear to be watching. Men getting quickly out of both sides of a car would set his pulses pounding. His home back in New Jersey had burned to the ground shortly after DeCarlo and Cecere were convicted, but before they were packed off to prison. Maris had often said it was their way of sending him a message.

During that period Maris usually carried a gun, and he found himself constantly in situations that pricked his suspicions enough to make him reach inside his pocket for the reassuring touch of the weapon. It was only a .25 caliber automatic, loaded with a clip of bullets so tiny that they seemed almost delicate. But the pistol was compact enough that he could carry it in the side pocket of his suit jacket without a revealing bulge. And having it there provided a necessary prop for a scenario that he had seared into his mind, to carry him through whatever surprise or numbing fear might possess him if his prior life should suddenly catch up with him.

Maris had promised himself that he would never let them lead him quietly away. That was the way it had happened to his friends Joe Green and Gil Beckley. Neither man was officially dead, just missing. But everybody believed they had been killed, and the stories that Maris had been told had an ominous similarity.

The last time Joe Green had been seen, he was walking out of a motel room in Miami. Maris was told that Green left his clothes, his room key, his car, and his money in the safe, and walked away with two men. He never came back. Gil Beckley's story was similar. He left his apartment one night to meet two men in a restaurant. He went away with them in a taxi and was never heard from again.

Maris had tried to drill the idea into his own mind, and that of Lillian and the other family members, that he would fight and die on the spot. Lillian was instructed that if a car pulled up beside them on the street and men jumped out, or if two or more strangers approached them in any out-of-the-way place, she was to run away as fast as she could, because it was going to happen right there. "I intend to die where I stand," he would say; "there's no way they are going to get me into a car and make me disappear. It is an absolute decision I have made."

At such times he would often mention Red Cecere, rarely Gyp De-Carlo. Cecere was an evil man, a sadistic animal, he would say. Cecere had enjoyed beating Saperstein. He liked violence. Maris had opened the Swiss bank accounts for Cecere and had deposited the money. He knew that Cecere could well afford to pay violent men to do things for him. Maris thought about it often, especially after Gerald Shur phoned one day to relay a warning that the FBI had picked up from its sources: that Red Cecere was telling the other cons in Atlanta Penitentiary that when he got out he intended to kill Gerry Zelmanowitz. When these thoughts would come to him, Maris would slip his hand inside his pocket to touch the gun, and Cecere's words would come back: ". . . *take him down into my cellar for three or four days.*"

Such fears were more often thought than spoken, and the thoughts could transform normal incidents into terrifying experiences. For Paul and Lillian Maris, once it turned a harmless husband-and-wife spat into a chilling incident. They were spending a weekend at Lake Tahoe, California, in the mountains near Nevada, and a dispute between them festered into a marathon argument. In the late afternoon, Maris decided that he had had enough; he would slip away to a restaurant across the lake, have a few drinks and a steak, and come back late after Lillian had gone to sleep. But for Lillian, as the hours passed with no word from him, anger turned increasingly to fear. She felt isolated and threatened in the strange place, and she became convinced that something had happened to him. Finally, in a panic, she telephoned Gerald Shur at his home. To Lillian it was a reasonable cry for help and reassurance — but to Shur, three hours deeper into the night in the Eastern time zone, it was a needless exercise in a woman's hysteria and jealousy disturbing his family's sleep. Shur put her off, arguing that there was no suggestion of foul play, that her husband would show up and it was premature to send for marshals.

147

Later Maris did wander in, oblivious to all the fuss. But the incident left another scar on his relations with the Justice Department. Shur and Bonomi had warned him to stay away from Las Vegas and the gambling centers of Nevada, where he might bump into people he had known in the mob. They had the impression — mistakenly, Maris claimed — that Lake Tahoe as an outpost of that Las Vegas culture. They felt that at least he had violated their instructions and needlessly disturbed Shur's sleep, or at worst, he had gone to Lake Tahoe to meet some of his old contacts in the Mafia.

Paul and Lillian Maris managed to laugh about Lake Tahoe later — but not about another frightening experience that happened when they were on another trip, this time to Montreal. They had gone there for business and pleasure, and Maris had routinely notified Shur of his plans, as he claimed he always did when he left the country. Maris knew it irked Shur to be reminded that the person whose identity he had programmed for a menial existence was back on the international circuit. Shur had not given Paul or Lillian Maris birth certificates or passports, because he did not want them traveling to places where they might serve as Mafia money couriers. But Maris had remedied that easily. He had Lillian obtain a passport, using her birth certificate as Lillian Ringel, but under her married name of Mrs. Paul Maris. Then Paul used *her* passport, plus his army card, to get a passport for himself. But he wanted to keep his skirts clean with the Justice Department, so he notified Shur before he took the Paul Maris fashion line to the Paris exhibition, before he and Lillian made a subsequent pleasure trip to England, and before they went to Montreal.

They arrived there on an earlier flight than the one Maris had mentioned to Shur, and a curious thing happened. The other passengers were passed quickly through customs, but Paul and Lillian were held for longer than an hour — long enough to slow them down to the schedule they would have kept if they had taken the later flight. The two of them finally cleared customs and bundled into a taxi for the long drive to their hotel, and Maris had an uneasy moment. As his taxi pulled away, he caught a glimpse of two men running to enter a car parked at the curb. He could not be sure, but it seemed to him that the car had then fallen into traffic behind them.

Maris realized, with growing apprehension, that as the taxi threaded its way through the streets toward the city, a pair of headlights seemed to be following behind. He had felt similar suspicions before and had dismissed them as false fears. But this time his fears, and the following headlights, did not drift away. Maris ordered the driver to hurry, but the driver, speaking with a thick French accent, seemed not to understand. By the time they approached the center of the city, the headlights seemed to be pulling closer, but Maris was able to push back the panic because he could see the sign on his hotel, the Queen Elizabeth, off to the right on the far side of a broad public park.

Just as his muscles were beginning to unknot, the driver passed the turn leading to the hotel, and continued on a direction that seemed to be taking them away. Maris swung around and saw that the headlights had pulled up close enough to make out the car behind them. It was the same car he had noticed at the airport, with two men inside.

Maris groped quickly for his pistol and then cursed, remembering that he had left it at home because of the customs inspection. Then he began to shout at the driver, forgetting what French he knew and yelling, "Turn right! Turn right!" repeatedly into his ear.

But the driver only jabbered incomprehensibly at Maris, and the car seemed to be closing the gap from behind. Maris quickly slipped off his belt, made a lariat, and threw it over the driver's head. He pulled it taut around the driver's neck and hissed: "Turn! Turn!"

The driver swerved into a one-way street leading to the right, and then made two more right turns that brought them to the ramp leading up to the hotel. The car behind disappeared, and Maris noticed that many of the side streets were one-way. He realized that this could have accounted for the indirect approach to the hotel, but he was certain that the car was following, with little effort to avoid detection. The frightened taxi driver quickly deposited Paul and Lillian at the door of the hotel. Maris tried to soothe him with an extravagant tip, but he was not sheepish about his strong-arm tactics, and he noticed that the man drove away without reporting the incident to the doorman at the hotel.

It was not until several years later that Maris learned the full story of that night in Montreal. He was to learn that the two men in the car were indeed following him, but that they were not emissaries of the

Mafia. But he did not know that story on that chilly spring night in 1973 when he walked his dog in the shadowy park in San Francisco. What he did know was that he had been followed in Canada, and that now men were sitting in a car in front of his home. Maybe it wouldn't be so paranoid, he thought, to perform a little test.

Maris walked the dog across the street to the apartment building and handed the leash to the doorman. With a wave, he turned and began walking rapidly down the street toward the heart of the city. Out of the corner of his eye, he saw the Corvette's door open. The man he remembered from the night before got out and started walking in the same direction as Maris. Paul angled across the street, so that he could glance back without turning his head.

The man stepped behind a tree.

"This is it!" Maris thought.

It was the stunning, dizzying moment that was the dread of every graduate of the alias program: the realization of disclosure. He had thought about it many times, had even dreamed about it in a recurrent nightmare about Red Cecere. He knew it was a fear he shared with all of the two thousand hidden Americans whom the Justice Department had sprinkled throughout the population, with only a change of identity to shield them from the vengeance of the past.

He wondered for an instant how many of them had confronted this moment, and how they had felt. Maris was surprised that his own reaction was so simple. He was furious. There was none of the confusion or fear that had seized him in Montreal, no mental flailing about for clues to the identity of his pursuer or how he had been found. Maris had spent three years building a new existence that had fulfilled his life's ambitions, and the man behind the tree represented a threat to that new life.

Maris slowed down to a casual pace, strolling along the walkway that would take him around the park and back toward his building's entrance. He forced himself to show no concern, no indication of his purpose. If the man left him alone, he would circle the park, retrieve the dog from the doorman, and go inside the building. Then he would rush to his apartment and get his pistol.

Maris was determined that if he made it that far, he would take the little automatic and return to the park. He had come too far, accomplished too much to do anything else. He would confront the man behind the tree.

When the government created the alias program, it had simply been assumed that those who testified against the likes of Gyp DeCarlo and Red Cecere would be killed if the mob could ever find them. But, because there was no testimony or debate in Congress over the program, this assumption was never tested. Robert Kennedy had mentioned in his testimony on organized crime in 1963 that the Justice Department had been so concerned about some witnesses' safety that it had sent them overseas or changed their names. But he didn't say why. The nearest thing to official documentation of the reasons for this concern came in 1965, when the new Attorney General, Nicholas deB. Katzenbach, came to Capitol Hill in an effort to cool the Senate's alarm over the recent disclosures of widespread wiretapping by the FBI, the IRS, and various other agencies.

Katzenbach's message was that organized crime was so horrible that the agents who had been fighting it occasionally got carried away and did improper things, such as planting illegal listening devices.

"It should not be hard to conceive of their frustration," Katzenbach remarked, "when after months or years on a case we find we are forced to dismiss it for reasons other than tainted evidence. We must dismiss it because key witnesses or informants suffer 'accidents' and turn up, for example, in a river wearing concrete boots."

Then Katzenbach dropped the remark that was to become, years later, the factual basis for creation of the alias program: "Such accidents are not unusual," he said; "we have lost more than twenty-five informants in this and similar ways in the past four years." Katzenbach then went on to what was the main purpose of his testimony, the justification for the government's illegal wiretapping, and nobody took any notice at that time of his aside about the mortality rate of government witnesses.

But five years later, when Senator McClellan rose in the Senate on January 21, 1970, to begin the debate on the Organized Crime Control Act, Katzenbach's remark suddenly became the factual underpinning of the alias program. "It is not necessary for me to recount horror stories showing the extent of torture and terrorism practiced by organized crime in its efforts to prevent unfavorable testimony," McClellan intoned; "suffice it for present purposes to note the testimony of the Attorney General that between 1961 and 1965, the organized crime program, despite attempts to offer protection, lost twenty-five informants. More need not be added."

There was, indeed, some reason to believe that the government could simply assume that people would be killed if they testified against Mafia criminals. Anyone involved with organized crime could recite gruesome tales of people gunned, garrotted, or dynamited to death on the eve of their grand jury appearances, or suspected snitchers found anchored in the river or laid out with dead canaries in their mouths.

The catch was that almost without exception, the victims had been potential witnesses who had been silenced before they could testify. Nobody would deny that the status of a future witness for the prosecution was a precarious one indeed. The point that had never been closely examined was whether the rough-hewn characters who made up organized crime were really organized enough to track down a witness after he had given his testimony, and after the presumably vengeful subject had spent a long stretch in prison. The DeCarlo tapes revealed that, for all their simpleminded brutality in dealing with rival gangsters or potential witnesses who were close at hand, the mobsters did not seem to have the attention span or sense of purpose to track down and kill anyone who was not then on the scene and giving them trouble.

The one clear instance to the contrary was one that virtually every hidden witness tends to recount, with a shudder, when the question of their safety is mentioned — the murder of the witness who turned in the notorious bank robber and escape artist, Willie "The Actor" Sutton. It was in 1952 that Sutton, who was living quietly in Brooklyn after having escaped from prison five years before, was spotted on a subway by a twenty-four-year-old clothing salesman named Arnold Schuster. Schuster played the part of the good citizen and tipped off the police, who seized the escaped convict. Two weeks later, Schuster was gunned down on the sidewalk near his Brooklyn home by John

"Chappy" Mazziotta, an ex-convict and small-time bookmaker. Mazziotta vanished and was never found, but the police were told by underworld sources that Mazziotta had not been sent as a mob hit man — he had been a volunteer. The arrest of Sutton had been a highly publicized event, and Mazziotta apparently concluded that if he killed Schuster, the squealer, Mazziotta would earn great respect and status in the criminal underworld.

The ultimate private hell of each relocated witness seems to be that somewhere he may be recognized by one such status-seeker, a mindless punk who would commit murder just to "become somebody" in the mob. But aside from this irrational threat, many hidden witnesses will concede that the tradition of *omertà* has been so eroded, and the government's retaliation against revenge killings so relentless, that a witness might well testify and then just brazen it out, and never suffer any retaliation.

Obviously, nobody would volunteer to test this out. But circumstances made Herbert Itkin/Atkin a test case, and to the continuing astonishment of the Justice Department, he has remained living proof that for a former witness against the Mafia, discovery is not necessarily the kiss of death.

Several years after his testimony, Itkin was in New York, strolling past the Waldorf-Astoria Hotel, when he came face-to-face with Anthony "Tony Ducks" Corallo, one of the Mafia figures convicted by his testimony who had served a prison sentence and had been released.

They looked at each other for a moment, and then both spoke:

"Hello," they said.

Then Tony Ducks spoke again.

"You did a hell of a job on us," he said.

Then he walked on.

A year later the *New York Times* printed a front page story, revealing that court records filed in Los Angeles had blown the cover of Herbert Atkin, a local private detective, and had identified him as a former witness, Herbert Itkin. The story added that Itkin/Atkin worked at the Continental Investigative Agency in Los Angeles.

After that, he and his wife and four children wearily pondered the miseries of another change of identity and relocation, and he decided,

"I couldn't put them through that again." So Herbert Atkin, who is known to be Herbert Itkin to anyone who can read the *Times*, stayed on at his job in L.A. No attempts were ever made on his life.

A similar end has come to the relocation story of Bourbon Street's gift to the alias program, the irrepressible Pershing Gervais. The fun-loving Cajun from New Orleans found life in a small Canadian town a bit bland for his taste, especially after his job for General Motors turned out to involve little more than picking up his weekly check. Gervais stuck it out for a year, and then he terminated his relocation with one bold stroke.

He arranged for a television journalist and camera crew from New Orleans to come to the town of Tsawwassen, where he had been relocated, for four days of filming and interviews. When the interviews with Gervais went on the air in New Orleans a few days later, they amounted to a public announcement that Pershing Gervais was coming home. His message was that his testimony had been false, obtained by lies and trickery by government agents, who had harassed him into entrapping District Attorney Jim Garrison on the bribery charges. By the time the series of broadcasts had run, the outcome of the Justice Department's expensive venture with Pershing Gervais was fore-doomed; Gervais's value as a witness had been tarnished, and the flamboyant "Jolly Green Giant" would be acquitted.

It was all so predictable that Gervais didn't even wait for the trial to be held. He, his family, and the surviving dozen Yorkshire terriers returned to New Orleans, where Gervais reclaimed his original name and went back to his old haunts in the French Quarter. So far as anyone knows, there have been no threats, no attacks, no murder plots. Pershing Gervais had returned home, just as if the alias program had never existed.

No one outside the government knows how many other relocated witnesses may have become homesick and gone home to take their chances, but a few other instances have come to light. Paddy Calabrese has resumed his true name, and he returns to Buffalo periodically and gives interviews to the press. Asked why such openness doesn't make him nervous, his reply is that the threat of retaliation by the mob has faded with the passage of years: "Those guys have all gotten old."

There have been reports of other relocated witnesses who have moved back home, lending credence to the theory held by some that the threat of Mafia revenge has been exaggerated by many witnesses, either out of fear or a desire to manipulate the Justice Department, and that much of the cloak-and-dagger activity of the alias program is simply not needed.

That would be very reassuring to the other alumni of the program, except that frightening, and sometimes deadly, incidents have dogged the heels of some relocated witnesses.

Several have found that, after their identities were compromised in their new locations, they were driven to move on by what they took to be ominous signs. Such a thing happened to Edmund Graifer, who was relocated in Virginia Beach after he testified against Mafia figures in New York. After the word somehow got around the neighborhood in Virginia Beach who he was (he said one of the marshals gossiped; they blamed his wife), a suspicious black car began to cruise the neighborhood. Graifer and his family were hustled away.

Officials in the Justice Department tend to pass off such incidents as frayed nerves and overreaction on the part of the witnesses, but things went beyond that for Frank Peroff, the witness who testified against financial manipulator Robert Vesco and others allegedly involved in the narcotics trade. After his cover was blown over the doctor's bill incident in Washington, Peroff was driving to his home one night when the inevitable black sedan pulled alongside and — according to the subsequent suit filed by Peroff against the government for allegedly disclosing his identity — a shotgun blast crashed through Peroff's side window, missing his face by inches. He was so frightened he had himself locked up in protective custody for several weeks in the Leesburg, Virginia, city jail.

A closer call happened to James Barrett, a former Baltimore policeman, who was relocated during a period of protracted testimony in New York against organized crime figures involved in the pornography trade. Barrett returned to Baltimore for a time, during which he traded in his Mercury for a new car. The day of the trade proved to be the luckiest day of Barrett's life. Barrett believed in reinforcing his luck with precautions. He had equipped the Mercury with special floodlights, which he always switched on each night to bathe the approach to his home with light as he drove up the long, dark driveway to his apartment house. It was protected by an eight-foot-high fence and around-the-clock security guards, so he felt safe in parking his car outside.

On the morning of the trade, Barrett climbed into his Mercury parked outside his apartment house, drove to the Packer Ford Company in Baltimore, and drove away in his new car. Meanwhile, a mechanic named Don Darrah was assigned the job of checking out the Mercury before it was put up for resale. Darrah was fascinated with the special switch for the floodlights, and so he tested it first. When he switched it on, there was an explosion in the undercarriage of the car, riddling his legs with shrapnel but leaving him alive.

The Baltimore police later found out that the Irish luck of both Barrett and Darrah had been running strong. Three sticks of dynamite had been wired to explode when Barrett switched on his floodlights that night. But the blasting caps had shaken loose from the dynamite sticks, so that when Darrah threw the switch, only the dynamite caps exploded. The police said that if the dynamite had gone off, it would have demolished the car and everything near it.

Most relocated witnesses know that in 1975, a dynamite blast did, in fact, demolish the car of a man who was living under an alias provided by the government in Tempe, Arizona. He was Louis Bombacino, the Justice Department's witness from Chicago, and the explosion was so powerful that pieces of his new Continental Mark IV sedan were thrown a quarter of a mile away. This gave the government much to explain, because Bombacino was in the car when the dynamite exploded.

Neighbors had noticed that Bombacino was a methodical man; that each night he taped shut the hood of his car, and each morning he checked to see that the tape had not been disturbed. On the morning of the blast he checked the hood, slid under the wheel, and threw the car into reverse. Then there was a shattering explosion. Dynamite had been packed into the car's trunk and wired to its back-up lights. The protective tape on the hood was left intact until the car blew up.

As so often happened, there were circumstances that might have explained the murder, short of a breakdown in the government's cover.

Bombacino had drifted back into criminal ways and had made contacts with small-time operators in bookmaking and prostitution who were said to have links to organized crime beyond Arizona. But there was no evidence that these petty crooks had any reason or capability to kill Bombacino, or that they knew or could have told anyone outside Tempe that he was not Joseph Nardi, as he claimed to be. It was also possible that Bombacino had — perhaps literally — blown his own cover, through an astonishingly foolish act. He had become involved in a lawsuit, and had testified in a deposition that he had once been an informer for the FBI.

But it was never explained how such an obscure gaffe on his part could have made its way back to the men in Chicago who presumably most wanted Bombacino dead — John "Jackie the Lackey" Cerone, operating chief of Chicago's rackets at the time of his bookmaking conviction as a result of Bombacino's testimony; James "Tar Baby" Cerone, "Jackie the Lackey's" cousin, who was also convicted; and Frank Aurelio and Joseph Ferriola, two childhood friends of Bombacino, who went to jail along with the Cerones on the strength of their childhood friend's testimony. All of them had been released from prison in the months preceding the bombing in Tempe.

Officials in the witness protection program did not deny that somehow the gangsters in Chicago might have learned where Bombacino was, but still they insisted that there was no evidence that their program had been penetrated or compromised. Their reason: Bombacino, they said, was never officially in the alias program. They insisted that the United States marshals had never heard of Bombacino until they were flooded with telephone calls from nervous hidden witnesses after his death. They explained that the FBI had instead relocated Bombacino, on the grounds that he did not qualify for the regular witness protection program because his testimony was given in May of 1970, five months before the Organized Crime Control Act was signed into law. This response failed to soothe the fears of some of the alumni of the alias program because they knew from the witness grapevine that Zelmanowitz, Calabrese, and a few others were relocated by the program, even though they testified before the Organized Crime Control Act became law.

Despite these near misses and Mafia hits, Gerald Shur and the Marshals' Service claim that no witness relocated by the witness protection program has been tracked down and killed. There is some artifice to that statement, because some relocated witnesses are known to have been tracked down but for various reasons not killed, and others have been killed but not, according to government officials, because they were tracked down.

The officials insist that in each case, the witness did something that played into the assassin's hands. No figures are given as to how many times this has happened, but John Partington, the United States Marshal official who runs the major witness protection program operation out of Providence, Rhode Island, says seven witnesses in the program have been murdered by gangland assassins — but only, he says, because they wouldn't obey the rules. "They tried to cut it on their own," he says; "they didn't fellow instructions. It's not how far we move them from the danger area but what they do when they get there."

That is the way the alias program has discounted the murder of its former witness from Gary, Indiana, James Berry. He was murdered, gangland-style, after he was relocated in Fort Worth. But nobody has denied the government's story that this was done by a gang that Berry joined after he moved to Texas.

A more difficult case is posed by the assassination of another protected witness, a small-time hood from Connecticut named Daniel LaPolla. LaPolla had agreed to testify against a group of Providence, Rhode Island, thugs who were allegedly stealing and selling some of the National Guard's guns. After the United States marshals whisked LaPolla away to a nearby safe house, it became obvious that the gunrunners were out to kill him before he could testify. First, they were spotted cruising in a car near LaPolla's home in Oneco, Connecticut. Then, after LaPolla's brother, a Catholic priest, died, federal officers saw the mobsters from Rhode Island sitting piously in the rear of the wake, scanning the mourners' ranks for LaPolla, who had prudently stayed away. Two of the gang even rented a private airplane on a couple of occasions and flew over the Oneco area, looking for LaPolla.

Five days after the second aerial reconnaissance, LaPolla made the fatal mistake of going to his home. When he opened the door, there was a massive blast that blew the upper half of Daniel LaPolla away. In speeches and interviews, Shur has pointed out that LaPolla was not tracked down; that he violated the government's warnings to all witnesses never, ever, to return to old haunts.

The government has a similar explanation for the sudden demise of Joseph "The Baron" Barboza, the hired gun from Boston who had been relocated by the alias program. He was a man who had given many people ample reason to wish him ill. Barboza had been the New England Mafia's "enforcer of enforcers" — a hulking, brutal killer who was brought in by the mob to kill other thugs who had become threatening to the top leaders. Barboza surfaced as a federal witness in the murder conspiracy trial that resulted in the conviction of New England's ruling Mafia chieftain, Raymond Patriarca.

As if he hadn't made enough high-level enemies, Barboza appeared in 1972 before a House Crime Committee hearing in Washington, where he testified that Frank Sinatra served as a front for mob interests in two hotels, and that he had a stake in a racetrack owned by Patriarca and other mobsters. Sinatra made an angry appearance before the committee to deny Barboza's charges, and the abashed Congressmen were unable to come up with corroborating proof.

Barboza's relocation in San Francisco as Joseph Bently collapsed when he was arrested for murder, in a case that made it clear that he had returned to a gangland style of existence in California. He was released from state prison in 1975, not long after Patriarca had been released from prison in the East. Rumors circulated in Boston that a $250,000 bounty had been put on Barboza by unnamed enemies in the mob. Soon, stories appeared in the San Francisco press and on local radio broadcasts that Barboza was back in the city under a new alias and that hit men from the East were there looking for him. Soon after, death caught up with Joe Barboza. He was entering his car on a San Francisco street when a van with two men inside pulled up. One man stuck a shotgun out the window and blew much of Barboza's head away with a blast to the face.

Tremors of fear rippled through the scattered ranks of the government's relocated witnesses. How did the hit men know where Barboza was? How did the press get the story in advance? Shur was reassuring.

159

There had been no slipup on the government's part. Barboza had triggered the publicity himself, by an inexplicable call to a San Francisco radio station. He would not have been hard for the underworld to find; he had left the home of a reputed bookmaker just before he was killed.

The hidden witnesses' fears were exacerbated by another incident that happened at about the same time, involving a witness named James Jelicks. His had been a typical story — a small-time car thief and bad-check artist, who gave grand jury testimony against a score of organized crime figures in Jersey City and then was given a false identity by the Justice Department and had lived in various cities in Pennsylvania, Kentucky, and Rhode Island during his months of court appearances. Then, his court testimony apparently at an end, Jelicks was seen no more in New Jersey and it was assumed that he had gone to his final reward in some sunny region selected by the Justice Department. But suddenly, Jelicks reappeared in New Jersey, charging that he had been found by the Mafia, under circumstances suggesting that the alias program had been penetrated by organized crime.

Jelicks's story was that after he had settled into his new life of supposed anonymity in Pittsburgh, he twice received warnings not to testify anymore. The third warning came in the form of a bullet in the night, which shattered his right arm and persuaded him to drop out of the alias program. Still using his government alias, he moved quietly back to a New Jersey coastal town, only to have two messengers from the mob appear on the scene. They brought an ultimatum: either he would feed the government false information to discredit the FBI and undermine some of the convictions he had helped secure, or his wife and children would be murdered. According to Jelicks, it would have been futile to flee again; one of the men had copies of confidential government documents relating to his supposedly secret activities and whereabouts while he was in the witness protection program. He agreed, and for months gave false information to the government.

When James Jelicks came in from the cold and told his story to a state grand jury in New Jersey, it at first seemed that every hidden witness might be in potential danger. If the hit men from Jersey City had found a chink in the Justice Department, others might do the same.

It was the most terrifying prospect that had ever confronted the alias program — that the Mafia might have found a source through which the program's secrets could be obtained, so that potentially any witness might be found and killed at any time.

Gerald Shur had an answer for those doubts, and in fact no string of discoveries and assassinations subsequently occurred. Shur agreed that Jelicks had blown his own cover through his own carelessness, and that the document he mentioned was one that the Marshals' Service had sent him. That left unexplained some loose ends, such as why Jelicks would concoct such a story, and the bullet scar on his arm. But whatever the true answer, Jelicks and the Justice Department seemed to have made their peace; he testified again, taking back all of the lies he had told while he was cooperating with the Mafia, and then James Jelicks disappeared again.

In fact, by the time of Paul Maris's incident in the park in San Francisco, the Justice Department had considerably tightened up its procedures for protecting witnesses' anonymity. The Marshals' Service had made its operation more professional by creating a special witness security unit staffed with fifteen relocation specialists. This group, operating out of an unlikely suite of offices in a shopping center in Falls Church, Virginia, outside Washington, had become the logistical center and command post for the alias program. Witnesses' files could be kept under tight security there, and procedures had been adopted to discourage gossip by keeping witnesses' identities secret even from the marshals who guarded them. The result was a cops-and-robbers jargon that the marshals thoroughly enjoyed, referring to witnesses by their file numbers ("Meet twelve sixty-three at the airport") or by code names ("Take Big Mack to the courthouse"). In a move to tighten up protective procedures, a series of orders were issued to govern the marshals while on bodyguard duty. ("Report to duty physically fit and mentally alert. . . ." "Dress in a conservative manner. . . ." "There will be no display of any firearms at any time. . . ." "The witness will not be posed for photographs. . . .") And finally, arrangements were made with the Social Security Administration to assign to families Social Security numbers that are not sequential.

The result appeared to be a mixed record of success and failure —

of an impressive number of lawbreakers hidden by the government among the law-abiding citizens of the nation, and an unanswered series of questions as to what the ultimate results of all this subterfuge might be. So many hidden witnesses were eventually scattered across the country that any person who traveled widely might stumble upon one; a Greyhound bus driver in Arizona was one, so was a desk clerk at an apartment building in the District of Columbia, a hooker on the streets of Los Angeles, and a bartender in San Diego. The Justice Department's hidden Americans were working as private detectives in a half-dozen cities; several were selling used cars; and a handful were drifting back and forth across the country, making their living as paid informers for government law enforcement agencies. These were some of the obscure witnesses from minor-league prosecutions, but the alias program had also managed to hide highly publicized witnesses whose faces had become well known in the course of important trials: Vincent Teresa, the three-hundred-pound loan shark who testified against thirty of his former colleagues and then dared to publish a book entitled *My Life in the Mafia;* Silous Huddleston and Annette Gilly, whose testimony linked the United Mine Workers' Union's leadership to the murders of union insurgent Joseph Yablonski and his family; Paul Rigo, the Newark engineer who told of bribing Mayor Hugh Addonizio; Tony "Big Bear" Stagg and Vinnie Capola, who set up the "Mount Kisco Sting" that led to the conviction of a Latin America–based ring that was plotting to sell ten thousand submachine guns to the American underworld. Even by the time that Paul Maris began to feel the hot breath of discovery on his neck, several thousand Americans had sensed something strange and distant about the new family that moved in next door, but had not been told enough to suspect that they were observing probably the most unusual service ever offered by any government in peacetime. No other nation has been known to create a special program to change the identities and then infiltrate back into society persons who had served justice by testifying for the government. Whether that was an unsung governmental accomplishment or a manifestation of grotesque forces in American society was for the future to show. But already it was clear that the program would involve the bureaucracy in life-and-death responsibilities that governments traditionally undertook only in matters of capital punishment and war. Given the fallibility of people in general, including those who earned their livelihood in government service, it was not surprising that questions had begun to surface as to whether the concept of an alias program was really a good idea, and whether its witnesses — sprinkled across the country with nothing between them and the hatred of men they had sent to prison but the efficiency of the program — were really safe.

It was doubts and fears such as these that tumbled through Paul Maris's mind as he circled the park and turned back toward his apartment building. By now he was convinced that the man behind the tree was watching him. But the man made no move to try to cut him off as Maris approached the building. Maris could feel the relaxing flow of relief in his legs and spine as he retrieved his dog from the doorman and walked into the lobby.

He had at least one advantage — the two men in the car didn't know he had seen them. He punched the elevator button and rose quickly to the third floor. Inside his apartment, Lillian was asleep, and he was able to slip the shiny little automatic out of the bedside table's drawer without awakening her. He left the dog in the kitchen, and returned to the elevator.

Maris knew his little popgun would provide puny firepower against what the men outside might have, but it never occurred to him to stop. He had thoroughly conditioned himself to fight as soon as he was discovered, and he was seething with fury at the man who threatened his new life from behind that tree.

Maris rushed out the front entrance, pointing the little pistol through his jacket pocket toward the tree. Nobody was there. The man was gone. So was the Corvette with the Oregon license plates.

Maris was relieved, but also puzzled. He was almost certain that the man behind the tree had been watching him, but if so, the two men's purpose was a mystery. If they had been sent to kill him, they had had their chance, two nights in a row. If they had not been sent by the Mafia, why had they been watching?

He could not fit the pieces together, but Maris sensed that events affecting his life had been set in motion, and that various recent incidents were related in ways that he could not yet comprehend. He returned to his apartment with a heavy sense of foreboding.

It would be months before he would learn enough to conclude that it was a government agent he had wanted to kill that night.

8......................................Quarry

When Hal Lipset left Milton Stewart's office on the Monday after the Good Friday Massacre, he seemed to be confronted with a mystery worthy of his reputation as San Francisco's foremost sleuth. He had just announced that Paul Maris was a phony, and he realized that he had climbed far out on a limb. Lipset knew he had showed off a bit with Stewart, playing the crafty and cynical private eye. But he also sensed that there was something about Maris that did not add up, and after all those years as a detective, he tended to respect the vibes picked up by his investigative antennae.

As Lipset drove back toward his town house office in Pacific Heights, he was already mentally mapping out what he would do. There was nothing mysterious about most detective work—just knowing which facts to check and how to check them. In this case, he even had a checklist to run down. He would examine every item on Maris's résumé to see if public records backed up each claim.

By the time he strode into his office, Lipset had worked out in his mind how to check each point on the résumé. This was where the experience came in. If the public knew how detective work was done most people wouldn't think it was very romantic, but if the average man tried to do it himself, he would thrash around in confusion. To Lipset, it was just a matter of falling back on old habits, old contacts.

Lipset flipped open his address book and dialed an area code and a number. A man answered.

"Hello, Gerry, this is Hal Lipset." Lipset had phoned an old friend, Gerald Ross, who did business with his brother in Philadelphia as the Ross Bureau of Investigation. There were a few routine pleasantries, and then the two men got down to business.

Lipset wanted to check out three facts on a man named Paul Maris: Did the city's birth records show that he was born in Philadelphia on January 12, 1935? Did the records of John Bertram High School show that he graduated in June of 1953? Did the city's real estate records show that the Maris family lived at 8916 Laycock Avenue in Philadelphia until 1953?

Ross said he would get right on it, and the men hung up.

Then Lipset flipped through his address book again, and dialed another area code and telephone number.

"Hello Ned, this is Hal Lipset." This time, he had called Ned Rogers of Brewster, Rogers & Associates in Kensington, Maryland, outside Washington. The conversation was much the same: Had a Captain Paul J. Maris been released from active duty from the army reserve in January of 1970? Had he served temporarily with the State Department? The Atomic Energy Agency?

Rogers said he would check it out.

There was just enough time to make one more telephone call to the Eastern time zone before people began drifting away from their offices toward their evening martinis, so Lipset made one final call. This one was placed with the aid of the information operator in Berea, Ohio, to the office of admissions of Baldwin Wallace College. A woman answered, and explained that all the men had left. But yes, she would check for the records of Paul J. Maris. There was a long silence. Then the woman came back on the phone again.

She said she could find no record that a Paul Maris had ever attended Baldwin Wallace College.

Lipset asked if she was certain, and she said she had checked the student lists for the mid-1950s, and had found no student named Maris. He asked her to take another look the next day, and to send him the results in writing. Then he hung up and immediately dictated a letter to Baldwin Wallace, asking again for the same information. Lipset thought for a moment, and then spread the Maris résumé and the Proudfoot report side by side on his desk.

He had not noticed it before, but Maris's résumé said that he attended Baldwin Wallace for only two years, from 1953 to 1955. But the Proudfoot report said: "From 1953 to 1957 subject attended Baldwin Wallace College, Berea, Ohio. The Registrar's Office of that educational institution verified that subject was awarded a Bachelor of Science degree in 1957."

Lipset shook his head over that. He had never known a person to claim only two years of college in his résumé, if he had in fact completed four years and earned a degree.

At odd moments during the next day, April 24, Lipset thumbed through a stack of standard books of corporations. None of them listed a Sound Enterprises, Inc. He knew that many corporations were too small to be listed, but if Sound Enterprises was so small, why had not Maris noted its location on his résumé? By then Lipset's curiosity had been thoroughly whetted, so he tried a long shot — a call to Geneva, Switzerland, to Allen Vogel, who operated a detective agency immodestly called Agence Privée Internationale. A man named Paul Maris had claimed to own a home in Lausanne, Switzerland, Lipset told Vogel; would Vogel check to see if Maris might have been associated with Bernard Cornfeld's Investors Overseas Services operation in Geneva? Cornfeld, and his IOS, were then much in the news. He had built the company from the ground up into a multimillion-dollar international corporate giant, only to have it taken away by the ubiquitous Robert Vesco. Vesco was ultimately accused by the Securities and Exchange Commission of looting the IOS treasury of $224 million. But despite a stretch in a Swiss jail, Cornfeld ended up as very rich, with his investors very poor. It was only a hunch, Lipset explained to his friend in Geneva — but from what he had seen of Maris, he and the high-rolling, wheeling-and-dealing Cornfeld could easily have been struck from the same mold. Lipset asked for a check of Cornfeld's business associates, to see if one might have been named Maris.

Detective work takes time, and Lipset had assumed that it would require weeks, or perhaps months, to find that one chink in Maris's story that he sensed was somewhere to be found. The negative response from the clerk at Baldwin Wallace had been surprising, but he had been an investigator for too many years, and had seen too many apparent breaks vanish under closer examination, to become overly excited over such an obvious contradiction in Maris's story. The clerk might not have known how to use the lists, or she might have overlooked Maris's name, or his records could have been misplaced. There could be many reasons why the Baldwin Wallace records did not immediately check out.

Thus Lipset was astounded when on Wednesday, April 25, just two days after he began to probe, Maris's story collapsed.

First, Gerald Ross phoned from Philadelphia. He had checked with the bureau of vital statistics. No Paul Maris had been born in Philadelphia on that date. He checked with John Bartram High School, assuming that Lipset had just slipped by calling it "Bertram." But the principal's office reported that they had no record of a Paul Maris ever having attended the school. Just to be sure, Ross checked the yearbook for 1953 in the school library. Again, no Paul Maris. Then he checked the home address, 8916 Laycock Avenue. It was a vacant lot, and had been for years. It was also in a South Philadelphia neighborhood that had been all black for decades. Nothing in Philadelphia checked out. Nothing.

Lipset quickly dialed Ned Rogers in Washington. He said there had been time to check only one point, Maris's army serial number. Rogers was puzzled — the Pentagon said that number had never been issued to anyone.

By the time Lipset completed that call and hung up, there was no doubt left in his mind. There was no Paul Maris.

Lipset next phoned Milton Stewart. It was all too sweet; Lipset could not restrain a note of triumph.

"I told you so," he began.

Lipset's message to Stewart was a negative one. Despite Maris's apparent credentials, despite his breezy confidence, despite the Proudfoot report, nothing in Maris's résumé checked out. But the unanimity of Lipset's negative findings only served to deepen the mystery. How could Maris have come so far on such a flimsy story? As vulnerable as his story was, why was Maris so confident? How could Proudfoot have been so wrong?

All Lipset and Stewart knew was that he was not the Paul Maris he claimed to be. They did not know who he was — and that proved to be a much tougher puzzle to untangle.

Lipset and Stewart might have been content to stop there, to leave the question unanswered. After his fast start, Lipset found out very little more about Maris. There was a subsequent letter from Baldwin Wallace College, confirming the clerk's telephone response: "We have made a thorough search and find no records in our files of a student by this name." Lipset also found Maris's old loan application, claiming ownership of the mansion on Embassy Row in Washington. A check of real estate records showed that no Maris had ever owned that property.

Then Lipset allowed himself to be drawn into a blind alley. Word came from the detective agency in Geneva that Bernard Cornfeld did, indeed, have a former associate named Maris. According to Swiss authorities, a Franklin Maris had been employed as a securities salesman for IOS. On the surface, Lipset seemed to have struck gold; Franklin Maris listed his home state as New Jersey and had worked in the Far East. But beyond that, nothing quite fit. According to passport records, Franklin Maris was only thirty-two years old and had worked in Formosa, not Japan. Lipset was never able to establish a link between the two Marises, but the coincidence appealed to his taste for intrigue and chicanery. For months he continued to probe the "Cornfeld connection," making no progress in cracking the riddle of who Paul Maris really was.

Milton Stewart might also have been content to drop the matter at that point. His company's main concern was not in solving the riddle of Paul Maris's identity but in trying to make the company turn a profit with Maris gone. Stewart might have been drawn totally into the day-to-day affairs of the business, leaving little time to puzzle over the mystery of Paul Maris.

But then Maris committed a colossal blunder. On Friday, April 30, he sued Stewart, Lipset, and the Creative Capital Corporation, for $5 million. Typically, Maris's blunder was carried out in grandiose style. He used San Francisco's largest and most prestigious law firm, Pillsbury, Madison & Sutro, and he accused the defendants of undertaking a broad scheme, using various illegal and improper means, to oust him from the Paul Maris Company just as it was about to become profitable. Against Stewart and other officials of Creative Capital he alleged breach of contract, conspiracy, wrongful firing, breach of fiduciary responsibility, and loss of future profits. Lipset was accused of illegal eavesdropping and breaking into Maris's Sonoma home to examine, among other things, the contents of a high-school yearbook. But the allegation that carried the seeds of Maris's downfall was a peripheral one, the kind of makeweight charge that lawyers tend to throw into court pleadings to further blacken the defendants and to serve as a possible parachute if everything else should somehow fail. In this case, Maris accused the defendants of libel, slander, and defamation of character. He had put his reputation on the line, and the defendants had no choice but to try to find out everything about his past life.

Maris explained later that he felt he had to bring the suit. He was then in the thick of negotiations to buy another women's apparel company to compete with the Paul Maris label, and he had received feelers from several major garment manufacturers, suggesting possible job offers. If he let Creative Capital kick him out without a challenge, that might be taken as a tacit admission that some of the charges of misappropriation of funds had been true. They were not true, Maris insisted — he had used accepted standards of ethics in the trade, and the board of directors had approved all of the expenditures that they were now denouncing as excessive or suspect. "I had no choice but to sue," he argued, even after his world had come tumbling down; "I had to stand behind my reputation in the business, I had to protect my good name."

For Gerald Zelmanowitz the identity of Paul Maris had finally become a trap. He had enjoyed the admiration of the respected business leader too much. The life of the swinging corporate entrepreneur had been too sweet. In his own mind he had become Paul Maris, and so he reacted as Paul Maris would have reacted if he had really been what he appeared to be. In hindsight, he added the thought that if he had not sued to clear his good name after the Good Friday Massacre, if he had just slunk away, it might have created more suspicion about his identity than the danger of a direct challenge in court. Also, Maris believed that his alias was airtight. It had been created by the government, by professionals, and he had the Proudfoot report to prove it.

But whatever the justifications, the timing could not have been more disastrous. The court papers in Maris's countersuit were served on Stewart and Lipset just as they were quietly punching the final holes through his identity. The suit only whetted the fighting instincts of the two men who were groping toward the key to his past.

Having easily discovered that their opponent was not Paul Maris, Lipset and Stewart ran into a blank wall in their efforts to find out who he was. Nothing of importance was learned during the first two weeks of May. Meanwhile, Maris was seizing the initiative. He had initiated the purchase of a dress company called Miss Pat, located in Los Angeles. The acquisition clearly posed a competitive threat to the Paul

Maris Company, for about a half-dozen of the Paul Maris Company's best salesmen and executives chose to follow Maris into the Miss Pat Company, which operated in the same market as the Paul Maris Company. Stewart protested that Miss Pat would be using style designs and customer lists developed by his company, and he was outraged by what he saw as unethical attempts by the new company to steal away his orders. The ethics of the new company were disputed, but not the fact that in the women's sportswear business, Paul Maris seemed to be making a comeback.

Two incidents happened during this period that might have served as warning flags to Paul Maris — cautioning him to slow down, to ease off his antagonists, to begin to watch his flanks. But his sales and promotional campaign for the new company was in full cry, and Maris was not receptive to notes of caution.

Maris had established a temporary office for his new company in San Francisco's most elegant and chic hotel, the Stanford Court. It served as a nerve center for his staff, the place where salesmen came and went and clothing designers worked on the new line. On a day in mid-May, Maris agreed to let Hal Lipset drop by and serve court papers on the entire new Maris team. Maris explained to his staff that it was all part of their struggle with the Paul Maris Company, which Maris intended to win anyway, and this would spare everybody the trouble and potential embarrassment of having the papers served at their homes and offices around the country.

Maris was in a relaxed, confident mood when Lipset arrived with the court documents, and Lipset found himself unexpectedly exchanging easy small talk with the man who was suing him for $5 million. Lipset had admired Maris's dignity and calm on the day of the Good Friday Massacre, and he was impressed with the businessman's obvious intelligence and ability. All of which intensified Lipset's curiosity over the mystery of the man's true identity, and so Lipset decided to give Maris a jolt, to see if it would shake loose more information about his past.

"You know, we're having a lot of trouble pinpointing your record," Lipset said. "I've written to Baldwin Wallace, and they don't have any record of your going to college there."

Maris's response was calm and deliberate. He said he couldn't understand that, except that he had spent his career in highly clandestine intelligence activities, and the Army Security Agency might have withdrawn his records for reasons of security. As Lipset recalled the conversation later, Maris went on to say that the ASA cover was so thorough that Lipset might just as well stop wasting his time by trying to crack it. Lipset said he took that as a challenge, and went away more determined than ever to penetrate Maris's story. Maris got the impression that Lipset was making a veiled offer to drop his investigation if Maris would withdraw his suit against Lipset. Maris, still believing his cover was operational, tried to steer Lipset to make queries with the government, where Maris assumed a satisfactory cover story would be told.

As soon as the two men parted, chatting casually, Maris rushed back to his telephone and punched out the area code and special number of Gerald Shur.

Later, Maris and Shur were to tell significantly differing versions of that conversation, Maris to say that he told about the detective's report that the Baldwin Wallace story did not check out, and Shur to insist that Maris did not mention Lipset but said only that he was being investigated and he needed a letter stating that he did attend that college. But under either version, it is clear that the two men — both with much at stake — became victims of their own self-images as calm, confident, in-charge operators.

It was, by any calculation, a crucial moment for both. Maris's very existence in his current identity was very much on the line. Shur's first effort at constructing an identity was being put to the test, one that could prove embarrassing for the man who was now in charge of the burgeoning, multimillion-dollar government alias program. And with all that at stake, a basic element of cover — an impostor's college record — was in question. Yet the talk between the two men was so casual, so larded with mutual self-confidence, that both went away soothed, without fully confronting the enormity of what might be happening.

Maris began with a phrase that both men were to recall later: that he had "a small problem." Maris meant by that to make it clear that he was not in trouble with the law — that this was a civil case, typical of lawsuits that businessmen sometimes encounter. He assumed that the news that he was being investigated and that there had been a slipup would be enough; that Shur would take action, locating the souce of the blunder, shoring up Maris's cover, and protecting his own program from a possible humiliating public disclosure. Maris also read Shur's easygoing responses as a reassurance that all was secure with the Maris background, that all the statements in his résumé were supported by records and that there was no reason for concern. Shur got the impression that Maris was in control of the situation in San Francisco, that there was some question about his college record, but that all that was needed was a letter saying he had attended Baldwin Wallace. It seemed so unimportant that Shur did nothing at all.

Maris ended the conversation irked, but not alarmed. So Stewart knew he didn't have a college education. Stewart couldn't pillory him for that. Creative Capital had bargained for expertise and drive — not a piece of paper from a college — and expertise and drive they had gotten. Maris was disgruntled and unhappy, but undeterred. It did not occur to him that other elements of his cover might also not check out.

A few days later, another incident happened at which Maris bridled, then which he brushed aside. Earlier, at about the same time that Milton Stewart had first attempted to fire Maris, and most of the company had walked out, Lipset had sent over one of his men to try to get evidence that the insurgents were removing books and records. The investigator was a stubby, roly-poly black man named Sam Webster, and he hung around, taking pictures of people who left carrying things in their arms. Webster stayed on after the Good Friday Massacre, on the lookout for what Stewart thought was an ongoing effort by Maris to woo away the key employees and accounts of the Paul Maris Company. Sam Webster took it as part of his job to keep tabs on the new Maris operation at the Stanford Court Hotel. He was also familiar with a well-worn story around the Paul Maris Company: about the occasion when a team from *California Apparel Magazine* appeared at the plant to do a major spread on the company, including — they thought — a picture of the firm's dashing young president. Maris hadn't been informed of this, and when they told him, there was a scene. He insisted that so long as he was still in the army reserves as an intelligence officer, he couldn't permit his photograph to be taken without the special permission of the Defense Department, and he sulked in his office out of range of the cameraman. The incident impressed on everybody Maris's phobia about photographs, and Sam Webster later took it as a challenge to get a picture of Maris.

Webster's chance came as he was cruising in his car near the Maris headquarters at the Stanford Court Hotel. Maris and several of his executives were standing at the curbside chatting, and Webster pulled up, clicked off a couple of exposures, and drove away. Some unpleasantness followed. Maris phoned Lipset to protest this response to his own cooperation in the serving of the papers, and Lipset chewed Webster out for needlessly troubling the waters.

Sam Webster felt so put down that at the time he didn't even bother to develop the pictures.

Those were the dog days of the Maris affair. At the Paul Maris Company, Milton Stewart was quietly struggling to make the corporation turn a profit, and was beginning to discover that the departure of Paul Maris had not cured the company's ills — that under the new management the losses were continuing.

For the new Paul Maris operation, it was a time for making preparations, and waiting. Throughout the month of May, Maris was putting his new team together and making contacts to begin operations. But the date set for final purchase of the Miss Pat Company was May 31, so until then there was little he could do but prepare. Even for the lawyers, there was a pause. The papers had been filed and served, but the hearings were for the future. Also, the quest for Paul Maris's true identity had bogged down. There were no new leads of importance, and the feeling was spreading throughout the ranks of Milton Stewart's staff that the cover story concealed no more than the spotty background of a wheeler-dealer from the East who had manufactured a clean slate to start life with in California.

Then, in the third week of May, the key to Paul Maris's identity fell into Stewart's hands. It came in the person of Charles Thompson, the burly ex-narcotics officer who had stuck close to Stewart on the day of the Good Friday Massacre.

Thompson first telephoned William Trautman, the San Francisco attorney who had obtained the court orders on the day of the Good Friday Massacre. Thompson had become acquainted with Trautman because both men had stayed close to Stewart that day, and there had

The only known photograph of Paul Maris, a.k.a. Gerald Zelmanowitz (left), *was snapped out of the window of a moving car by Sam Webster, an investigator employed by Harold Lipset.*

Former San Francisco police officer and federal narcotics agent Charles Thompson was a private investigator when he provided a tip which led to the unmasking of Paul Maris.

been a good deal of conversation about Paul Maris. So Thompson called the lawyer, Trautman, and said he had some information to sell. He said he thought he knew who Paul Maris really was. Trautman told him to come right over to his office.

At first, Thompson's story seemed fuzzy and intuitive. He had heard, the big man told Trautman, that Paul Maris was really somebody else, and that had set Thompson to thinking. Something jogged his memory, and he recalled that when he was a narcotics agent for the United States Justice Department, he had been told of a mysterious program to give false identities to witnesses who needed protection. Thompson said he had thought about that a good deal, along with bits and pieces of information he knew about Paul Maris.

By this time, Trautman was beginning to shuffle his feet with impatience, and Thompson hit him with his punch line: Paul Maris was a relocated government witness; he had testified in a Mafia trial in the East some time around the late 1960s, and his real name had been something like "Malowitz."

As Trautman later remembered it, Thompson said he had overheard from some United States marshals the part about Maris being a relocated government witness, and the name "Malowitz." But for the moment, he cared nothing about the source. All that mattered was whether the information was true. If so, it would probably unlock the full story of the identity of Paul Maris. Stewart thanked Thompson, and said that if his information proved accurate, he would be paid.

Several days later, Thompson received an envelope in the mail from William Trautman. It contained a check for $2,000.

When Charles Thompson walked out of the lawyer's office, Paul Maris was unmasked. Thompson had set in motion forces that would inexorably lead to the public disclosure that Paul Maris was a figment of fertile imaginations within the Justice Department, and that the man who had dazzled San Francisco's fashion world was really Gerald Zelmanowitz of Brooklyn.

United States Deputy Marshal Glen Robinson (left, guarding Patricia Hearst during her 1976 trial) *was implicated in but denied responsibility for the unmasking of Paul Maris.*

The reverberations from Thompson's disclosure were to be felt in many ways, and thus the question of how he found out was to become crucial to a number of people. Thompson was to tell his story many times — to lawyers, congressional investigators, and journalists, and it never seemed to come out quite the same with each telling. Essentially, Thompson gave two inconsistent versions, neither reflecting any degree of credit on him.

One version was the explanation that Thompson had given to Trautman, and which Thompson told later in detail to investigators for the United States Senate Permanent Subcommittee on Investigations. According to this version, ordinary cocktail party gossip by one of the United States Marshals' Service's most trusted and promising deputies blew Paul Maris's cover. Thompson said he was attending a party at the home of Glen E. Robinson, Supervisor of Field Operations for the United States Marshals' Office in Northern California, when, in the heat of a bull session about the much-publicized Paul Maris litigation, Robinson blurted out that the man wasn't Paul Maris at all, that he was a government witness from the East, with a name something like "Malowitz."

Thompson later recanted this version, and said he was sorry he ever told it. He and Robinson had been longtime, if not close, friends, with much in common. Both were black men ambitious to get ahead in the white-dominated world of law enforcement, and both had moved to the comfortable suburb of Mill Valley, where few other blacks lived.

But Robinson had greater dreams beyond his family life in Mill Valley, and these ambitions were shattered by his friend's testimony to the Senate investigators. Robinson had generally been considered a good bet to become the first black man to head the United States Marshals' Office in San Francisco, but after Thompson's allegation, the promotion didn't come. Robinson denied that the cocktail party conversation ever happened, but the charge took the glow off his prospects. "It tarnished my reputation, everything I worked for all those years," Robinson said later. "My career will never be what it would have been."

Thompson version number two, which was given under oath in a deposition growing out of Maris's suit against the government for allegedly blowing his cover, said that version number one was a lie. He said he told it out of bitterness toward his friend, Glen Robinson, who had talked him into leaving the security of the San Francisco Police Department for the Justice Department's Narcotics Bureau — from which Thompson felt he had been wrongfully discharged because of race prejudice. According to this explanation by Thompson, he figured out the entire riddle by himself, using his investigator's powers of deduction to conclude that the mysterious Paul Maris was a product of the government's alias program.

Thompson claimed that the fact that Maris was from the East and had popped up in San Francisco in 1970 was well known. Thompson also deduced that the trial that propelled Maris to the West Coast occurred in the late 1960s.

Thompson recalled being in Hal Lipset's office one day, where he spotted, on Lipset's desk, a list of six names that someone had jotted down, apparently playing with the possible names from which "Maris" could have been derived. One of the names was "Malowitz," and Thompson said he passed it on, together with his other hunches about Maris, to William Trautman for $2,000.

In attempting to decide which one of Thompson's versions was true, officials felt that the simplest and most coherent was that Thompson had overheard the truth about Paul Maris at the marshals' party. To accept the second story, it was necessary to believe that Thompson had independently figured out that Maris was a relocated witness, had then seen the list of hypothetical names, and had somehow picked out the one of the six that did sound something like the name "Zelmanowitz."

The latter account was almost too much to swallow, until Hal Lipset, angry at Thompson and pleased with himself, turned up with a list he said he had written down while casting about for family names and sound-alikes that might have been the inspiration for Paul Maris's choice of a name. The list read:

MARIS, MARKS, MARANTZ, MARKOWITZ, MALOWITZ, BALABAN

At that, the officials threw up their hands, resigned to the fact that they would never know whether Paul Maris's cover was destroyed by a

United States marshal's indiscretion, by shrewd guesses by Thompson and Lipset, or — perhaps most likely — by a combination of both.

In any event, Thompson had been able to tell Milton Stewart *what* Paul Maris was, and Stewart set out to find out *who* he was. It was a quest that was to be carried out with remarkable ingenuity and determination.

Stewart issued orders to the Creative Capital Corporation's staff in New York to comb the *New York Times* for reports of Mafia trials in the late 1960s. They were to look for a witness fitting the description of Paul Maris, but with a name something like "Malowitz." A further hunch: the search should concentrate on New Jersey, in the Newark area, where Maris's daughter might have attended high school. One of Stewart's San Francisco attorneys, William Chandler, added another suggestion. Maris had once given as a reference the name of a Newark lawyer, Thomas Campion. Chandler had looked Campion up in the legal profession's basic list of attorneys, Martindale-Hubbell, and had noted that Campion's law firm, Shanley & Fisher, had also once had as a partner an attorney named Frederick Lacey. Lacey had become a nationally known prosecutor of corrupt politicians and Mafia leaders, and Chandler knew of his reputation. He advised the searchers in New York to be on the lookout for a trial involving Lacey.

The next day, Stewart received a call from William Ragals, a vice president of Creative Capital in New York, who had drawn the assignment of combing the *Times* for leads. Ragals said he quickly found a report of a trial that might be the one.

It was the trial of Angelo "Gyp" DeCarlo in Newark, which had been given front-page coverage in the *Times*. Frederick Lacey had prosecuted the case, and his star witness bore several striking resemblances to Paul Maris. He was lean, curly-haired, intense, and articulate. He had a wife named Lillian, and she had a daughter named Cynthia Balaban. And the witness's name did sound something like "Malowitz": it was Gerald Martin Zelmanowitz.

Milton Stewart knew that he had found his man.

But Stewart had to be certain, and he had to have proof. Stewart remembered the flap over Sam Webster's sneak photographing of Paul Maris, and he called Hal Lipset.

Lipset phoned Webster about the picture for the second time, this time in a more affirmative mood. That was good work, snapping the picture. Did it show Maris's face clearly? And how soon could Webster get it over to Stewart?

As it turned out, the snapshot was perfect for identification purposes. Maris was standing talking to another man, whose back was to the camera and slightly to the right of Maris in the photograph. It left a clear view of Maris's face, turned three-quarters toward the camera.

The rest was easy. Stewart retained a private detective in Newark to make the final identification. His name was John F. Kelly, and he had a cozy relationship with the small suburban police force that served Short Hills, where the Zelmanowitz family used to live. Kelly took the snapshot to police Captain Leo Wallace.

"Oh sure, that's Gerry Zelmanowitz," said Wallace. Stewart had his proof.

Before he took action, Stewart had one more move to make. He had a friend in Washington named Charles A. Noone, a lawyer who was perfectly suited to the task of plumbing the depths of a Justice Department undercover operation. Noone was a former FBI agent, a member in good standing of the old-boy network of former G-men who hold key positions throughout government and private industry. This had come in handy earlier, when Stewart was trying to check out Maris's murky intelligence story. Noone had once been president of the Society of Former Agents of the FBI, and he had telephoned another ex-president of that organization, Francis X. Plant, who happened to be an assistant to the Under Secretary of the Army. Plant had been able to negate any possibility that Maris's military background was genuine, by telephoning the center in St. Louis where all army records are kept. The word came back: there was no record that the person named Paul J. Maris had ever been in the United States army. Noone had made a similar contact with an old friend at the Atomic Energy Commission, with the same results: no Paul Maris had ever worked for the AEC.

Now, Stewart wanted Noone to reach deeper into his past associations with the FBI, to go directly to the bureau for information about Paul Maris. He told Noone what they had discovered about Maris's double life, and he asked for the answer to two questons: did Maris still work for the government, and would unmasking him damage any government operation?

It was the sort of delicate information that an outsider might never have been able to wring from the FBI bureaucracy. But Noone knew where the levers of power were. On May 17, he went to the hulking Justice Department building, to the FBI area three floors above the sealed-off wing where Paul Maris had learned his identity three years before. Noone went to the office of William Cleveland, a veteran FBI official who was in charge of investigating criminal activities. When Noone explained that his business involved a relocated witness, Cleveland quickly turned him over to Alvin Staffeld, Jr., who served as liaison between the FBI and Gerald Shur. Noone swore later that he did not ask for confirmation that Paul Maris was Gerald Zelmanowitz and that the FBI men did not volunteer that he was.

Noone did, however, go away with the answers to Stewart's two questions. Paul Maris was no longer a witness, and to disclose his identity would not interfere with any government operation. Staffeld had disposed of both questions with one answer: "We have no interest in the matter."

If Staffeld or Gerald Shur was concerned to learn that the cover of one of his prize hidden witnesses was about to be spectacularly blown, neither gave any outward sign. Shur said later that he did not believe that Maris would be publicly unmasked, although he would not say why. In any event, nobody asked Stewart to keep silent. No attempt was made to find out how he had cracked Maris's alias or how many other persons might know. And no one told Paul Maris what had to be assumed from Charles Noone's visit to the FBI — that Maris's bright new life was about to be abruptly demolished.

If Paul Maris had been told what the Justice Department learned on May 17, he could have taken steps in the days that followed to salvage his business investments and his personal possessions, and to protect himself and his family from possible danger. He had been urged by Justice Department agents and attorneys to testify and accept a government alias, and he had put three years of work into making a success of his new life. It seemed fair to assume that if the Justice Department learned that Maris's true identity was about to be revealed, he would be the first to be told. But the days went by after May 17, and Paul Maris continued his hectic efforts to build a new business in California, including laying out most of his savings toward the purchase of the Miss Pat Company. And from the Justice Department came only silence.

Milton Stewart had operated brilliantly in tracking down the true identity of Paul Maris, but at the end of his quest he capped it with an oddly simplistic act. Having discovered Maris's secret, Stewart held the whip hand. By using his information subtly, he could have got all he wanted from Paul Maris. To keep his identity a secret, Maris would gladly have settled the litigation on Stewart's terms, returned any records, customer lists, or patterns belonging to the Paul Maris Company, abandoned his own competing company, and faded quietly into the woodwork. But Stewart put out no feelers for a settlement, gave no hints that he had scored a breakthrough, and invited no offers of compromise. Having learned that the man to whom he had loaned more than $2 million was a former hood with no business experience, Stewart was in a mood to play rough. By the fourth week in May, he had documented all of his findings, and Milton Stewart was ready to make his last move.

On the afternoon of May 29, Paul Maris sat in his room at the Beverly Wilshire Hotel in Beverly Hills and counted his blessings.

On the morning after the following day, at 11 on May 31, he would achieve his highest ambition — to own a business of his own. As he thought about it, he had to shrug off a temptation to cross his fingers and knock on wood, because it was a situation so perfectly suited to him that it was as if fate had designed it with him in mind. The name of the company was Miss Pat, Inc., and it was in many ways a Los Angeles version of the deal he had encountered three years before, when he met Alvin Duskin.

Miss Pat was a small company that operated a chain of shops called Beno's, as well as a separate manufacturing division that was strikingly like the onetime Alvin Duskin Company. It manufactured women's sportswear in a factory much like the Duskin plant, had five showrooms scattered around the country, and employed a national sales force. It had sold about $5 million in clothing in the previous year, but still had not managed to make a profit, so the parent corporation was ready to let the manufacturing division go cheaply. As a result, Maris had an opportunity to buy it, as he loved to say, "for a song and a dance." After all of the high living of the past three years Maris didn't have much cash, but he and Joe Miller managed to scrape up $50,000 — mostly composed of Joe's life savings — for the down payment. To close the deal, they had to come up with $200,000 more by May 31, or, according to the contract, they would forfeit their $50,000 as penalty damages.

It was a Draconian arrangement, but Maris had thrown himself into the effort with his special mix of ingenuity and salesmanship, and everything seemed to fall together. He had opened the office in the Stanford Court Hotel to serve as a magnet to draw away talent from the Paul Maris Company, and many of the best people had come. They had put together a spring line of chic women's sportswear — the type of knitted casuals with a young look that had been the mainstay of the

Paul Maris Company — and put their booth near the Paul Maris display at the annual Dallas show. Maris estimated that they outsold Stewart's company, ten to one. His competitors claimed that Maris was undercutting prices to get started with a bang, but for whatever reason, it was working. Orders started to flow in, Maris's staff began to move into actual control at the Miss Pat plant in Los Angeles, and in the showrooms around the country, and it was obvious that he would have a promising business operation under way by the May 31 deadline for closing the deal. Then the last element fell into place when Maris got a $200,000 loan from the United California Bank. That meant that the deal would go through. Nothing could stop him now.

Maris didn't know it then, but the shoestring character of his purchase had indirectly contributed to a problem of another nature. Two weeks before, when the news of his contract to purchase Miss Pat had made headlines in *Women's Wear Daily,* the article had made much of the mystery of who was putting up the money for Maris. Not wanting to admit that he had borrowed most of it from his father-in-law and that he didn't know where he would get the rest, Maris laughed during an interview and remarked; "My family, they're backing me."

He had no way of knowing that, back in Washington, his joshing quote about his "family" would add fuel to the charge that his business career was being financed by the Mafia.

Maris considered that his suit against Stewart, Lipset, and Creative Capital to be a face-saving device — he planned to even the score with them through Miss Pat. His strategy was to let the litigation bog down, then offer to drop his suit in exchange for the cancellation of Stewart's claims against him. Meanwhile, he would be beating them to death in the marketplace.

Sweetest of all to Maris, the pivotal incident — the happening that shifted the momentum of the whole venture in his favor — did not turn on his persuasive powers or his business finesse, but, of all things, his character.

It happened early in the affair, when Maris began to approach key personnel of the Paul Maris Company to leave the firm and join Miss Pat. Maris had already formed the nucleus of his new executive staff out of the loyalists from the old Paul Maris Company. These were mostly office executives — James Shornick, who had supervised the office operation, production men Don Lurie, Larry Rosenbloom, and Jay Stern, and computer specialist Marshal Parton. And as his executive assistant, there was, of course, Kat Walker.

But to make the new company go, Maris needed the top sales staff of the Paul Maris Company, the men with the contacts and sales know-how of the women's sportswear market to channel business away quickly from the Paul Maris Company to Miss Pat. Maris took a characteristically bold approach. He offered jobs with his shoestring company to the entire sales hierarchy of the Paul Maris Company: Paul Shenkman, eastern regional sales manager; Martin Thall, West Coast regional sales manager; Mike Day, in charge of sales for the Midwest; and Dave King, director for sales in northern California. There were offers of small holdings of stock in the new company, and talk of quickly expanding into men's and women's shirts and other garment lines, but essentially the appeal to the four men was to leave the well-paid security of the Milton Stewart enterprise and cast their futures with the visionary Paul Maris.

All four indicated that their answer would be "yes," but Stewart pleaded for a showdown meeting, an opportunity for him to demonstrate to these critical employees that they were being lured by a dishonest pied piper whom they could not trust. The sales executives told Maris that they would meet with Stewart and hear him out. If Stewart failed to prove his case, they would cast their lot with Maris.

They met on a Sunday afternoon at the home of Ken Bernard, a vice president of the Maris Company who had sided against Maris from the start. Creative Capital called in its big guns: Milton Stewart, Richard Banks, the new president of the Paul Maris Company, and Peter van Oosterhout, the new chairman of the board of Creative Capital.

The thrust of their case against Paul Maris was that he had misused company funds. It was said that he had used corporate money and company employees to beautify his Sonoma ranch; that he had purchased, with company funds, tape recorders, radios, phonographs, and other items for his personal enjoyment; and that he had squandered company money on expensive cars and extravagant parties. Shenkman, Thall, Day, and King were not persuaded. They knew that, technically, some of the expenditures were for Maris's pleasure rather than the stockholders' profit, but they had been around corporations enough to know that for company officials to pleasure themselves at the expense of the corporate till was the norm of corporate morality — not the exception. Stewart himself had known of some of the expenditures and had said little, until the profit picture turned consistently sour.

But Stewart insisted that Maris had exceeded the bounds by spending corporate funds on items that could serve no possible function around the office, and could only be for his personal use. As an example, he disclosed that Maris had taken company funds to purchase a $2,300 trailer for his own use. This did shake the four salesmen. If Maris had spent company money to buy a trailer, which could not possibly contribute to the manufacture or sale of women's sportswear, then he was clearly capable of other, perhaps greater, misuse of the corporation's funds. The trailer became the symbol of Stewart's allegations, and the four men trooped solemnly back to Maris's apartment to hear his response.

When they broached the matter of the trailer, Maris answered with a confident smile. He explained that there had often been times when he had spent long stretches on the road, unable to tend to banking and other personal chores, and personal obligations would come due. At such times he would call Kat Walker, he explained, and ask her to pay a bill with a company check. By the same token, he said he had sometimes covered company expenses with his own checks. Then as soon as he could get back to San Francisco and get everything in order, he would reimburse the corporation for any payment it had made for him.

Then Maris dipped into a file and came up with a canceled check for $2,300 from him to the Paul Maris Company. It had been, he explained, only a "loan." That had been the turning point. The four men quit their jobs with the Paul Maris Company, and Miss Pat was on its way.

As Maris thought about it later at the Beverly Wilshire Hotel, the crucial difference in this venture would be that with Miss Pat, any money squandered would be his money or his family's. He knew that he had played fast and loose with Creative Capital's money. Maris had been astounded when Creative Capital continued to pump money into his company beyond the $1.25 million mark. He didn't think its prospects justified more than that, and he developed an attitude of almost overt contempt toward Stewart's complaints that such an investment wasn't paying dividends. Maris realized that it had turned into a poisonous, destructive relationship, and he knew that now, with Miss Pat, the major stake was his. He would have to keep expenses in check and sales high. If not, the main loser would be his family and he. It was a shift in responsibility that he actually liked; he knew that he could meet this test and make the business a success, and that he then would be the beneficiary of it all.

Maris's thoughts were interrupted by the ringing of his hotel room phone.

It was a call from San Francisco, from Dennis Bromley, the young partner of Pillsbury, Madison & Sutro who was handling Maris's suit against Stewart. A younger associate of Bromley's was scheduled to handle the closing of the Miss Pat purchase, and Maris immediately felt it odd that Bromley should be calling then. Bromley always projected the lean and hungry intensity of a first-rate litigator, but when he came on the line this time, there was an extra edge of emotion to his voice.

As Maris remembered the conversation later, Bromley was so excited he started out stuttering: "Paul, I, I, I've just come from a conversation with our senior partner, and he's talking with Creative Capital's attorneys." Maris had never heard Bromley stutter before, and he braced himself for his next line.

"Paul, it's a weird thing I've got to tell you."

Cindy is in Oakland. Shelley and Bobby are together, in San Francisco. Lillian's safe, here, and so are Joe and Evelyn. But I didn't bring my pistol. I've got to get a gun. . . . Maris's mind raced through a checklist of protective measures as he waited for Bromley to get to the point.

"All right, Dennis, what is it — what is this weird story?"

"Paul, they say that's not your name at all. They say your name is Gerald Martin Zelmanowitz and you were a witness in a Mafia trial. . . ."

There was a long silence.

On the other end of the line, Dennis Bromley was taking notes. He was a methodical man, and he had firmly in mind what the situation required of him: to find out if the story was true, and if so, to decide how to salvage as much as possible from the wreckage of Paul Maris.

If there was any stuttering on his part he did not recall it later, but only that he got quickly to the point: "Our opponents have told us they think you are a man named Gerald Martin Zelmanowitz."

Bromley, also, recalled the long silence, before Maris replied: "I've never heard of him." And then, after a few more denials, increasingly vague — "Have they done anything about it yet? It could hurt them."

With that, the situation spoke for itself. Bromley had hurled an incredible charge at Maris, and instead of exploding with indignation, Maris was parrying with weak denials. Then he shifted the conversation to the Miss Pat closing, only a day and a half away. Maris pointedly reminded Bromley that Maris had laid out $50,000 as a pledge that he would be there to complete the deal. Bromley was sure, then, that Maris was in deep trouble. Bromley noted the time, 5:45 P.M., and said that he would grab the air shuttle to Los Angeles and would be at Maris's hotel by nine.

The hour-long flight to Los Angeles gave Bromley time to scribble more notes and pull together his thoughts about where they were and how they should proceed from there.

About an hour before he placed his call to Maris, Bromley had been summoned to the office of the senior partner of the Pillsbury firm, an Oxford-educated patrician of the San Francisco bar named Turner McBain. The older man came to the point quickly with his thirty-three-year-old subordinate. McBain said he had just been paid a visit by the senior partner of Chickering & Gregory — whom Bromley knew to be a lawyer with the equally patrician name of Burleigh Pattee — accompanied by a younger member of the Chickering firm, William Trautman. They had told McBain an extraordinary story — that one of his firm's clients was not a businessman at all but a former Mafia employee living under an alias provided by the Justice Department. Turner McBain re-created the scene for Bromley: how Burleigh Pattee had sat in his elegant office high above San Francisco and the Bay and told the story of the gangster from Brooklyn named Gerald Zelmanowitz who had come to be a client of Pillsbury, Madison & Sutro. In the gentlemanly manner in which high-priced corporate attorneys deal

190

with each other, Pattee had informed McBain — so that he would not learn about it for the first time when the papers were filed in court — that the Chickering firm was about to blow the Pillsbury firm's client out of the water. Chickering & Gregory planned to disclose its information in court papers soon, and Pattee said he wanted McBain to know in advance so that Maris's life would not be endangered.

As he had related the story to Bromley, McBain was irked that his law firm had been caught in an impossible position. The firm had filed court papers alleging defamation of Paul Maris's character, based on statements of facts about his character that were not true. Of course, the Pillsbury firm had not lied knowingly, and McBain would deal with the situation a few days later with flawless advocate's reflexes — by issuing a statement blaming the entire flap on his firm's adversary: "When we commenced representing Mr. Maris," McBain's statement declared, "we assumed Creative Capital would not have retained him as the principal executive officer and made him a director of their subsidiary and invested millions of dollars in an enterprise to be run by Mr. Maris without first thoroughly investigating his background and business experience."

As McBain would recount the story later, his only reactions were concern for Maris's safety, and chagrin that Maris had lied to the firm and put it in an impossible position. He said he was not embarrassed to have the Pillsbury firm's name headlined in the press in connection with a former Mafia criminal, and insisted that he issued no orders to Bromley to get rid of Maris as a client. Bromley could not recall later if McBain had given the order to dump Maris as a client, but he felt that in any event he had reasons enough to do it himself: Maris had lied to him and given the firm for one of his fee payments a $5,000 check that had bounced, and he would have to be on the run and would therefore be unable to keep in contact with his attorneys.

It was about nine o'clock when Dennis Bromley arrived at Maris's suite in the Beverly Hilton. He was immediately struck with the atmosphere of fear. Earlier in the day, Maris had noticed a man in the lobby who seemed to be watching him — now he was wracked with suspicion as to who the man might have been or if he had really been watching Maris at all. Maris was ashen and agitated, and Lillian was tense and obviously fearful and quickly withdrew into her parents' suite down the hall.

"This is a matter of life and death," Maris said, and then he began an explanation that started with the development of a program under Attorney General Robert Kennedy to protect witnesses who testified against the Mafia. He told about arbitrage, about Saperstein, The Barn, the beating, the DeCarlo tapes and the disclosures of the Mafia murders, and the blunders by a defense lawyer named Querques.

Finally, Maris was ready to say it: "I was a witness in the DeCarlo case. I am the guy."

He repeated that it was a matter of life and death, but said that he had telephoned a Justice Department official in Washington named Gerald Shur and had told him what happened. "He was flabbergasted," Maris said, and had promised to send United States marshals to Maris's hotel room right away and to try to persuade Milton Stewart to delay filing his court papers long enough to give Maris time to get his affairs in order and move his family to safety. The marshals should be there at any moment, Maris said.

Meanwhile, Maris and Bromley decided to try to find out how many people knew, and what Maris's exposure to danger might be. Maris phoned Trautman with a volley of questions: How had they found out? How many people knew? How much time did he have before it hit the papers?

Trautman was very lawyerlike and correct, but not very reassuring. As to the identity of the informer, he said, "Milt Stewart has a friend in Washington," an ex-FBI agent who had confirmed that Maris was Zelmanowitz. Trautman's firm had tried to avoid leaks until they told Maris, but he could not say who else might know. If Mr. Zelmanowitz wanted more information, it would have to come from Milton Stewart.

Maris slammed down the receiver and then quickly dialed Stewart's number. Stewart's voice had the cool assurance of one who held all the cards, and was enjoying nestling them close to his chest. Could the word of Maris's identity have somehow leaked to dangerous quarters? "There is cause for alarm," he said. "We tried to limit who knows, but we have to assume that enough people know to possibly permit a leak to organized crime. At least five people know," he said, and possibly, "dozens of people."

But assuming the word hadn't leaked, would he hold off filing his papers until Maris had closed the Miss Pat deal and made a getaway with his family? "I'm not going to be responsible for such a delay," Stewart replied. "There is a three-million-dollar risk here. I will file the papers and it will become known."

Again, Maris slammed down the telephone. They had him in a corner, and they were not giving him an inch. There was no way he could be sure that the story would not be in the morning newspapers, no way to be certain there was enough time to give somebody his power of attorney to sell his house, move his furniture, or find a new home. And there was no way he could be sure that he and his family would be safe if he stayed to close the Miss Pat deal. But if he didn't stay, he would forfeit the $50,000 that represented his life's savings and Joe Miller's.

Bromley saw to it that Maris had sound legal advice on the last point. He got him on the phone with Robert Herr, the young lawyer who was handling the Miss Pat deal for the Pillsbury firm back in San Francisco. The talk was instructive, but not very helpful. Herr explained that under California law, the owners of Miss Pat were not entitled to keep all of the $50,000, even though the contract said it was to be forfeited if Maris did not close the deal on the thirty-first. Actually, the owners could keep only as much of the $50,000 as they had lost by virtue of Maris's default. But to get the remainder back, he'd have to sue, and the Pillsbury firm would have none of that.

Then he would just have to forfeit the $50,000, Maris replied. There was no way he could close the transaction on the thirty-first. Now that the word was out, he had no alternative but to run for his life. Maris agreed that since he wasn't going to be there for the closing, Herr could cancel his plans to come down to Los Angeles on that day. Without Maris there, the papers couldn't be signed and the deal couldn't be closed. Nothing could stop the $50,000 from going, uncontested, down the drain. On that gloomy note they ended their conversation.

At no point did either of the attorneys challenge the factual assumption underlying all of Maris's actions — that his life was in danger, and that it was necessary for him to run for cover. Was there time for him to close the deal before the story broke? Could he stay around, even after his identity became known, and operate the business from the background? Could he at least stick around long enough to take ownership and try to salvage something? Was it certain that anybody was gunning for him; that he couldn't just be careful, keep a low profile, and go on with the Miss Pat deal?

Nobody raised any of these questions, and Paul Maris, his judgment numbed by panic, thought only of flight.

There seemed to be nothing more for Dennis Bromley to do, so shortly before midnight, he made his preparations to leave. Even as he went through the ritual of the final handshake and regrets, Bromley saw that Maris had become increasingly distracted and nervous. The fear was infectious, and Bromley noted that the promised United States marshals had not arrived. He mumbled something about not being eager to rush out the door, perhaps to stumble into a team of hit men who might be outside, preparing to burst in. That brought back a flash of the old Maris: "Don't worry," he laughed, "they never kill a person's lawyer."

Bromley recalled later that as he walked out of the Beverly Wilshire Hotel into the dark and silent city, he was suddenly seized by fear. After all, he did look much like Maris — the same lean build and curly mop of hair, the same conservative dark suit, the same briefcase. What if they should be there, waiting, and should shoot him down by mistake?

He hurried out the door and away from the hotel, half-expecting to see the dreaded automobile pull away from the curb or the sinister men start to follow. Nothing happened, and Bromley walked quickly down the street and away from the hotel.

It was a few minutes later that the president of Miss Pat, Inc., was awakened by a telephone call: "Max, this is Paul Maris. Something has happened that affects our closing on Friday. I must talk with you tonight. Can you come to the Beverly Wilshire?" Max Salter said he would come. He had found Maris to be engaging and attractive, but mostly he had found him to be desirable as a purchaser for Miss Pat's manufacturing division. Max Salter was a retail man; he knew little about the design, manufacture, and mass marketing of clothing. He had lost money on his flyer in the manufacturing division from the start, and he had been delighted to find a purchaser to take it off his hands.

There was more to it than that. Maris had impressed him as a man who had been a success in the trade, although Salter thought that when Maris started to move his people in, he had been a little heavy on staff — "the Maris entourage," Salter called the newcomers, who were younger by years and style than his own office group. Salter hadn't checked his purchaser out. Maris was represented by Pillsbury, Madison & Sutro, a law firm that dealt with only the best people, and he had a loan from the United Bank of California. Salter assumed that the UBC must have been satisfied with Maris's credentials. Despite the irregular circumstances, Max Salter phoned his attorney, Robert Weil, and arranged to meet him that night at the Beverly Wilshire.

When they arrived at Maris's door, there was a man standing guard outside, with a pistol strapped to his hip. He ushered them inside, where there were another armed guard and Paul Maris.

Maris explained that the men with pistols were United States marshals, and he sat Salter and Weil down and began to talk. "My mouth was hanging open," Salter said later, as Maris told the story of Robert Kennedy's plan to encourage witnesses to testify against the Mafia, of the DeCarlo trial, of his relocation to San Francisco, and of his discovery that night that his identity was about to be revealed.

Then Maris said he could not be present for the closing, and he mentioned the deposit. "My life is on the line. The Mafia is after me and it's all I've got." Maris wanted his $50,000 back.

Paul Maris said later he had begun to suspect that Max Salter would not be easily moved when the older man's jaw dropped at the start of the story, and when Salter's coma seemed to deepen as Maris went on, rather than turning to concern. Maris had felt that he had a warm relationship with Max Salter, whom Maris had come to respect and admire for his business sense and his straight-dealing character. He hoped that Salter would comprehend his inability to close the deal and his need for the $50,000 now that his family would be in hiding. But Salter said he couldn't return the money because it was in escrow until closing. Anyway, he had incurred expenses — accountants and lawyers. Finally, insisting that there was nothing he could do, Salter strode into the corridor and was gone. Maris stood for a long moment, gaping at the door and knowing that his $50,000 was gone, too.

Maris told the marshals they could lock up for the night. They would all get up early in the morning and slip away from Los Angeles.

Kat Walker woke the next morning in a bright and happy mood. She dressed quickly and then hurried down to the Miss Pat plant. There was much to be done, and Kat went at it with even more than her usual bounce: on the following morning Paul would be closing the Miss Pat deal, and before that day was over, they would be officially back in business.

Then the phone rang, and it was Bob Levine, their accountant, asking her and the other Maris representatives in the plant to come over to his office in the Century Tower. She located Larry Rosenbloom, Don Lurie, and Jay Stern, and they went together to see Levine, puzzled at the need for a meeting on this day.

When they got there, Levine got quickly to the point.

"Paul Maris doesn't exist. He is a man who testified against the Mafia and now his true identity has been found out. He is running for his life," Levine said. There was a long silence, and then Levine added: "You will never see him again."

There was little more for the accountant to say. The Miss Pat deal was dead, and they were unemployed. They might as well go back to San Francisco.

Kat went to her hotel and packed her things. She was so numbed by what Levine had said that there was little feeling of surprise or hurt. She had never suspected that he was anyone other than Paul Maris. He had never hinted to her that he was not what he pretended to be, and she had not glimpsed anything behind the facade of the dynamic and acquisitive businessman — if there was anything there to be seen — to make her suspect he was anyone else. Her gullibility was like that of the businessmen who had trusted him with their money and their corporations. She wanted him to be the Paul Maris that he appeared to her to be, and she did not look for signs that he was anyone else.

A few hours later the four of them — Kat Walker, Larry Rosenbloom, Don Lurie, and Jay Stern — boarded the air shuttle for San

Francisco. They talked quietly as the flight began, betraying their emotions only by the rapid rounds of drinks they ordered from the stewardess. Then the conversation dwindled away, and the others passed their unopened little bottles over to Kat Walker. She sat without speaking the rest of the way, and drank them all.

At 11 the next morning, there was a tense little ceremony in the office of Max Salter's attorney, Robert Weil. Salter was there, all the papers for the closing were there, and all the other signatories were there — except Paul Maris. They waited a few minutes, and then attorney Weil announced that the time for the closing had passed. Everybody left, and Weil dictated a letter to the offices of Pillsbury, Madison & Sutro, giving notice that the $50,000 deposit of Paul Maris, also known as Gerald Martin Zelmanowitz, had been forfeited.

Paul Maris's team of crack sales executives was spread around the country, poised to launch the Miss Pat sales blitz, when the bottom fell out. Paul Shenkman, Martin Thall, Mike Day, and Dave King were already working in Miss Pat showrooms in their various territories when, late in the afternoon of May 31, the word went out from Max Salter that Maris had not appeared that morning to close the deal. The four men were ordered to leave the Miss Pat showrooms — the deal was off, and they were unemployed.

None of the four had ever had a hint of Paul Maris's past life, and they were totally unprepared for the collapse of his plans. In New York, Shenkman had already arranged a sale of $260,000 in new Miss Pat fashions to the J. C. Penney Company, and was just waiting until after the closing to wrap up the deal. The thirty-year-old Shenkman had abandoned a prospect of $60,000 in commissions with the Paul Maris Company to follow Maris out of the company, and he had spent his own money on travel expenses while they were setting up the new company.

A few days after their world caved in, a reporter for *Women's Wear Daily* checked on the four to sample their reactions to the debacle. The result was a mildly bemused article that catalogued their misfortunes, noted that they had not heard from Maris, and puzzled over the lack of rancor on their part.

When Shenkman was asked for his view of Maris from the rubble of the Miss Pat disaster, his response was upbeat: "The guy was terrific. He had charisma, a dynamic personality, was fair and a terrific guy to work with. He did a great job with the company."

At about the same time, the *Financial News Service* carried a similar article, which summed up the reaction of the abandoned Miss Pat executives with this quote from one of them, who was not named: "I don't know Gerald Martin Zelmanowitz, I never met him. The only man I knew was Paul Maris.

"Would I go back with him again? Yes!

"If he showed up in this room and said OK, the Mafia doesn't want me any more, let's get back to work, I'd be there in a flash."

10 . . . . Nontaxpayer

On the morning after he learned that his secret was out, Paul Maris woke up after a few hours of sleep, still haggard and exhausted. It was May 30, the eve of what was supposed to have been his big day — the closing of the Miss Pat deal — but Maris was thinking only of getting back to San Francisco and organizing his next moves before Milton Stewart publicly blew his cover. The two marshals were rumpled and unshaven after sleeping out the shank of the night in chairs, but they threw water on their faces and helped with the packing as the Marises and Millers glumly prepared to leave.

There was a bad omen at the start. Lillian went to the lobby to pay the bill, and somehow the marshal who had gone along as her guard got separated from her. She spent a harrowing fifteen minutes searching for him, fearful that every strange man she saw was a hit man from New Jersey. Then on the way to the airport they lost the marshals' two cars, and Maris, Lillian, and the Millers drove in panic, fearful that every car that trailed along behind was following them. At the airport they rushed aboard the shuttle, and sat, white-knuckled, until the plane took off.

When they landed at Los Angeles, the first sight they saw was the broad, smiling face of Deputy United States Marshal Gary Bricker. Bricker was an open, friendly young man with the muscular, scrubbed look of a high-school football coach, and the worldly bearing of a veteran cop. He had first met Maris four years before, when Bricker was sent to New Jersey to help protect an informer named Gerald Zelmanowitz. Bricker had started the assignment with the same near-contempt for Zelmanowitz that he had for the other hoodlums he had guarded as prisoners. But gradually that attitude had changed, and with it there was a subtle shift in their relationship. Bricker found himself liking Zelmanowitz, admiring his mind and respecting his character. Before long, Bricker began to defer to the judgment of the man he was guarding, accepting his guidance in important matters and letting him take the lead in day-to-day affairs. Bricker became the

Private detective Gary Bricker was long a United States deputy marshal charged with guarding Gerald Zelmanowitz's life. Gerry was a guest when Linda and Gary Bricker married.

unofficial bodyguard of Zelmanowitz and later Maris, often drawing the assignment to direct the team of marshals who were periodically needed to guard him when he would appear to testify.

At the airport the beleagured Maris family threw themselves at their old friend Gary Bricker. At last, they told each other, they would be safe. In the excitement, nobody but Bricker noticed a man surreptitiously take a photograph of Paul Maris. Bricker said nothing. The family and Bricker's team of guards piled into the marshals' automobiles, and they had barely pulled onto the freeway when Bricker spotted two cars following. He mentally catalogued them for future reference; a small yellow Camaro, license number GQL-241, and a Corvette with Oregon license plates.

Bricker's marshals drove to the Pacific Heights building, where the guards ushered the family up to their apartment. It had been decided that Maris and his family could be more easily guarded at the isolated house in Sonoma than in the apartment building, so the plan was to pack as quickly as possible and leave the city. Maris was moody and distracted as the job of selecting and packing the items to be taken got under way, but his street-savvy instincts led him to make one crucial move.

He immediately sent Lillian and a marshal to a downtown office of the United California Bank to withdraw all of the family's assets. There she presented a teller with an assortment of passbooks, checkbooks, and safety deposit box keys, and announced that she wanted to take everything. There was a tense scene as the teller, sensing that something was wrong, declined to turn over the money without the approval of the assistant bank manager. Lillian persuaded him that everything was all right, that they just needed all their cash for business reasons. The manager, still obviously puzzled and not quite convinced, finally gave her the money and extracted a promise that the bank had done nothing to displease her and that she would be careful with so much cash. Lillian crammed into her purse the papers and jewelry from the lockboxes and a thick stack of bills — almost $50,000, two-thirds of which belonged to her parents — and, walking close beside the wide-eyed deputy marshal, hurried from the bank.

Once outside, Lillian heaved a long sigh of relief and clutched her purse to her side. The weight of it gave her a feeling of security, even though she had no way of knowing that her act of withdrawing the money that day had saved her family from near-poverty and absolute dependence on the government — that within a matter of hours all of the family's bank accounts and safe deposit boxes would be frozen to satisfy the unpaid taxes of a criminal named Gerald Zelmanowitz.

Meanwhile, the bustle at the apartment was compounded by the arrival of a team of FBI agents, dropping by to offer their help. Maris tried to persuade them to take over the assembling of his property, so that he could bolt immediately for the Sonoma hills. There followed a long conversation as Maris listed the various items that would have to be located and stored. The FBI men finally concluded that they had no authority to undertake such a task and left, and it was not until later that Maris learned that discussing his assets in such detail in the presence of the various federal agents in the room could have been a trap. The person who was soon to find that out was Maris's friend and bodyguard, Deputy Marshal Gary Bricker.

At one point during the confusion of the packing, Bricker slipped quietly out of the apartment and rode the elevator to the lobby. A glance out of the front door confirmed his suspicions: the yellow Camaro and the Corvette with Oregon plates were parked a discreet distance away.

Bricker walked out the entrance and sauntered toward the cars. He walked casually, and did not loosen the .38 police revolver in the holster on his hip. He knew that such precautions were unnecessary, because Bricker had realized from the instant he spotted the photographer that the men surveilling Paul Maris were not Mafia executioners.

Bricker had recognized the photographer at the airport as an agent in the San Francisco office of the IRS Intelligence Division. He saw that agent following them on the freeway in the Corvette with Oregon plates, and he assumed that the driver of the yellow Camaro was also with the IRS. From what he had been told of the actions of the man who had seemed to be watching Maris the day before in the Beverly Wilshire Hotel, Bricker assumed that he, too, had been an IRS man on a stakeout. Bricker was puzzled to discover IRS intelligence agents shadowing Paul Maris, but he was not altogether surprised. The Internal Revenue Service had a broad mandate to investigate matters related to taxes, which could mean almost any activity involving money, and Gary Bricker had crossed paths with the IRS many times in his career in law enforcement. Bricker decided to inquire what had brought them to Maris's door, at a time when the Mafia might be thought more likely to be closing in.

"Hello, Steve, let's go have a talk," Bricker said to the agent whom he had recognized. The three of them went to a nearby cafe for cups of coffee, and the man Bricker knew as Steve explained. He said that the IRS had been watching Maris, off and on, for some time. They knew he had complained to the Senate Permanent Investigations Subcommittee about his treatment by the Justice Department and the Internal Revenue Service, and they believed he might have hidden assets that he owed the government for unpaid taxes. Steve said he had been part of a team of agents who had surveilled Maris's home, and that the agent had hidden in some bushes one night to be ready to follow Maris in case he left. The agent named Steve did not say — and Bricker had no reason to ask — if he had also hidden behind a tree in the park. Steve and the other IRS man asked Bricker not to tell the FBI about their surveillance. They said it would complicate things, and in the live-and-let-live tradition of police agencies, Bricker agreed and did not ask why.

The problem, Steve explained, was that they hadn't managed to get close enough to find out what possessions Maris had. But they thought they had a solution. If Bricker would give them badges and credentials as United States marshals, and then assign them to the detail guarding Maris, they could get inside the apartment and look and listen, and they might manage to find out everything.

Bricker said no — no way. Then he went back to the apartment, and the IRS agents went back to watching the building. The incident bothered Bricker, because he knew he had a responsibility to the federal government as well as to Maris. He was concerned that he might be forced into a painful conflict of interest, between his friendship for Maris and the IRS agents' claim that Maris owed the government unpaid taxes.

That night, Bricker took his problem to the United States marshal for the Northern District of California, George Tobin. The young deputy explained what the IRS men had asked him to do, and said that he had refused. Had he done the right thing? Tobin said yes, their assignment was only to protect Maris. If the IRS agents had been assigned to collect back taxes from Maris, they would have to work that out in their own way.

A few hours later, a teletype came from Washington, authorizing Tobin to issue marshals' badges and credentials to the IRS agents. Tobin sent a message back, saying he was fresh out of badges. The matter was never raised again.

Meanwhile, Gary Bricker said nothing about any of this to Paul Maris, who clearly had enough on his mind already. Bricker realized that Maris was in much greater difficulty than he knew — so much so that Maris probably couldn't help himself if Bricker told him what he had learned. For the news that IRS intelligence agents had been watching Maris almost from the time he reached San Francisco meant that his problems with the government were far more complicated than just his feud with the men who ran the alias program. Bricker had been around law enforcement long enough to sense that the misery in store for Paul Maris after his cover was blown would be not death, but taxes.

Gerald Zelmanowitz's troubles with the Internal Revenue Service began long before the Department of Justice ever heard of him. Zelmanowitz was not a taxpaying man. He had rarely filed income tax returns or paid income taxes. His reason, as he expressed it later, was that he had no legal income and thus could not declare his earnings without incriminating himself or somebody else. Part of that was undoubtedly so; he could not have truthfully declared his income from the DeCarlo-Cecere-Polverino venture without exposing his three partners, who distinctly wished to remain silent and might have broken his legs for his candor.

Beyond that, Gerry's special talent, the international arbitraging of securities, required the systematic evasion of interest equalization taxes. In the typical transaction, he would purchase a large block of shares in Geneva and simultaneously sell them in New York, where the market was often stronger and the selling price was about 2 percent higher. Thus he could make a profit only if he could evade the 18 percent interest equalization tax on sales of securities purchased overseas from foreigners — a trick that Gerry regularly pulled off with ease, by forging documents showing that he had bought the foreign stocks from Americans, who presumably had paid the 18 percent tax when they had purchased the shares.

As a result of such ingenuity by Zelmanowitz and many other dedicated nontaxpayers, by the mid–nineteen sixties the government found its interest equalization tax program to be a sieve. The nub of this problem was the IRS Form 3625, which the government accepted as proof that a security purchased overseas had been previously owned by an American and thus was exempt from the tax. Form 3625 was a simple declaration signed by the alleged prior owner of the shares, with his signature certified as genuine by his banker or broker, stating that he was a citizen of the United States. Zelmanowitz found that in dealing in bulk transactions of securities that were difficult to trace, he could simply sign a Form 3625 with a fictitious name, attach the Form 3625 to securities that he had purchased overseas and resold at a profit, and thus "prove" that the prior owner was an American who had presumably paid the tax. Never one to think small, Zelmanowitz obtained hundreds of Form 3625's, signed them in blank with various fictitious names, and persuaded complaisant executives of two of the nation's most prestigious banks, Chase Manhattan and First National City, to certify the signatures as genuine. Thus, when Gerry spotted a certain security that was ripe for arbitrage, his confederates in Switzerland could simply purchase the stock, fill in one of Gerry's signed Form 3625's with the name of that stock, and thus exempt that arbitrage transaction from the interest equalization tax.

Gerry's dodge was, obviously, too good to be true. In July of 1967 the IRS put into effect new regulations, specifying that no overseas transactions could be exempted from the tax unless the IRS was satisfied that the prior owner was a United States citizen, and until the District Director of Internal Revenue gave a signed document to that effect. It seemed to chop international arbitrage off at the knees, for the massive, hair-trigger purchases of stock involved in arbitraging could hardly be justified to the IRS as bona fide purchases of shares from prior American owners.

Thus when Gerald Zelmanowitz assured three of New Jersey's meanest gangsters in the fall of 1967 that he would multiply their money through arbitrage, he obviously became a man in need of a creative idea. As it turned out, he had one. With consummate chutzpah, Gerry made a trade, and then simply took his forged and fraudulent Form 3625's to the local IRS office and presented them as proof of the prior American ownership of his newly purchased stocks. The IRS had not anticipated such a brazen maneuver to subvert the new system with the old one, and, after a period of stunned inaction, the Newark IRS office issued the newly required document, exempting that transaction from the tax. It was a bold stroke (and apparently a felonious one; Zelmanowitz testified later that he greased that transaction with a $1,000 tip to two IRS agents), and Gerald Zelmanowitz was back in business.

He traded briskly through November and the early days of December, at a time when other overseas purchases by Americans had bogged down in the new IRS procedure. By late December, it had become too obvious; the IRS froze the securities trading account at Hayden Stone, and issued a declaration that it would no longer approve tax exemptions on the basis of Form 3625's. Gerry appeared, again, to be out of business. But he came under intense pressure to resume. Saperstein was pleading for more money to keep DeCarlo and Cecere at bay, and Gerry was tiptoeing around the Saperstein-DeCarlo relationship, dreading the moment when the racketeers learned that Saperstein had siphoned off some of their capital.

It was then that Gerry made one of the breathtaking plunges that were to mark the course of his roller-coaster career. He acted, typically, as if he was in fact the international dealer in corporate securities that he claimed to be, and not a systematic law violator, a front for a trio of notorious racketeers, a man who had not paid taxes in years.

He sued the IRS. He brought a court action to force the IRS to continue accepting his Form 3625's as proof that his arbitrage trades should not be taxed.

Rarely has a government bureaucracy reacted with such lightning speed. Within a matter of days, IRS agents sifted through the records of Hayden Stone dating back to 1965, locating a series of transactions that had been exempted from interest equalization taxes because they had been accomplished by the distinctly forged Form 3625's that were the trademark of a Zelmanowitz arbitrage. Then they assessed the full amount of interest equalization taxes on all those trades against Gerald Zelmanowitz. The total came to $1.7 million, and the IRS used this assessment to seize the $104,000 balance in Gerry's personal securities trading account at Hayden Stone.

At that point, the average nontaxpayer who had traded millions of dollars' worth of securities annually, who lived in obvious two-Cadillac affluence, and who had failed to file tax returns or pay taxes in years would have thrown up his hands and conceded that the IRS had him. Zelmanowitz began to study his mountainous financial records for possible weaknesses in the IRS's case. He made an intriguing discovery — that the Swiss brokers who had been allied with him in his larcenous scheme were not totally honest men. Unknown to him, they had been using some of his bogus IRS Form 3625 certificates to carry out illegal deals of their own. Zelmanowitz discovered that most, if not all, of the transactions that the IRS had cited as the basis for its assessment against him were these sales. Since he had received none of the money from these transactions, he owed none of the taxes. He was undoubtedly guilty of failing to file income tax returns, nonpayment of income taxes, and filing false official statements, among other malfeasances — but the IRS had bypassed all of that to hit him with the whopping assessment for unpaid interest equalization taxes. It had mistakenly tried to skin Zelmanowitz for a wolf instead of the fox he was. Gerry gleefully sued to get his $104,000 back, and he seemed to have the IRS on the ropes when he was arrested and became a protected government witness.

As intricate as his dealings had been with the IRS before, the situation became many times more complicated when Gerald Zelmanowitz, nontaxpayer, became Paul Maris, secret ward of the government. This was eventually to play a key role in making Zelmanowitz a classic example of the many things that can go wrong when the government enters into a complex relationship with a citizen requiring systematic governmental deception — with the stakes not merely dollars but also possible life or death.

When Gerry agreed to become a witness for the prosecution, the commitments on neither side were spelled out. He handled the arrangements himself — his defense attorney had also been representing the thugs from The Barn and could not be told that Zelmanowitz had switched sides, and Gerry did not hire another lawyer to pin down his agreement with the government. Thus it only gradually dawned on him that his grand jury testimony foredoomed him to bearing witness against DeCarlo in open court, and he did not require the prosecutors to write down what the government owed him in return. Generally, it was understood that the government would drop all legal proceedings against Gerry. This raised no problems where criminal cases were involved; the Justice Department had full control over them, and it arranged to obtain leniency for Zelmanowitz in each case. But where the IRS was involved, the Justice Department could only make requests, and that is where the trouble began.

The Justice Department promised at the outset to try to get the IRS to return Gerry's $104,000, and the two local United States attorneys involved, David Satz and Frederick Lacey, both attempted and failed to have this done. Then Zelmanowitz agreed to drop his tangled litigation against the IRS, and again he believed that the IRS had agreed in return to release his money. Again, the IRS refused to budge. It became obvious that extracting from the IRS money that it had already collected was like pulling crocodile teeth, but Zelmanowitz still assumed that the IRS would not go after him for more. One reason was that he believed that the government's promise not to pursue him further in court included civil actions to collect back taxes, as well as criminal prosecutions. In any event, it seemed to follow that if the Justice Department intended to relocate him in a new city as Paul Maris, the IRS would hardly follow him to that place and sue him for taxes owed by a criminal named Gerald Zelmanowitz.

Thus when Zelmanowitz completed his debriefing in Washington and flew off to San Francisco as Paul Maris, he assumed that he was finally at peace with the United States government, including the Internal Revenue Service. In fact, had the IRS been left to follow its own institutional instincts, it very likely would have been content at that point to keep Gerald Zelmanowitz's $104,000 and forget Gerald Zelmanowitz. But a seed of distrust and suspicion had been planted during his interrogation in Washington that was to bear bitter fruit for him later on. It happened during the cat-and-mouse routine that occurred when Shur and Bonomi delayed Gerry's relocation in an effort to wring more information from him, and he enticed them with tidbits about Mafia overlords in an attempt to shake loose his $104,000. Never one to underplay his role, Gerry dropped enough notorious names to persuade Shur and Bonomi that if he would just come clean, he could be the greatest Mafia canary since Joe Valachi. He was so persuasive thal even after his relocation, Shur and Bonomi flew to California to see him with authorization to pay him $10,000 — informer funds to be paid in return for the number of Meyer Lansky's Swiss bank account. But Gerry did not come through with that information or with enough evidence to make a single additional case. He said he wouldn't get involved as a witness again until they returned his $104,000, but Shur and Bonomi saw a more sinister motive — that Gerry was holding back because he was still allied with the Mafia.

"I was always suspicious of him," Shur explained later. "I believed that he was concealing assets and that he might be engaging in illegal activities." Shur was bitter that Zelmanowitz had been spared going to jail, had been given a new identity, had been granted numerous reviews of his tax assessment, and yet appeared to be withholding evidence. "We thought the government had been put upon," he said; "we were used."

Shur had said nothing about this when he sent Paul Maris off to his new life in California. But almost immediately, his office initiated a program of surveillance, spearheaded by the IRS and designed to find out if Maris was still serving as a conduit for mob money or concealing ill-gotten funds. In retrospect, there appeared to be a built-in contradiction to this effort by the government to investigate a person whom it was also seeking to conceal. It involved, for instance, having IRS agents skulk about, shadowing and photographing a man whom the Justice Department was seeking to blend into the population. In addition, there were other awkward and sometimes ridiculous governmental actions, which remained a secret until much later, when the litigation by the unmasked Paul Maris brought them to light.

Most significant of all, these efforts proved to be fruitless. In the end, there was no evidence that Paul Maris ever had any contact with the Mafia after he went to California. But in the meantime, the government's clandestine effort to prove the opposite was silently eroding Maris's position, setting him up for a harder fall when his identity was finally pulled out from under him. Later, even Gerry's closest friends could not say whether or not he had actually been deeply enough involved with the top crime syndicate figures — other than those he had already helped convict — to be able to give evidence against them, even if he had wanted to, or dared. They agreed that he might have been a victim of a final irony — that he might have exaggerated and oversold his Mafia connection to Shur and Bonomi, and that when he failed to back it up with evidence, they believed that he had betrayed them and instituted the program of surveillance that was eventually to contribute to his ruin.

The first move made against Paul Maris after he went to California proved symptomatic of the fiascos that were to follow from the government's use of the IRS to investigate a man being hidden by the Justice Department. The IRS decided to seize for taxes the home Zelmanowitz had left in New Jersey. The Justice Department objected, on the grounds that the government would never have known that the property was really owned by Zelmanowitz and not his father-in-law if Gerry hadn't admitted that fact as a government witness in the De-Carlo trial. But the IRS replied that *how* it knew about a tax cheat's assets wasn't important — just that it *did* know — and it commenced proceedings to seize the house for taxes. Later, after the house burned, the IRS decided to file papers with the insurance companies to place a lien on the proceeds, so that when the claims were paid the money would go to the government to help satisfy the $1.7 million tax assessment. The IRS did so, sending notices of the liens to the insurance companies and thus blocking them from paying Zelmanowitz. The law required that a notice also be sent to the owner, which the IRS did by mailing a letter to Gerald Zelmanowitz at the New Jersey address. Since neither Gerald Zelmanowitz nor his house existed anymore, Paul Maris predictably did not soon receive the word that the IRS was again pressing its tax claim.

But, in fact, the IRS was not pressing its claim with notable success.

First, while the tax men were freezing the insurance proceeds on the burned-out house, they did not place a lien on the insurance proceeds for the house's furnishings, apparently because that policy was in Lillian Zelmanowitz's name. The company offered Zelmanowitz $32,000 through attorney Thomas Campion, and Shur first learned about the offer when Paul Maris telephoned to say he had accepted the settlement and wanted Shur to receive the $32,000 check and forward the money to him. Shur said fine, and then telephoned the insurance broker and told him to hold the check until they heard from him again. But then Shur forgot to tell the IRS: the check gathered dust until it lapsed; the $32,000 reverted to the insurance company; and neither Paul Maris nor the IRS got anything.

Then, Paul Maris learned that the IRS had placed liens on any proceeds he might get from the sale of the house, and he quit making payments on his mortgage. Under normal circumstances, the IRS and the tax debtor would have seen to it that the property was sold for as much money as possible, so that whichever side prevailed in the disputed tax case, there would be as much money as possible to go to the winner. But here, with Zelmanowitz in hiding and out of touch, the burden fell on the IRS to protect the interests of both, and the result was a disaster. Zelmanowitz had an equity of about $110,000 in the property, based on a total worth of $180,000 (a cash offer of $55,000 for the burned-out building and the land, plus an insurance claim of $125,000 based on the lowest bid from a contractor to repair the house), minus $70,000 in first and second mortgages. Yet the IRS did nothing to protect this equity: the mortgages went into default; the house was sold without Paul Maris's knowledge at a quiet sheriff's sale; it was purchased for the bare amount of the second mortgage — only $23,000 — by the lawyer who had been recommended by De-Carlo to represent Zelmanowitz before he turned state's evidence; and the insurance companies were able to settle the fire claim with the new purchaser for the rock-bottom price of $10,000. Thus Paul Maris got nothing, the IRS got nothing, the insurance companies got a windfall, and the sole party to profit clearly from the deal was an attorney with close ties to the organized crime elements that the government had originally set out to combat.

Meanwhile, Paul Maris was prospering in California. But unknown to him, there was a dark side to his success — for as Maris's star rose in the garment business, so did Gerald Shur's suspicion that he was being bankrolled by Mafia money. Thus the government's surveillance of Paul Maris escalated, along with his rising fortunes.

The surveillance began in 1971, at about the time the press carried the story of Maris's takeover of the Paul Maris Company. Word went out from Washington to the United States marshals who served as guards for Paul Maris during his trips and his testimony to watch him closely and submit detailed reports on his comings and goings. They took it to heart, and, because the nature of their work kept them in intimate proximity with the man they were guarding, they were able to supply Gerald Shur with pages of irrelevant details — where Maris went, whom he saw, what telephone calls he placed, and even how much money he had in his pocket. But with all the writing and filing away of surveillance reports, there was no evidence that he had taken up with old and unsavory friends or had violated any laws.

In 1972, Paul and Lillian Maris went to London, and Shur learned of the trip. It seemed likely to him that Maris had reverted to old ways, and had gone on a courier run to bring home some Mafia cash. Shur alerted the United States Customs Service to search the Marises upon their return, and Paul and Lillian were given the full customs treatment — complete with a strip search and anal inspection. Nothing illegal was found.

Then, on the occasion in 1972 when Maris informed Shur that he was going to Montreal on business, Shur warned the Royal Canadian Mounted Police that Maris might be coming to make contact with organized crime elements in Canada. The team of Mounties assigned to follow Maris did it so clumsily, that Maris spotted them and caused the panicky scene with the taxi driver, out of fear that the Mafia might have found him. Yet all the Mounties' surveillance produced was a flurry of late-night telephone calls from Maris to disturb the peace of Justice Department officials at home.

So far the surveillance had produced nothing, but the Justice Department, instead of concluding that there was nothing to find, decided that what was needed was more surveillance. So in the spring of 1972, Shur and Bonomi convened a meeting of about fifteen representatives of key federal law-enforcement agencies — the Justice Department, FBI, Intelligence Division of IRS, organized crime strike forces and the Marshals' Service. It was agreed that the Paul Maris situation had become increasingly suspicious. How could a person achieve such a meteoric rise in business and in the community in such a short period of time? Where did Maris get the money? The consensus was that an investigation was in order. It was decided that the IRS Intelligence Division would take over the case, and would initiate close surveillance of all of Paul Maris's activities in San Francisco. Apparently no one thought to place a telephone call to Alvin Duskin, who could have explained that Maris's takeover of the company did not require a large bundle of cash, but only the $5,000, borrowed partly from his in-laws. Also, no one checked to find out that Maris' high style of life was made possible by a steady flow of loans from his ever-hopeful backers in New York. Whether this failure to try the obvious was due to the Justice Department's long-standing suspicion of Gerry, or the built-in problem of investigating a person whom one is hiding, or simply a zest for cloak-and-dagger activity, on May 3, 1972, IRS agents began a night-and-day surveillance of Paul Maris.

For the next fifteen days Maris was watched and followed, people coming and going from the Paul Maris Company and from Maris's two homes were photographed, and the telephone records of the Paul Maris Company were examined. On May 18, nothing apparently having been discovered, the surveillance was discontinued. A Justice Department official summed up the agency's frustration in a brief memo notation: "The surveillance did not result in any investigative leads, but the Internal Revenue Service report was disseminated to the FBI for them to check out any leads which may have been developed during the course of the surveillance."

There the matter rested until October of 1972, when Gerry failed to recognize Fat Tony Salerno in court. As a Justice Department official put it in an interoffice memorandum: "Feelings prevailed that perhaps Zelmanowitz had used the Department of Justice to his advantage without fulfilling his promise to the Government. This lack of cooperation and follow through was evidenced by the failure of Zelmanowitz to provide Gerald Shur and Dan Bonomi with Lansky's Swiss bank account number. This was promised, but Zelmanowitz would not produce it when the two went to San Francisco to pick it up."

The resentment at the Justice Department continued to fester, but nothing happened until about the third week of May 1973, when the IRS was again turned loose against Maris — and why the government suddenly began to move secretly against him at just that time was later to become a subject of much bitterness and dispute. For on May 23,

Shur and Bonomi met again with the same groups that had planned the surveillance of Paul Maris the year before, and it was decided that the IRS would resume its surveillance. But in addition to the search for illegal activities on Maris's part, there was an important second reason for the decision to resume surveillance: the agents were instructed to find out what assets Maris had, so that collection activities could be commenced by the Internal Revenue Service.

The timing of this decision to prepare to seize Paul Maris's assets, just as his cover was about to be blown, was to prompt Zelmanowitz later to accuse the men who ran the alias program of deliberately betraying a person whom they were supposed to protect. Gerald Shur denied this; he said he did not believe that Paul Maris's cover would be blown. But the coincidences were striking. Early in May, Maris had phoned Shur to report that his college cover had not checked out. Shur did nothing about Maris's cover, but began to coordinate government plans to seize his assets. On May 17, Milton Stewart's emissary, Charles Noone, told the Justice Department that Paul Maris's true identity was known, and was given assurances that no governmental interest would be damaged if that identity was disclosed. Shur did not tell Maris, and a few days later, Maris placed a check for $50,000 in escrow, as a pledge that he would complete the purchase of the Miss Pat Company on May 31. Meanwhile, IRS agents were watching Maris and cataloguing his assets. At the same time, they were preparing documents to use in seizing those assets, to satisfy taxes assessed against Gerald Martin Zelmanowitz. On the day that the San Francisco newspapers stunned the city with the news that Paul Maris was a former Mafia employee, the IRS began to serve the papers to attach Maris's bank accounts, cars, homes, furnishings, and personal effects. The documents had been signed and dated the previous day, before the story broke.

Shur was to testify later that the government did not make its preparations in anticipation of its hidden witness being unmasked, but rather as part of a plan to quietly enforce the Zelmanowitz tax assessments against Maris. He did not fully explain how the Justice Department expected to take garment executive Paul Maris to court to force him to pay the tax debts of Mafia courier Gerald Zelmanowitz, without raising some eyebrows in San Francisco.

In the wake of all of the charges, denials, and unconvincing explanations that eventually surrounded this incident, the temptation was strong to conclude that the government decided to administer what it saw as rough justice in this case: that Gerald Zelmanowitz had betrayed the government in the Salerno trial, and the Justice Department paid him back in kind.

But as it turned out, Zelmanowitz got, if not the last laugh, at least the final snicker. Unfortunately for the IRS, its subsequent moves against Gerald Zelmanowitz proved almost as futile as its ill-fated first assessment. The initial IRS levy, for $1.7 million, had been voided by the Appellate Division of the IRS, when it was shown that the stock transactions had not been made by Zelmanowitz, but by his Swiss partners-in-crime, using false Form 3625's forged in blank by him. Then the resourceful IRS assessed Gerry for the identical $1.7 million again, under a law that made persons liable for the tax if they made a misrepresentation of material fact on a Form 3625 as to the prior ownership of the stock. That was to be thrown out in United States District Court in San Francisco on the grounds that Gerry only forged the signatures on blank forms, and others misrepresented the facts. But the IRS struck again, this time assessing Zelmanowitz $570,000 for interest equalization taxes owed on the DeCarlo-Cecere-Polverino arbitrage transactions. This was declared invalid by the District Court on the ground that Gerry was only an agent and received none of the profits from those trades. The IRS made one last try. It accused Zelmanowitz of owing $612,000 in income taxes for the years 1965, 1966, and 1967, when he had filed no income tax returns. However, the only income cited by the IRS was the profits from the two sets of arbitrage transactions that Zelmanowitz denied having been a party to — the $1.7 million that was the free-lance work of Swiss brokers and the $570,000 on the DeCarlo trades. Logically, it followed that Zelmanowitz didn't owe any income taxes on the profits from these arbitrage transactions, as it had already been decided that others were responsible for them. But at this point, United States District Judge Spencer Williams in San Francisco broke Zelmanowitz's winning streak against the IRS by invoking what lawyers sometimes refer to as curbstone justice. Judge Williams observed that Zelmanowitz had admitted doing quite well for himself during that period, and had also admitted paying no income taxes. Therefore, the judge concluded that even though Zelmanowitz didn't owe the exact taxes that had been assessed, he probably owed some taxes, and the burden would be on him to prove that he didn't owe at least the amount of taxes claimed by the IRS for one year — 1967. This was obviously impossible for a confirmed non-taxpayer such as Zelmanowitz. The judge concluded that the amount of taxes Zelmanowitz owed roughly canceled out the value of the property that the IRS had seized from Paul Maris. Thus the marathon dispute between Gerald Zelmanowitz and the IRS ended, after much expense and wear and tear on both sides, in a virtual standoff.

It was to be many months before all of this would be untangled in court, and in the meantime, the original $104,000 seizure by the IRS was to remain an obsession with Gerry. He argued to anyone who would listen that if the IRS had only released the money to him at the outset, he could have used it to take his family to Europe, and there would have been for him no costly government relocation, no blundering alias program, and no final bitterness.

But there was to be a point in time, shortly after he returned to Washington, when beleaguered officials would consider his demand for one final review of the $104,000 misunderstanding. For Gerry to bother to seek such a formality after the IRS had operated for so long on the assumption that the $104,000 had been properly seized was a measure of his incurable naïveté about the function of government. But in one respect, Zelmanowitz then held the whip hand. He had not told his side of the events that led to the demise of Paul Maris, and there were many allegations in that story that the government could have wished to remain untold.

So Zelmanowitz was promised a hearing before an objective IRS official, who would review the case and decide. On the appointed day about a month after Maris's cover had been blown, Gerald Zelmanowitz slipped into the IRS building across the street from the Justice Department in Washington and entered the office where the special arbitrator was to hear and decide his case.

"You've got to be kidding!" Zelmanowitz shouted, when he saw the hearing officer. He was Joseph Fontenella, one of the agents Zelmanowitz had accused of taking bribes from him, back in New Jersey.

Zelmanowitz stormed out of the hearing room raving that the whole

216

scene had been crazy, insane, perverse. He could hardly expect an impartial hearing, he shouted, from a man whom he had accused of taking bribes, in connection with the same transactions that were the subject of Zelmanowitz's claim.

It was at that point that Zelmanowitz realized that he could never persuade the government to grant him justice, as he saw it, through sweet reason. He decided then that he had nothing to lose by telling his side of the story, by testifying before the Senate Permanent Investigations Subcommittee. After he did, Senator Joseph Montoya of New Mexico became intrigued by the telling of the Fontenella incident. Senator Montoya was chairman of a subcommittee that controlled the purse strings of the IRS, and as such he had the clout to attract the attention of the highest levels of the IRS toward matters that piqued his interest.

On August 3, 1973, Montoya sent the IRS a statement of Zelmanowitz's charges and asked for an explanation. On June 24, 1974, more than four years after Zelmanowitz had first told the Justice Department his story about the bribes, IRS Commissioner Donald C. Alexander sent a letter to Senator Montoya with the government's final report on the case. Alexander explained that as to Joseph Fontenella, the matter had become moot — he had recently died. As for the other IRS agent accused by Zelmanowitz, the Justice Department had declined prosecution, but Alexander reported, "He has been severely reprimanded and we are in the process of reducing him in grade." Alexander concluded by expressing his appreciation to the Senator for "bringing this matter to [their] attention and giving [them] the opportunity to inquire into this situation."

Meanwhile, on May 30, 1973, Paul and Lillian Maris had spent their last night in their Pacific Heights apartment, and the next day they finished packing and the marshals drove them out to the country retreat in Sonoma. That evening all the relatives came, called together to be forewarned of the blow that was about to fall. It was a depressing family reunion, made worse by the realization that it was supposed to have been the day when Maris would realize his ambition to finally own a company of his own.

The next day, June 1, Milton Stewart's lawyers filed their court papers and distributed copies to the startled reporters at the courthouse. There was a scramble to contact Maris, but the telephone in his apartment had been disconnected. Most of the reporters gave up, but one recalled an article about a country fair at a home owned by Maris in Sonoma County. The reporter got the number from information, and the man who answered said that he was Paul Maris.

According to the article, the man became excited and shouted that many lives — his whole family — were in danger and that irresponsible lawyers and reporters were making it worse. In the cold type of the article that appeared in print the next day, his reaction came across as almost hysterical: "My whole cover is being destroyed. . . . At this moment, I am traveling very far and very fast."

It was clear enough from the earliest press reports that the scene had grown untenable for Paul Maris in San Francisco. The press in the city and in the garment trade, which had fawned so gullibly over him for so long, turned the tables with a series of articles, fed by Creative Capital and Hal Lipset, which painted Maris as a much darker figure than subsequent testimony showed him to be. The San Francisco *Chronicle*'s gossip columnist, Herb Caen, published a column attributed to "a source," declaring as a fact Hal Lipset's theory that Paul Maris once worked for Bernard Cornfeld in the Orient, where he was "able to launder some of his dirty money." It was also published that Superior Court Judge Ira Brown, Jr., had given attorney Dennis Bromley permission for Pillsbury, Madison & Sutro to withdraw as Maris's counsel, as soon as Maris could obtain a new lawyer. Judge Brown issued an order to the absent Paul Maris to obtain new counsel within thirty days or have his litigation dismissed.

But Paul Maris did not have to read the papers to know that he was through in San Francisco. After the telephone call from the reporter on the day that Stewart dropped his bombshell, Maris saw that he and Lillian were isolated, with no source of income, no usable identity papers, no coherent communication with Washington about the future, and a growing sense of stationary vulnerability to anyone who might want to take their lives.

That last point was brought home to them late that night in the stillness of the rambling country house — they discovered that their bodyguards, exhausted, had all fallen asleep.

After a whispered telephone call into the city, the two of them packed their bags and slipped past the sleeping marshals, out of the house and down the long drive to the highway. There they found Lillian's son-in-law, Bobby Stricker, as arranged, waiting in his station wagon.

He drove them into San Francisco, to a car rental agency. Gerald Zelmanowitz rented a car and turned east, toward Washington.

11......Gerald Martin Zelmanowitz

On Friday the thirteenth of July, 1973, Gerald Martin Zelmanowitz walked, unaccompanied by United States marshals and petrified, into the Dirksen Senate Office Building to testify before the Senate Permanent Subcommittee on Investigations. On the surface, his appearance as a witness was to be for much the same purpose as his testimony at the DeCarlo and Salerno trials — to give evidence about organized crime. But in fact, his Senate testimony was motivated by fundamentally different reasons. As he took the oath and gave the routine assurance that no "promise, representation or threats" had been used to persuade him to testify, this time he was telling the literal truth.

Before that day, Gerald Zelmanowitz could have combed his entire life — excluding, possibly, some events in the life of Paul Maris — without being able to point to a single act he had taken at a heavy personal cost and with no possible benefit to himself. Yet his appearance as a witness that day was such an act. But so tangled were the happenings that had brought him there that it was impossible to know whether his basic motivation was to help the government in its efforts to combat organized crime, to expose the alias program for its ruinous handling of his case, or simply because events had brought Gerry Zelmanowitz to the point where he could not be hurt anymore.

He had first contacted the subcommittee about two years before, when he was struggling to establish himself in San Francisco as Paul Maris. He had read a newspaper report of a speech by one of the subcommittee's members, Senator Charles Percy, about an upcoming investigation into the crime syndicate's traffic in stolen securities. There followed a series of guarded telephone calls, in which an anonymous voice contacted Senator Percy's office, was directed to the Permanent Investigations Subcommittee staff, and was finally put on the line with one of the subcommittee's veteran investigators, Philip Manuel.

As soon as the anonymous telephone caller identified himself as Gerald Zelmanowitz, Manuel knew it was a stroke of luck. Manuel was a bullnecked, barrel-chested, cigar-chomping investigator who spent long hours on the telephone spouting broken Italian to contacts around the country, and he was the subcommittee's resident expert on organized crime. He knew all about Zelmanowitz, because he had tried to find him after the DeCarlo trial. As one of the most prolific paperhangers of stolen securities in the business, Zelmanowitz could have told the Senate more about how the racket really worked than its investigators could ever find out from the outside, so Manuel had leaned hard on the Justice Department to let the subcommittee staff pick Zelmanowitz's brains. But Zelmanowitz had mysteriously disappeared immediately after his testimony, and the chief of the Newark Strike Force, John Bartels, stonewalled Manuel's requests to interview him. The word was that Zelmanowitz was just not available. Then one day, the telephone rang and he fell into Phil Manuel's hands.

Manuel flew to Los Angeles and met Zelmanowitz at the Airport Marina Motel. They talked for eight hours, and it provided the subcommittee with a goldmine of information. Zelmanowitz said he had contacted the Senate because he felt that the government was missing the mark in its efforts against organized crime. It was a mistake, he said, to concentrate on locking up notorious characters with Italian names, while ignoring the businessmen and bureaucrats who made it possible for the mafiosi to get by with their crimes.

Zelmanowitz backed it up with names and examples: brokerage houses that studiously failed to spot stolen securities because the commissions on the trades were so lucrative; bankers who signed blank stock ownership certificates for customers with large accounts; IRS agents who overlooked phony tax forms in exchange for monthly bribes. To Zelmanowitz, the best way to choke off the flow of funds from white-collar crimes to the Mafia would be to pass laws focusing legal responsibility on businessmen and bureaucrats whose laxity permitted the lawbreaking to flourish. Zelmanowitz felt that ponderous criminal trials against the racketeers were secondary, but he did say that the Justice Department had a new program that could make those trials more successful, except that it was being botched. Then Manuel heard for the first time complaints he was to receive increasingly as time went on, allegations of bungling by the men who ran the alias program.

Most congressional investigations are one-half fact-gathering, one-half theatre. Manuel explained that as helpful as Zelmanowitz's information was, the subcommittee needed his testimony, dramatically and in person, to put his message across to the public. He mentioned a possible appearance with Zelmanowitz wearing a mask. That was out of the question, Zelmanowitz explained. He was starting to get ahead in business in the city where he was living, and somebody might put together his absence and the voice behind the mask. Zelmanowitz said he might testify before the Senators in a secret hearing someday, and he promised to phone Manuel from time to time, but the investigator left Los Angeles that day in 1971 believing that he had lost Zelmanowitz as a live witness.

When Gerald Zelmanowitz arrived in Washington in late June of 1973, about three weeks after he had been unmasked, he telephoned Phil Manuel with the word that the time for that sensational hearing might have come. He had driven cautiously across the country from San Francisco, swinging down through the Southwest and staying in out-of-the-way motels. As he went he tried to reestablish contact with Washington by telephone, to find out how his cover had been blown, whether any hit men were known to be looking for him, and what would be done about his identity now. But he was having trouble getting through to the government. Gerald Shur's home number was now unlisted, and his secretary referred calls to the Marshals' Service, which she said was handling all witness security matters. Zelmanowitz told Manuel it might have become impossible for him to go through another government relocation, and that if so, he would have nothing to lose by telling his story in an open hearing.

In the days that followed, Zelmanowitz was subjected to an experience known in the capital city as "the Washington runaround." He was a problem and an embarrassment, and nobody seemed to be responsible for his case. When he first phoned to establish contact with the Justice Department, his call was transferred several times, until finally it came to rest with the secretary of the acting duty officer for the Marshals' Service. She explained that the duty officer was unavailable, and would the caller explain his business.

For once in his life, Gerald Zelmanowitz was almost speechless. How could he explain to this faceless young woman that he had just arrived

United States Marshal John Partington (right center, with radio) *provided Gerald and Lillian Zelmanowitz with documents for new false identities in 1973.*

in the capital with his family, frightened, exhausted, running out of money, and with no identity papers except those bearing the name of a notorious fraud, Paul Maris? Where would he start to relate the story that four weeks before he had been a well-known businessman in California, but that now he was nameless and vulnerable, and that he did not even know how it had happened? How could he tell her that he had suddenly become a nonperson, and he had come to Washington to ask them to make him a person again?

After a protracted pause, he said that it was a long story, and that he would call back when the duty officer was in.

Zelmanowitz soon learned that the Marshals' Service apparently had made no provisions for handling the case of a witness whose cover had been blown. He was immediately assigned a new team of bodyguards, but nobody seemed to be responsible for putting his identity back together again. He was referred to one minor official for his new Social Security card, to another for a driver's license, a third for requests for money. The person in charge of Social Security cards said there would be a delay in obtaining new documents from the Social Security Administration. The official responsible for drivers' licenses said he couldn't act until the new Social Security card came through. The man in charge of money said he had no authority to pay someone who had already been relocated. Gerry was spending long, exhausting days seeing many people, but nothing was happening.

Finally, the government dealt with the situation by flying Gerry and Lillian to another state, where they were met at a secret location by John Partington, the Marshals' Service official who specialized in emergency relocations. Partington managed to obtain two items of identification for each of them in their new names, and they were back in Washington in two days.

Meanwhile, Gerry had been having increasing contacts with the Permanent Investigation Subcommittee. He talked frequently with Phil Manuel, then told his story to the subcommittee chairman, Senator Henry M. Jackson, and finally testified in a locked room before the entire subcommittee. The Senators were startled by his disclosures of the then little-known heavy volume of organized crime activity funneled through Swiss banks and brokerage houses. Gerry suspected that Swiss officialdom would be considerably less surprised than the Senators to hear this, but at the subcommittee's request, he went to the Swiss embassy and briefed the Swiss minister to the United States, Oliver Exchaquet, on the details of the crime syndicate's operations in his country.

But Gerry was also talking to the subcommittee about his frustrations with the alias program, and he visualized his proposed testimony as having a dual purpose — to dramatize to the country how the government's anti–organized crime campaign was failing to come to grips with the roots of white-collar crime; and also to warn that a potentially valuable tool, the witness protection program, was being bungled.

Meanwhile, the Justice Department seemed to have been almost paralyzed at the prospect of Gerald Zelmanowitz on the loose in Washington. Some officials apparently clung to the belief that he was still on the payroll of the crime syndicate — he learned later that he had been surveilled by his marshal bodyguard and a report was sent to Shur about his visit to the Swiss embassy. Others in the government wanted to satisfy Zelmanowitz if they could, and they pressured the IRS to grant him the special hearing he wanted on his $104,000 claim. They gnashed their teeth when the IRS blew it by assigning Joseph Fontenella to conduct the hearing. But the overriding attitude seemed to be that Zelmanowitz's presence in Washington was not to be desired, and that he should be moved elsewhere as quickly as possible.

As his contacts with the Senate subcommittee increased, so did the suggestions that he get out of town. But Gerry could not have left if he wished to. The strain had finally become too much for Lillian, and on the Monday before her husband's planned Senate testimony, she was hospitalized with a stomach disorder. The doctors operated immediately, and there was no way that Gerry Zelmanowitz could consider leaving the city, at least for several weeks.

But when Thursday came and Senator Jackson announced the hearing for the next day, the Justice Department decreed that the danger to Gerry in Washington had become too great; he would have to leave the capital that day. Gerry said that was insane: his wife was in the hospital; it had been announced that he would testify the next day; and there was no reason why the marshals could protect him any better in Nebraska than in Washington. But the men who were calling the shots in the Justice Department decreed that the danger was too great.

225

If Gerry insisted on staying in Washington, they said they could not continue to be responsible for his safety. He said he would stay, and testify. That night, the team of marshals that had been guarding Zelmanowitz was withdrawn.

Thus the next morning it was Phil Manuel, feeling alternately protective and foolish with a pistol in his belt, who escorted Zelmanowitz and his lawyer, Neil Bloomfield, into the Dirksen Senate Office Building. The occasion had all the ingredients of high Washington drama, with Senator Jackson instructing the news media not to photograph the witness's face, and then thundering indignation at the Justice Department for its refusal to protect Zelmanowitz after it learned that he intended to testify.

For his part, Zelmanowitz lived up to his billing as the master-criminal-turned-informer.

He began with a humble disclaimer; then quickly turned up the pitch: "I was born in Brooklyn, N.Y., January 12, 1937. My formal education is not great. I left high school at an early age to go to work. . . . My military background is poor. I was undesirably discharged from the Marine Corps.

"I cannot truly state that prior to 1970 I was ever gainfully employed except for small periods of my life. I do have a criminal record; I have been convicted three times of crimes, including the sale of stolen securities, and a scheme to defraud banks in New York City by the use of fraudulent checking accounts.

"I have been involved with members of organized crime in various schemes to sell stolen securities and to arbitrage foreign securities with the intent of avoiding and evading interest equalization taxes. . . ."

That launched him into an hour-long lecture on the intricacies of evading interest equalization taxes, of fencing stolen and counterfeit securities, of violating the tax laws through the good offices of Swiss banks. He spiced his testimony with tidbits of felony and scandal — of a telephone call placed on Zelmanowitz's behalf by New Jersey political

No photographs of Gerald Zelmanowitz's face were permitted when he testified before Senator Henry Jackson's Senate Permanent Subcommittee on Investigations, July 13, 1973.

boss John V. Kenney to the federal judge who was handling Zelmanowitz's $104,000 tax claim; of New York Mafia figure Christopher Furnari having so many stacks of stolen securities in the back room of his Brooklyn bar that Zelmanowitz managed to slip out $200,000 in IBM stock without Furnari even missing it; of flying to London to cash $200,000 in stolen American Express checks in two of the city's swankiest casinos, the Colony Club and the Victoria Sporting Club.

Then when Zelmanowitz mentioned giving $50 or $100 "tips" to officers of two leading New York banks, Chase Manhattan and First National City, in exchange for signatures on bogus stock ownership certificates, Senator Percy called for proof. Percy explained that he was a former member of the board of directors of Chase Manhattan, and he wanted the names of any such officers. Of course, the witness replied. Zelmanowitz just happened to have some of the forms signed by those bank officials, and he passsed them to Senator Percy with an invitation to take the matter up with the two banks.

Zelmanowitz was also eloquent in his denunciation of the alias program. He reeled off a point-by-point indictment of the Justice Department in his case, and raised the possibility that hundreds of relocated witnesses could be in danger across the country, mistakenly believing that their government aliases would stand up under scrutiny. But for the government's mistakes, Zelmanowitz claimed, he could have won his suit against Creative Capital for kicking him out of a prospering company.

Again, Senator Percy pressed the witness for details, and again the answers were persuasive — but, unknown to Percy, not as credible as they appeared on the surface. Percy, a former businessman, refused to accept ambiguous claims of prosperity from Zelmanowitz, and finally wrung from him an estimate that in the current year, the Paul Maris Company would have made a net profit of $800,000, before taxes. It was a claim that would have brought justifiable hoots of disbelief from the officers of the Creative Capital Corporation.

But still, Gerald Zelmanowitz held his own during that long day of grilling before the Senate committee. He demonstrated detailed and accurate knowledge of the securities market and tax legislation, and late in the day, Senator Percy invited his suggestions on how the government should deal with the complex problem of white-collar crime: "Obviously, you do not have a Harvard degree," Percy said, "but you certainly have a degree of sophistication which goes way beyond what I have seen in many people who have schooled themselves at Harvard, Yale, and Princeton, and have had years of business experience."

So Zelmanowitz, the high-school dropout from Brooklyn, conducted an informal seminar, instructing the Senate committee on reforms that should be made — legislative changes, sharpening of corporate responsibility, upgrading of business ethics, and negotiating changes with the Swiss bankers to reduce some of the secrecy that protects American gangsters. Then Zelmanowitz, with a perfectly straight face, added that he would be pleased to meet at greater length with top officials of the IRS to expand on this advice.

It was a scene that under normal circumstances would have caused a sensation in Washington and across the country. There was the former stockbroker for the Mafia being praised by one potential presidential candidate, Henry "Scoop" Jackson, and then grilled and finally complimented by a leading Republican hopeful, Chuck Percy. There were charges of bribery and corruption in leading New York banks and in the IRS. There was the first public discussion of a mysterious new Justice Department program that had already infiltrated hundreds of former hoodlums into society under false identities. Normally, it would have been only the beginning of a series of investigations, hearings, and exposés.

But those were not normal times, and that was not an ordinary day. It was the summer when Watergate was in full fever, and much of the nation watched on television that day as the Senate Watergate Commitee questioned President Nixon's White House legal advisor, Richard Moore.

Late in the afternoon, the Senators on the subcommittee began to drift away. Taking that as a signal, most of the reporters left too. The cameramen slipped out, and the bright television lights were turned off, leaving the hearing room gloomy and dark in the dwindling afternoon light. The chamber was almost empty, and the only Senator left was a freshman, Walter ("Dee") Huddleston of Kentucky, who found himself in the unaccustomed role of acting chairman.

Senator Huddleston, a sincere, round-faced young man with all the

229

dash of a Kentucky Rotarian, was plainly uncomfortable. He stated that he had run out of questions, but he was obviously reluctant to end the hearing with the witness having said that he feared for his life, and with the Justice Department having withdrawn his protection.

Under the circumstances, the most reassuring thing that Huddleston could do was invoke the majesty of the Senate. He reminded Zelmanowitz that Senator Jackson had stated earlier that he had complained to Attorney General Elliot Richardson about the withdrawal of the marshals, and that Jackson expected to hear from the department before the end of the day. "I can say to you, I think without fear of contradiction, that our Subcommittee chairman is a man of some means here on Capitol Hill who doesn't make idle statements, and a man who can accomplish things," Huddleston said, finishing on the upbeat; "Hopefully before you leave here today you will have some more reassurance than you had when you came in."

From Zelmanowitz's point of view there was less cause for optimism; "I am in fear for my life. I do not know where to go or what to do when this is over. I leave here now and that is it."

But there was nothing more to be said. Senator Huddleston banged down the gavel and the hearing was over.

Everybody left except Zelmanowitz and the Capitol Hill policemen who had been on duty that day in the hearing room. They had heard Senator Jackson's blast at the Justice Department, had listened to Zelmanowitz's testimony, and then had passed the word to their brother officers standing guard over caucus rooms, parking lots, and Congressmen's hideaways across Capitol Hill that a threatened person needed their help. Gerry was persuaded to wait in the empty hearing room, and gradually a volunteer squad of Capitol Hill police began to form. But before they could organize their detail, a team of guards from the United States Marshals' Service rushed into the room. Zelmanowitz had been taken back by the alias program, and he was escorted away.

12..................Plaintiff

On September 26, 1973, the United States was sued for the first time in its history on charges of issuing a worthless alias. In Federal District Court in San Francisco, a $12.5 million suit was filed under the title of *Gerald Martin Zelmanowitz, a/k/a Paul Maris, and Lillian Zelmanowitz, a/k/a Lillian Maris* v. *United States*. In it, the plaintiffs related the events that led to the creation and destruction of the identity of Paul Maris, and they alleged that as a result of the government's negligence and blundering, Maris had lost his fortune and his chance for a decent life. In lawyers' terms, they were alleging that the government had committed wrongs against them by enticing Gerry to testify in return for a new identity, and then by the ineptitude and carelessness of Shur, Bonomi, Glen Robinson, and others, that the government had caused Gerry to lose his business and future employment prospects, the insurance proceeds from his home in New Jersey, his $104,000 Hayden Stone account and his homes in San Francisco and Sonoma. Lillian alleged that the same acts had "injured her health, strength and activity, sustaining severe shock and injury which has caused and will cause her great pain, suffering and mental anguish."

It was what many lawyers would call a hard case. As the government pointed out in its answer, Zelmanowitz had made a free choice to join the alias program and should have understood its risks; in any event, he had increased his own hazards by his freewheeling style of life as Paul Maris.

But by the time the suit was filed, Zelmanowitz had severed all of his ties with the government and had nothing to lose. Several weeks after Gerry's Senate testimony, Lillian recovered her health to the point where she could travel. They boarded a plane and flew to Canada, to reenter the United States at a time and place of their own choosing. Zelmanowitz returned under the second alias provided by the government, the one that John Partington had thrown together during Gerry and Lillian's hectic two-day sortie out of Washington. So the Justice Department knew the names they were using — but once they disappeared, the government had no way of finding out where they were or what they were doing. In the course of the early legal skirmishing, the Justice Department demanded that the plaintiff's lawyers tell where Gerry was living, and how well. The government's lawyers suspected that his capacity to make money — or at least to spend it — had not been diminished to the extent charged in his suit. But that tactic failed, and Gerry and Lillian's whereabouts during those years remained a mystery.

Then in March of 1976, the government won a major battle. Federal District Judge Spencer Williams ruled in San Francisco that the suit should be dismissed. The government had undertaken only to protect Zelmanowitz, Judge Williams declared, not to give him a serviceable false identity. The plaintiff had not, in fact, been physically harmed — thus the government had not failed in its obligations, regardless of how rocky the plaintiff's life had been since then.

It was the first ruling by a federal judge on the obligations of the alias program toward its witnesses, and it came in such unequivocal terms that further appeals by Zelmanowitz might have seemed hopeless, except for a more obscure case that was decided at about the same time in Atlanta, Georgia.

It was a suit that told a familiar story. The plaintiff was an automobile dealer in Philadelphia who fell into the clutches of loan sharks and agreed to testify against them in exchange for relocation under a new identity. After the trial he was given the name of William Rolland, and he and his family were sent to Atlanta. But in Atlanta the Marshals' Service had never heard of Rolland, had no file on him, and did nothing. According to Rolland's allegations, he received no help in finding work or housing; the promised documentation for him and his children never arrived; and his furniture was broken or stolen in transit. He moved into a motel but couldn't find work, and when he was facing eviction from the motel and was almost penniless, the government bailed him out with a small settlement but forced him to sign the "death warrant" release. His demands were more modest than Zelmanowitz's suit — he asked $9,500 for breach of his initial agreement with the government, and $25,000 in punitive damages.

The government sought to have the suit dismissed, but this time the United States district judge, Richard C. Freeman, ruled for the witness. On November 24, 1975, Judge Freeman issued an opinion that held that although the Organized Crime Control Act gives the Attorney General broad power to "provide for the health, safety and welfare of witnesses," it is not broad enough to permit Justice Department personnel to treat witnesses the way they allegedly did Rolland and his family. So the judge ordered a full-scale trial to test Rolland's allegations.

When two federal trial judges have ruled in opposite ways on an untested point of law, the result usually is to encourage appeals by all parties concerned. Thus Zelmanowitz's lawyer took his case to the United States court of appeals in San Francisco, citing the judge's decision in the Rolland case. Meanwhile, both sides were preparing for the trial in Atlanta, with a strong likelihood that if the government should lose, it would appeal to the United States court of appeals in New Orleans, relying upon its victory over Zelmanowitz. Both appeals would take years to decide, and should the two courts of appeal also come down with opposite decisions, an appeal to the Supreme Court would then become necessary to determine finally what responsibility the alias program owes to witnesses who testify for the government against vengeful men.

Thus it appears probable that the issues that were concealed and not confronted when the witness protection program was created will be raised and decided, ultimately, in court. The conflicts that existed in theory have now developed in fact, and those who have been aggrieved by the results have resorted to litigation. The courts may be called upon to determine the extent of the government's duties to its endangered witnesses; whether promising government witnesses new lives is fair to the persons they testify against; the rights of parents whose children are swallowed up into the program; and the government's obligations to citizens who are cheated, swindled, or robbed by relocated witnesses.

As these questions are resolved, either in favor of the program or of those who claim to have been wronged by it, for the first time it will be possible to know whether the concept of a witness relocation program is a defensible idea. There will finally be criteria by which to calculate the costs of giving former criminals good names and infiltrating them back into society and to balance those costs against the accomplishments of the program. Only then will it be possible to determine if it would be better to have those who testify for the prosecution arrange their own lives; in short, whether there should even have been an alias program at all — and whether it should continue.

In the meantime, the witness protection program has completed a metamorphosis that had been under way almost from the start. The program had been created under the chapter of the Organized Crime Control Act headed "Title V — Protected Facilities for Housing Government Witnesses," and despite the Justice Department's ingenuity in stretching this authorization to permit the creation of the alias program, it was clear that Congress intended only to empower the government to provide "safe houses" for prosecution witnesses.

So the purchase and renovation of a group of safe houses was undertaken. They were to be scattered around the country — inconspicuous buildings that would give unsentenced witnesses the anonymity to come and go without notice and where witness-prisoners could be kept safely under guard. Above all, safe houses were to be secret — placed where the witnesses could feel secure because the Mafia did not know where they were.

There proved to be a flaw in that theory, which began to emerge after a network of safe houses was established. Permanent facilities were dotted around the country on Staten Island, in Providence, Sacramento, and Fort Holabird, Maryland, and temporary establishments were located in such places as San Diego, Miami, Boston, Manhattan, and Bowling Green, Kentucky. The problem was that, once a few recently converted gangsters had enjoyed the hospitality of these secret safe houses, they were neither very secret nor very safe anymore.

Not long after the Staten Island safe house was established, the government got a tip that it was about to be blown up by the mob. That safe house was closed down, and the witnesses were hustled up to the more secure facility outside Providence, which had been constructed in an old mill house with thick, bullet-proof, bomb-proof granite walls. But then that safe house lost its anonymity and, gradually, so did all the others.

It became common knowledge in the criminal underworld where the safe houses were and, often, who was in them. Once a witness who was holed up in a supposedly secret safe house in the West was startled to hear a rap on the door and be confronted with the lawyer for the racketeer against whom the witness was going to testify. The lawyer walked in, popped open a briefcase, and began to question the witness in preparation for the trial. There were also a series of fights between the cooped-up witnesses and, sometimes, between witnesses and marshals.

So gradually, the Justice Department began to close the safe houses down. It was safer and simpler to rent apartments or motel rooms when each need arose, and to keep imprisoned witnesses in separate facilities within regular prisons. The last holdout was the safe house at Fort Holabird, which was kept in operation for the use of the Watergate Special Prosecutor to house such celebrity witnesses as John Dean, Egil Krogh, Jeb Stuart Magruder, E. Howard Hunt, and Charles Colson. When Watergate subsided and the government prepared to close that safe house and disperse the remaining witness-prisoners to jails and prisons around the country, the inmates became so irate that they decided to go to court. They felt that the safe house was being closed down because the famous Watergate figures were gone, and they thought that it was unfair to move them out of the relatively cushy surroundings of Fort Holabird into the cold reality of ordinary jails. They filed a suit in federal court in Baltimore and succeeded in blocking the closing for a time. But eventually they lost and the Fort Holabird safe house was shut down.

Thus the witness protection program, which was created by Congress to establish safe houses for witnesses, ended up with no permanent safe house at all.

13 .... Visitor

On a crisp autumn morning in 1975 an airliner arrived at San Francisco International Airport carrying a lean, curly-haired man wearing dark glasses and a conservative gray suit. The man traveled first class.

As soon as the jet docked, the man pushed his way out of the boarding area and walked with long, nervous strides down the corridor past the antihijack metal detectors to the baggage pickup area. He stood fidgeting until the luggage arrived from the airplane's baggage compartment, where it had been checked through without being X-rayed for weapons. The man snatched up a medium-sized valise and ducked into the nearest rest room.

In a few moments he emerged and walked toward the Hertz Car Rental counter, moving with a more relaxed, casual gait. There was a slight bulge in his right-hand jacket pocket that upon close observation might have been discerned as the outline of a small automatic pistol. But the man had a confident, expensive air about him that would have discouraged such a close examination, unless the observer could have known that despite the name on the credit card that the man presented to the Hertz clerk, there was a tattoo high on his right arm that spelled "JERRY."

Soon after, the visitor, his attorney, and a vacationing television journalist drove north into the rolling hills of Sonoma County. They drove to a church in Healdsburg, where people were gathering for a wedding. The bride was a tanned, black-haired young woman named Linda, who was introduced to friends of the groom as the star of the local women's baseball team. The groom was Gary Bricker, a former deputy United States marshal who had quit the government in disillusionment, grown a mod mustache, and was trying to make a new start as a private detective. Bricker had a couple of good, steady department store clients that had been suffering from shoplifting, but there seemed to be an odd, erratic quality to his availability. He disappeared periodically from northern California — to act as a bodyguard, it was said, for an old friend.

After the wedding and the handshakes and congratulations outside the church, the man in the dark glasses and his two companions returned to the rented car, and there was an awkward moment. Someone laughed and mentioned that the car had been left unguarded while everyone was in the church — it would have been a perfect time to tamper with the car, someone joked, with the bodyguard at the altar. The visitor didn't laugh. He said he had a recurring nightmare, of an explosion under his car, blasting up and tearing away his testicles and buttocks. There was a short, nervous laugh from someone, and then an awkward silence. Then the visitor in the dark glasses quickly started the car, and drove to a clubhouse on a hill outside of the town, where the wedding guests had gathered to drink champagne.

Many of the guests were the big, beefy types with bulges on their hips who seem to predominate whenever policemen get together. Several recognized the man in the dark glasses, shook his hand, and called him Gerry. Somebody wisecracked that a marshal's wedding was the safest place in northern California for him to be.

The visitor chatted easily with the men, and disclosed bits and pieces of his present life. He was still living under a name that had been given him by marshal John Partington after the Paul Maris debacle. But he worried that other people in the government knew that name, and he said he was slowly constructing, on his own, another identity. This identity would stand up under close examination, he said, because it was supported by background documentation — birth records, Social Security numbers that fit, medical records. He was slowly and methodically creating an intricate credit and business background for this nonexistent person, he said, by maintaining active bank accounts, credit card use, store accounts, and occasional trips under that name to the doctor and dentist. Nobody, he said — especially not the government — knows the name of the "person" whose financial stability and personal credibility is being so patiently constructed in some faraway place.

Meanwhile, he said, he was making it all over again in the business world. His new enterprise was strictly legitimate, he declared, and much bigger than the Paul Maris venture. He added that, this time, there would be no misunderstandings, because his new business associates would know about his past. Soon he would make his big score, he said, and then he and his family would disappear forever into that final alias.

The man the wedding guests called Gerry didn't disclose much more. He just chatted and laughed and continued to sip champagne.

.... Afterword

Four years after the Good Friday Massacre:

Kat Walker is a vice president of a small garment manufacturing company in San Francisco.

Milton Stewart is president of the National Small Business Association.

Dante Bonomi is teaching courses in law enforcement at the community college of Beaver County, Pennsylvania.

Daniel "Red" Cecere is a newly released ex-convict.

Alvin Duskin is knitting cloth for women's fashions again in the Paul Maris Company building.

Paul Maris's former executive office in that building is being used by the government as a center to rehabilitate convicts.

Gerald Martin Zelmanowitz is still in hiding.

And Gerald Shur is still in charge of the alias program.

F.G.
April 20, 1977